Good Luntving !

This edition is

limited to 1,500 copies

of which this is

No. 1292

CAUGHLEY
AND WORCESTER
PORCELAINS
1775-1800

GEOFFREY A. GODDEN

F.R.S.A.

CAUGHLEY AND WORCESTER PORCELAINS 1775-1800

1775-1800

ANTIQUE COLLECTORS' CLUB

First published in 1969 by
Herbert Jenkins Ltd
2 Clement's Inn, London WC2

ISBN 0 907462 01 4

Reprinted, with a new introduction, in 1981
for the Antique Collectors' Club
by the Antique Collectors' Club Ltd.
Woodbridge, Suffolk, England

British Library CIP Data
Godden, Geoffrey A.
  Caughley and Worcester porcelains 1775-1800
  1. Caughley porcelain
  2. Worcester porcelain
  I. Title
  738.27   NK4399.C3

Printed in England by Baron Publishing, Woodbridge, Suffolk

By the same author

Victorian Porcelain
Encyclopaedia of British Pottery and Porcelain Marks
An Illustrated Encyclopaedia of British Pottery and Porcelain
The Handbook of British Pottery and Porcelain Marks
Minton Pottery and Porcelain of the First Period
Coalport and Coalbrookdale Porcelains
Stevengraphs and other Victorian Silk Pictures
Jewitt's Ceramic Art of Great Britain 1800-1900 (Revised
    and re-illustrated edition, 1972)
The Illustrated Guide to Lowestoft Porcelain
The Illustrated Guide to Mason's Patent Ironstone China
The Illustrated Guide to Ridgway Porcelains
British Porcelain, an Illustrated Guide
British Pottery, an Illustrated Guide
Godden's Guide to English Porcelain
Oriental Export Market Porcelain and its influence on European wares
Godden's Guide to Mason's China and the Ironstone Wares

CONTENTS

COLOUR PLATES

BLACK & WHITE PLATES

The general arrangement of the black and white illustrations is that Plates 14 to 82 show the standard Caughley patterns discussed in Chapters II to VI. Plates 85 to 217 illustrate the standard shapes made at the Caughley factory, as listed alphabetically in Chapter VII.

Following these we have in Plates 230 to 314 the Worcester porcelains that have, in the main, formerly been attributed to Caughley and several of these illustrations show by comparison the slight differences between the designs or shapes used at each factory.

ACKNOWLEDGEMENTS

I am deeply grateful for the help given to me by a large number of people over a period of several years, for without this assistance this book would not have been written. Much of the new information is the result of discoveries made on the site of the Caughley factory, and the many interesting hours I have spent on the site have been made possible, and more rewarding, by the assistance given to me by the management and staff of Messrs Coalmoor Refractories (Horsehay) Ltd, who are at present working there. In particular I should mention Mr A. McCall and Mr R. Minton.

I have also enjoyed the co-operation of Museum Curators and collectors, who have selections of factory 'wasters' (fragments of spoilt or unfinished wares) found on the site, and who have kindly permitted me to view their finds, and in some cases to illustrate these key pieces in this book. These include Mr R. J. Charleston (Keeper of the Department of Ceramics at the Victoria and Albert Museum); Mr H. Tait (Assistant Keeper of the Department of British and Medieval Antiquities at the British Museum); Mr R. James and Mr M. F. Messenger (of the Shrewsbury Museum); Lady Benthall; Mr E. Gnapp; Mr and Mrs D. Holgate; Mr and Mrs D. Roberts and Dr B. Watney. I am also greatly indebted to Mr Henry Sandon's most interesting excavations of part of the Worcester factory site, and for the ready assistance he has given me in making the 'wasters' available to be photographed for inclusion in the Worcester section of this book. In this respect I must also acknowledge the kind co-operation of the Directors of the Worcester Royal Porcelain Co Ltd, the Trustees of the Dyson Perrins Museum Trust and the Corporation of the City of Worcester.

The several reproductions of designs taken from the original engraved copper-plates used at the Caughley factory between 1775 and 1799 have in the main been taken from a most interesting old 'rag' book of Caughley and Coalport designs. This book of 'pulls' has, fortunately, been preserved, although the copper-plates from which they were printed have now been destroyed, and I am indebted to Mr W. E. Brain, Managing Director of Messrs Coalport China Ltd, for permission to reproduce so many of these designs from this unique source. Other 'pulls' from Thomas Turner's engraved copper-plates are in the British Museum and the Victoria and Albert Museum, and some of these have also been reproduced.

The other main source of contemporary eighteenth century material incorporated in this book comprises the original Chamberlain accounts (see Chapter V), and again I am indebted to the Directors of the Worcester Royal

Porcelain Co Ltd, the Trustees of the Dyson Perrins Museum Trust and Mr Cyril Shingler (Mr Sandon's predecessor, as Curator of the Worcester Works Museum), for permission to use these records. Information from local church registers has been kindly supplied by the Revd. J. Glover and the Revd. L. F. Peltor and further contemporary information has been gleaned from the local newspaper, the *Salopian Journal*. The records contained in Appendix I have been quoted from the eighteenth and early nineteenth century sale catalogues of Messrs Christies and Messrs Phillips, Son & Neale (by permission of the Directors), while the extracts from the Joseph Lygo correspondence (given in Appendix II) have been made available through Mr A. Green and are quoted by permission of the Derby Librarian, Mr E. Bletcher, F.L.A.

The inclusion of so many illustrations has been made possible through the kindness of many members of the Trade, of the leading auctioneers and of private collectors. Several of the latter have generously permitted me to borrow specimens so that I could photograph them with matching 'wasters' found on the factory site, and my especial thanks are extended to the following collectors: Mr F. Baxendale; Lady Benthall; Mr and Mrs J. Cronk; Mrs N. Findlay; Mrs P. G. Ferriday; Mrs R. J. Green; Mr and Mrs D. Holgate; Mr H. L. Lloyd; Dr G. Loxton; Mr and Mrs J. Manning; Mr K. Middlemas; Mr J. Riley; Mr and Mrs D. Roberts; Mr S. Spero; Mr C. Staal; Dr B. Watney, and Miss N. Wilson.

Other porcelains have been illustrated from the collections housed in the British Museum; the Castle Museum, Norwich; the Victoria and Albert Museum, and the Dyson Perrins Museum at the Worcester Royal Porcelain factory, and I extend my thanks to their Directors and staff, for generous and prompt attention to my many requests for photographs. Several other examples have been photographed for me while on the premises of Messrs Christie, Manson & Woods Ltd, and Messrs Sotheby & Co, the London auctioneers, although pieces included in photographs credited to these firms have now passed on to other hands. I am also most grateful to my many friends in the Trade, who have supplied photographs of Caughley porcelain in their stock, and who include:

Chanctonbury Gallery (Washington, Sussex)
Chichester Antiques Ltd (Porcelain Department)
Delomosne & Son Ltd (London)
Godden of Worthing Ltd
Martin Hutton (Battle, Sussex)
Newman & Newman (Antiques) Ltd (London)
Mrs Stewart-Browne (Messrs 'Margaret Cadman', Brighton)
Stuart & Turner Ltd (Newbury)
J. Waring (Brighton)
W. W. Warner (Antiques) Ltd (London)
Miss N. Wilson (Harrogate)

My very personal thanks go to my wife for sharing my enthusiasm for the subject; to Derek Gardiner, A.I.B.P., for photographing, to such good effect, the porcelains from my own collection (and from the stock of Messrs Godden of Worthing Ltd); to Mrs B. Magness and Miss J. Print for interpreting and typing my notes, and to Mr D. Knox for checking this material.

GEOFFREY A. GODDEN

PREFACE

It was originally intended to confine the subject matter of this book entirely to pre-1799 Caughley porcelain, using as a basis the great number of factory wasters that have been found on the site during the past three years. This original idea seemed simple and straightforward.

However, a careful study of the factory wasters and of porcelains that have been attributed to the Caughley factory for over one hundred years, suggested that our accustomed idea of the Caughley products was based on tradition rather than fact. It soon became clear that all previous books had falsely attributed a range of Worcester porcelains to the Caughley factory.

Having separated the Worcester porcelains from the true Caughley examples, it then became necessary to show both, in the same work, so that the often slight differences in shape and pattern could be clearly demonstrated. This book therefore includes many illustrations of Worcester porcelains of the 1770–90 period, and the reason for the new title with the two names, Caughley and Worcester, becomes obvious.

The reader will find much new information in this book as well as statements which contradict those of previous writers. To give but two examples—it can now be affirmed that the series of blue printed disguised Chinese-style numeral marks signifies a Worcester origin, not the Caughley one given in all previous books, and that the filled-in or shaded crescent mark also denotes a Worcester origin, so that, contrary to earlier belief, the Caughley factory did not copy the Worcester printed crescent mark and indeed much of the Caughley output shows no Worcester influence whatsoever.

Much still remains to be discovered about the Caughley products, for new shapes are continually being found and these Shropshire porcelains offer much scope to the new collector. The prices are normally much lower than those asked for more fashionable porcelains in the standard blue printed designs and examples may still be found without too much difficulty (although in recent years prices have risen and examples have become more scarce) while the rarer patterns and shapes turn up from time to time to encourage and reward the diligent collector.

The book illustrates a large range of the factories' productions and I hope, shows the wares in a new light, as being individually attractive and interesting, not mere copies of the contemporary Worcester pieces.

INTRODUCTION TO THE 1981 EDITION

This book was first published in 1969 and was out of print by 1974, since then it has been in very great demand and copies have been sold to my knowledge for £80!

It remains the standard work on these Shropshire porcelains and on the related Worcester shapes and patterns and in view of its special coverage and continuing demand I have been pleased to agree to a limited reprint by the Antique Collectors' Club.

This second printing of specially numbered copies carries, together with this new introduction, additional illustrations as well as other minor amendments, so that it is unique in its own right. It is, however, a reprint of the original book not a revised work. Indeed, I give notice that I hope to publish a completely revised edition devoted entirely to the Caughley wares (excluding the Worcester section present in this edition) at a time subsequent to 1985. I will be very grateful to hear from any readers who may have, or know of, hitherto unrecorded shapes or designs, or who can offer corrections and new information.

I am pleased to be able to claim that no major errors have come to light since this book was published in 1969, although, of course, many hitherto unrecorded shapes and designs have been discovered as interest in the Caughley porcelains spreads.

The one great change — one perhaps occasioned by the book — lies in the new respectability of the Caughley productions and in the great increase in price. Comparing Caughley pieces with similar Worcester examples of the same post-1775 period, one very often now finds the Caughley to be more highly regarded by collectors and such pieces to be higher in price than the Worcester!

A blue-printed bowl similar to that shown in Plate 36 has recently been sold at auction for over £1,000 whereas in the 1950s this illustrated example remained unsold in our shop at £25!

The increases in prices may be expected to continue as more and more collectors open their eyes to the charms and interest of these items and as the available supply continues to diminish. Such little joys as the custard-cups (Plate 111), the eye-baths (Plates 121-122), the ink pots (Plates 127-128), the pounce pots (Plates 162-163), the spoons (Plates 178-179), the delightful miniature pieces (Plates 193-194) or the rare egg cups of the type here illustrated in the additional Plate A, will in price continue to astound the new collector and amuse the older collector who purchased at the low prices current some few years ago.

A. Two rare Caughley porcelain egg cups. The smaller painted with the popular blue 'Royal Lily' design, the other with blue-printed 'Fisherman' design. 1¾ and 2½ in. high. 'S' mark. *c.* 1780-90. *Godden Reference Collection.*

My original revelation that a whole class of blue-printed porcelains bearing one of the series of mock-Chinese so-called disguised numeral marks (see Chapter IX) were of Worcester origin not Caughley has now been universally accepted and such pieces are now proudly on display in the Dyson Perrins Museum at the Worcester Royal Porcelain factory and in the new reference books on Worcester porcelain. I show in additional Plate B one such blue-printed Worcester dessert service dish with its companion reversed to show the mark.

Now that we can see in the various collections a large range of Caughley porcelains, the quality of some of the classes which have been rather neglected by collectors is evident. In particular the rather rare pieces in the style of the then fashionable French porcelains are often of superb quality,

B. A blue-printed Worcester dessert dish, illustrated with its pair reversed to show one of the typical mock-Chinese numeral marks, see Chapter IX. 10½ x 7½ in. *c.* 1780-5. *Godden of Worthing Ltd.*

witness the 'S' marked blue-painted soup plate shown here in Plate C. Were complete matching dinner services made with tureens and such objects? Certainly these restrained French taste designs merit more attention than they have received in the past.

I find many of the gilt patterns particularly tasteful but such designs tend to be rather neglected by collectors. These gold designs occur mainly on tea-wares (see Plates 78-79, 82, 102-103 and 180) and on dessert services and their components. The dessert tureen and ladle shown in my new illustration,

C. A finely moulded Caughley soup plate after a French design. Also painted
in underglaze-blue in the prevailing French taste. Diameter 8¾ in. 'S' mark in
underglaze-blue. *c.* 1780-5. *Godden Reference Collection.*

Plate D, bears witness to the quality of the gilding, much of which was
probably added in the Chamberlain works at Worcester (Chapter V).

The general quality of the gilt Caughley porcelains can also be seen in my
next two illustrations. First in Plate E we have an elegant and workmanlike
mug decorated with an underglaze-blue inner border and insect motif, all enriched with gold. This piece bears the blue 'S' mark. The recorded number of

D. A typical Caughley tureen and ladle from a dessert service, attractively decorated with a gilt design perhaps at the Chamberlain Studio at Worcester. Tureen 5½ in. long. Unmarked. *c.* 1875-90. *Godden of Worthing Ltd.*

these tasteful blue and gold designs is growing almost weekly and such patterns warrant more attention than they are normally given.

The vase-like object depicted in Plate F is, of course, the tea canister from a 'new fluted' tea service. The pattern is in green enamel and gold; such designs are, of course, far rarer than the standard blue-printed wares, indeed, this tea canister is the only specimen bearing this design known to me.

Since the first edition of this book was published some styles which were then thought to be extremely rare have now been proved to be rather less so. I refer to the dessert wares finely hand-painted in under-glaze blue with European landscapes, as Colour Plate V and Plate 38. Some at least of these

E. A most attractive and well potted Caughley mug decorated with underglaze-blue enriched with gilding — probably added at Worcester. 4¼ in. high. 'S' mark in underglaze-blue. *c.* 1785-90. *Godden Reference Collection.*

F. A charming Caughley tea canister and cover from a tea service attractively decorated with a green and gold design probably added by the Chamberlains at Worcester. 4½ in. high. Unmarked. *c.* 1785-90. *Godden Reference Collection.*

designs were copied from originals by Paul Sandby. A magnificent service has recently been brought back to England from America by Miss P. Klaber of Klaber & Klaber, the London dealers. The kidney-shaped dish shown in Plate G is from this set and is one of several pieces now in the Godden collection. Pieces from a related dessert service made for the Darby family are currently on loan to the Ironbridge Gorge Museum collection at the old Coalport factory. The great question remains who painted these dessert wares? The talented hand seems only to appear on these few dessert services. Were they decorated at the Caughley factory? They appear to be painted in underglaze-blue and therefore factory productions but where did the painter come from and where did he go to? Could he have been Thomas Turner himself who reputedly as an engraver would have enjoyed some talent as a draftsman or artist?

The major amendment which will be found in the forthcoming revised edition concerns the last ten years of the Caughley story and the dating of these later pieces.

My own researches in the Chamberlain-Worcester archives indicate

G. An imposing Caughley dish from a dessert service, the scenic centres of which are painted in underglaze-blue by a hand not found on other types of Caughley porcelain. The borders are gilt, see also Colour Plate V. 10¼ x 8 in. Unmarked. *c.* 1785. *Godden Reference Collection.*

strongly that a radical change came over the Caughley teaware shapes in the early 1790s but the scarcity of these pieces suggests that the production was rapidly decreasing. In part this may be due to the Chamberlains making their own porcelains and their seeming break with Thomas Turner of the Caughley factory in 1793.

From about 1790 we have the fashion for spiral-fluted teaware forms apparently introduced by the Flight-Worcester management. Soon the Caughley factory was supplying the Chamberlains with very similar spiral-fluted pieces to which the description 'shankered' or 'shank'd' was applied. In 1792 the Chamberlain accounts include Caughley tea services of this basic type, painted by the Chamberlain decorators with various patterns, such as:

1 complete sett, new shank'd gold edge and line £3. 13. 6.

New shankered Angoulême pattern £5. 5. 0.

1 complete sett tea china, shank'd, different landscapes £8. 8. 0.

Representative pieces from such a landscape panelled teaset are shown here in Plate H. Similar shapes also bear the dove or 'Amitie' pattern seen on the 'new fluted' teaset in my original Plate 75, but these new spiral-fluted shapes will slightly post-date the straight-fluted version which was still being supplied in May 1792, though the new shankered forms were available by at least December 1792 when, for example, we find listed:

1 complete sett, shank'd, Doves, new £6. 6. 0.

H. Representative pieces from a spiral-fluted Caughley tea service of the early 1790s decorated at the Chamberlain Studio in Worcester and sold at £8. 8s. per complete service. Length of spoon tray 6¾ in. Unmarked. *c.* 1792-5. *Godden Reference Collection.*

Interestingly we can, I believe, very closely date one Chamberlain decorated set of Caughley spiral-fluted tewares. We can also show from one Chamberlain letter dated January 12th 1793 that the tea canisters from such sets were being sent down from the Caughley factory by May 31st 1792. This letter quoted in my book on *Chamberlain Worcester Porcelains* lists the 'shank'd canisters' received on various dates in May, June and July 1792.

Such a spiral-fluted Caughley tea canister is shown here in Plate I. This comes from a particularly interesting Caughley tea service, parts of which are in the Godden Reference Collection. The full story of this set is told in my article 'Caughley teawares painted by Fidelle Duvivier' (*Collectors Guide* magazine, August 1978), but here it is necessary only to state that the painting on most pieces is almost certainly by the former New Hall painter Fidelle Duvivier who was apparently only working for the Chamberlains for two weeks in October 1792. Related pieces and shapes of the 1792 period are here shown in Plates J, K and L. They are all relatively thinly potted and are quite different to the traditional blue-printed Caughley porcelains. The undecorated 'wasters' shown in Plate K were found on the Caughley factory site and although the covered sugar bowl is very similar in form to the contemporary Flight-Worcester one, it has several differences particularly in the manner in which the spiral-fluting ends near the edge of the rim of the cover as seen in the site wasters and in the simpler form of the Caughley knob.

I. A most attractive and rare Caughley spiral-fluted tea canister being part of a service believed to have been painted at Worcester by Fidelle Duvivier in October 1792. 4¾ in. high. Unmarked. *c.* 1792. *Godden Reference Collection.*

J. One of two spiral-fluted Caughley bread and butter plates from the service painted at Worcester by Fidelle Duvivier in October 1792. Such shapes emulated the contemporary Flight-Worcester forms. Diameter 7½ in. Unmarked. *c.* 1792. *Godden Reference Collection.*

K. A Caughley sugar bowl and cover (similar to a Flight-Worcester model) shown with undecorated broken wasters from the Caughley factory site. 5 in. high. Unmarked. *c.* 1792. *Godden Reference Collection.*

L. A rare form of Caughley spiral-fluted teapot matching in shape tewares shown in Plates H, J and K. The undecorated knob was found on the Caughley factory site. 6 in. high. Unmarked. *c.* 1792. *Godden Reference Collection.*

These circular spiral-fluted teawares of the 1792 period are very rare and were apparently quickly out of fashion as the new mode oval teapots were coming into use with their oval-plan sugar basins and jugs as is evidenced by accounts and sales lists of the 1792-3 period.

Did the Caughley management follow the fashion for oval teapots and related pieces? The factory site contained numerous broken pieces of such wares but I had attributed these to the post-1799 Coalport management which took over Turner's factory.

I may well have been wrong in this regard for we have about six years from 1793 when these oval teawares were in general fashion. Articles similar to and matching the pieces shown in my additional Plates M, N, O and P are most probably late Caughley rather than early John Rose.

M. A rare spiral-fluted oval-plan Caughley teapot of the form that would have followed that shown in Plate L. 9¼ in. long. Unmarked. *c.* 1792-5. *Mr. and Mrs. P. Miller Collection.*

N. A rare oval covered sugar bowl in a hybrid hard-paste body and bearing the impressed Royal Arms mark, examples of which were found on the factory site. 5½ in. high. *c.* 1795-9. *Godden Reference Collection.*

O. A hybrid hard-paste porcelain oval teapot decorated in underglaze-blue and shown with matching 'wasters' from the factory site; see also Plate 217. Teapot 6½ in. high. Unmarked. *c.* 1795-9. *Godden Reference Collection.*

If this is the case it should follow that the earlier circular plan teapots and the related articles pre-date c.1793.

Most of these shankered oval form teawares are of a harder looking body than the standard early Caughley soap-rock body. The pieces that I would now date to about 1795 onwards are of an even harder looking body and are thickly potted and heavy in weight, quite unlike the traditional Caughley porcelains. We still need, however, to fix the date of this change in paste and dated examples of the 1793-9 period are urgently required to help solve this problem.

The period of the Caughley factory's greatest strength would seem to be in the 1780s with a very real falling off in production from the early 1790s until the factory was taken over by the Coalport management in October 1799, see page 4.

P. Representative pieces of a spiral-fluted teaset of the type previously attributed to the post-1800 John Rose period but now believed to be late Thomas Turner. Teapot 6½ in. high. Unmarked. *c.* 1795-9. *Godden of Worthing Ltd.*

The original items illustrated in Plates 195, 277 and 309 have been replaced with similar articles.

It should be noted that the pattern which I termed the 'Pagoda' pattern (page 18) has now been termed the 'Two Temples Pattern' by Robert Copeland in his excellent book on these popular mock-Chinese blue-printed designs, entitled *Spode's Willow Pattern and other designs after the Chinese* (Studio Vista, 1980).

The blue-printed 'Conversation' pattern (page 21) has now been recorded on teawares, as well as the more usual dinner wares. The popular 'Fisherman' print does occur on the moulded salad dishes (see page 34) of the form shown in Plate 167.

I would now like to draw the reader's attention to some of the new books that have been written since 1969. The following titles should be added to the original bibliography.

Firstly we have the new revised 1973 edition of Dr. Bernard Watney's standard work *English Blue and White Porcelain of the Eighteenth Century* (Faber), a work which features the Caughley porcelains in comparison with the other manufacturer's productions, as does my *Illustrated Encyclopaedia of British Pottery & Porcelain* (Barrie & Jenkins).

We were in 1972 treated to a large exhibition of Caughley porcelains at the Shrewsbury Museum and Art Gallery. This event, called a 'Bicentenary Exhibition', was supported by an excellent catalogue prepared by Michael Messenger, the then Curator.

Also from the pen of Michael Messenger there was published in 1976 a descriptive catalogue of the *Caughley and Coalport Porcelain in Clive House Museum, Shrewsbury*.

As I have explained in Chapter II very many of the blue Caughley designs were copied from, or inspired by, the very popular Chinese porcelains which were flowing into England in vast quantities up to the 1790s. These hard-paste hand-painted (not printed) Chinese wares are illustrated and discussed in detail in my book *Oriental Export Market Porcelain and its influence on European Wares* (Granada Publishing, 1979).

Since 1969 Henry Sandon's excellent book *The Illustrated Guide to Worcester Porcelain* (Barrie & Jenkins) has run to three editions. This book gives a fine review of the Worcester porcelains, the later examples of which were contemporary with the Caughley productions.

As explained in Chapter V Robert Chamberlain in Worcester decorated much of the Caughley porcelains with various gilt and enamelled designs. This important aspect of the Caughley story is related in my 1981 book on *Chamberlain Worcester Porcelain* (Barrie & Jenkins).

In addition to these books a number of papers or articles have been published which will be of interest to the Caughley collector. In chronological order these are:

Polychrome and Hard Paste Caughley Porcelain, by D. Holgate, *Transactions of the English Ceramic Circle,* Vol. 7, No. 1, 1968.

Sources of Decoration on an unrecorded Caughley Dessert Service, by G.B. Roberts, *Transactions of the English Ceramic Circle,* Vol. 10, No. 1, 1976.

Caughley Porcelain — some new shapes and designs, by G.B. Roberts, *The Antique Dealer & Collector's Guide,* May 1976.

Caughley teawares painted by Fidelle Duvivier — The Missing Link, by Geoffrey Godden, *The Antique Dealer & Collector's Guide,* August 1978.

Caughley's shanked shapes, by Geoffrey Godden, *Antiques & Art Monitor,* September 23rd-29th, 1978.

French-style patterns of Caughley, by Michael Messenger, *Antique Dealer and Collector's Guide,* January 1979.

Caughley blue and gold, by Michael Messenger, *Antique Collecting,* January, 1980.

I also take the opportunity of mentioning my tape-recorded talks, one of which is on Caughley; the subjects are Dr. Wall period Worcester, Chamberlain-Worcester, Lowestoft and the Mason wares. Each cassette runs for approximately eighty minutes and is supported by a slim booklet illustrating in group poses typical pieces discussed in the talk. These tapes are available at £5 each from Geoffrey Godden, 17-19 Crescent Road, Worthing, West Sussex. We can also supply details of available reference books and particulars of our Study Meetings.

For those who wish to see collections of Caughley porcelains, since the publication of my book in 1969 and perhaps because of it, the large selection at the Victoria & Albert Museum in London has been rearranged and is both interesting and instructive. The collections housed at Clive House Museum, Shrewsbury are well worth a lengthy detour. Likewise you should not miss the collection now displayed in the new Darby Gallery at the former Coalport factory which is part of the Ironbridge Museum Trust (telephone 0952 580627 for opening hours). Pieces from the Godden Reference Collection are available for inspection, by appointment, at our Worthing showrooms (telephone 0903 35958) which are only open Mondays to Fridays.

I trust you will obtain as much interest and enjoyment from your collecting as I have from mine.

Good hunting!

19 Crescent Road   Geoffrey Godden
Worthing, Sussex, England

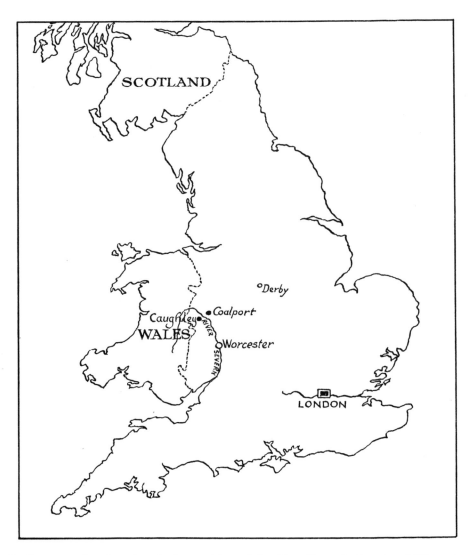

Outline map showing the relative position of the Caughley, Coalport and Worcester factories.

CHAPTER I

GENERAL HISTORY AND MARKS

The site of the porcelain factory at Caughley (pronounced Calf-ley), which is not to be found on any present-day map, not even the standard Ordnance Survey map, is in open country about two miles south of Broseley in Shropshire, in the Parish of Barrow, and not, as some writers have suggested, on the banks of the River Severn for, in fact, the river cannot be seen from any part of the site. The estate map reproduced in Plate I shows clearly its location which is, even today, accessible only along an unmade-up farm track cutting through countryside substantially the same as it was in the eighteenth century.

According to tradition, there was a pottery at Caughley on the estate of Edward Browne[1] from about 1751 to the early 1770s, when Thomas Turner came from the Worcester Porcelain Company to rebuild, or enlarge, the existing pottery and establish on its site the now famous 'Caughley' or 'Salopian' porcelain factory. I have been unable to discover any fresh facts relating to the Caughley pottery or to confirm that there was one on the site before the porcelain factory was established. However, several facts tend to substantiate the tradition:

(a) The site is well situated for a pottery, the underlying clay being suitable for the manufacture of coarse pottery and for the saggers in which it was fired.

(b) Fuel in the form of coal lies under the clay on the site and was later used by Thomas Turner to 'fire' his porcelain.

(c) Fragments of coarse country-styled pottery were found on the site, see Plate 5.

(d) The site is so isolated that it would appear unlikely that Thomas Turner would have chosen it for the site of his porcelain factory if a pottery had not already flourished there. For convenience of transportation he would probably have chosen a situation near to Broseley and a main road, or one nearer the River Severn with its water transport.

[1] The property passed, on Edward Browne's death, to Jane Browne, then in a Will made in 1779 to Ralph Browne Wylde Browne.

1

None of the above points affords conclusive proof that there was a pottery at Caughley between 1751 and 1770, even the discovery of fragments of pottery leaves the subject open to some doubt, for these could have been the broken utilitarian wares used by the workmen at the later porcelain factory, and as they are of the traditional styles of English pottery produced over many years, one cannot state whether they are of the 1760s or of the late 1770s. However, there is nothing to indicate that the tradition is incorrect, and it seems likely that the fragments shown in Plate 5 do represent factory 'wasters' of Caughley pottery of the 1751–70 period.

At one time the original lease for the Pottery may have been in existence, for an article in the *Art Journal* of March 1862 (based in part on material supplied by R. Thursfield of Broseley) states that an Ambrose Gallimore was granted a sixty-two-year lease in 1754. The name Gallimore is associated with that of Thomas Turner, the owner of the Caughley porcelain factory, in some rare 'Caughley' porcelain marks, and it is therefore probable that Turner at first entered into a form of partnership with Gallimore, who had the tenancy of the former Caughley Pottery.

Thomas Turner was born in 1749, the son of Revd. Richard Turner, Rector of Comberton, Worcestershire. He was apprenticed to the Worcester Porcelain Company in the mid-1760s, where he learnt the art of engraving on copper-plates, for the transferring of the design on to porcelain, and probably served under the most famous of all ceramic engravers, Robert Hancock, who was subsequently to be associated with his former pupil's Caughley factory (see below). This training as a ceramic engraver was to prove of the utmost value to him, for some two thirds of his own Caughley porcelain was decorated by this method, which enabled him to undersell the similar products of the Worcester factory. Thomas Turner would appear to have been also a china dealer at Worcester up to at least 1772.

The nineteenth century ceramic historians stated that Thomas Turner left the Worcester company in 1772 and that he built the Caughley porcelain factory on the site of an old pottery on the Browne estate, see Page 1. This date of 1772 is partly substantiated by the recollections of a Caughley workman named Perry (as related in Chaffers' *Marks & Monograms on Pottery & Porcelain* 15th revised edition. Vol. 2, page 135), for Perry remembered seeing a slab on the front of the building 'stating the date of its foundation, 1772'. On the other hand, the first known references to the new Caughley or 'Salopian' porcelain occur in 1775 and are so worded as to suggest, to us now, that in 1775 the Salopian porcelain was a novelty. The first reference appears in Aris's *Birmingham Gazette* of July 3rd, 1775:

SALOPIAN CHINA WAREHOUSE
BRIDGNORTH.

R. Hancock begs leave to acquaint the public and particularly the considerable dealers in china ware, that having disposed of his share in the Worcester work, he is now engaged in the Salopian China Manufactory,

on such terms as enable him to serve the trade at the most moderate rates.
He has already an ample assortment of the blue and white, and will with all
possible expedition proceed in the enamelled or burnt-in china. The sole
province of dealing in this manufactory, except in the London trade, being
assigned over by Mr T. Turner & Co . . . .

The next recorded reference was published on November 1st, 1775, a newspaper
account which read in parts:

. . . The Porcelain Manufactory erected near Bridgnorth, in this County,
is now quite completed, and the proprietors have received and completed
orders to a very large amount. Lately we saw some of their productions,
which in colour and fineness are truly elegant and beautiful, and have the
bright and lovely white of the so much extolled Oriental.

In the absence of other information, it can be presumed that porcelain was not
made on a commercial scale before 1775, when the above-mentioned notices
appeared. The use of the plural term 'proprietors' in this November 1775 notice
is interesting and probably refers to Thomas Turner and Ambrose Gallimore.
As previously stated, the latter is believed to have worked the Pottery on the
site from 1754 and Turner would appear to have entered into partnership with
him, rebuilt the Pottery and commenced the manufacture of transparent porcelain. Some very rare specimens bear marks incorporating the two names—
'Gallimore.Turner.Salopian'.

Caughley transparent porcelain, therefore, dates from 1775 until Thomas
Turner sold the leases to the Coalport porcelain manufacturers, John Rose,
Edward Blakeway and Richard Rose, in October 1799 (Pages 4 and 114).

Some eighty per cent of these Caughley or Salopian porcelains were decorated
in underglaze blue, usually by transferring the inked design from specially engraved copper-plates.

Several of these blue and white designs were close copies of the already
fashionable Worcester patterns and sometimes bore a 'C' initial mark which
may be mistaken for the standard Worcester crescent mark (see Page 8). It
would seem that the Caughley, Worcester-styled, porcelains undersold those of
Worcester and soon Thomas Turner had built up a steady demand for his new
'Salopian' porcelain, both in London and in the County, one of his most important customers being Messrs Chamberlains of Worcester (see Chapter V).

A further source of inspiration was the Chinese porcelains of Nankin-type,
decorated in underglaze blue with Chinese landscape designs. These were flooding into England and were extremely cheap, underselling most of our native
porcelains until high import duties were levied upon the Oriental wares. The link
between these Chinese porcelains and the Caughley factory is very strong and is
enlarged upon in Chapter II.

Not all Caughley shapes or modes of decoration owe their origin to Worcester or Oriental originals, some designs were original. For example, a class of
meticulously painted European landscape patterns in a light, bright blue, seem
unique to Caughley (see Colour Plate V and Plate 38).

3

By about 1780, although the old, standard blue-printed designs were continued, a new style of decoration came into favour, which mainly comprised
floral sprays and borders painted in underglaze-blue with leaves and borders
picked out in burnished gold. These new blue and gold designs were very popular,
being tasteful and reasonably priced, and typical examples are shown in Plates
80–81, 96–97, 114, 125, 145, 196, 206 and 207. The teawares bearing these new
designs are often fluted, and are very neat in their general appearance. Dessert
wares and other objects were also decorated in this style. Of the same period,
c. 1780–90, is a class of wares decorated only with gilding, gold flowers or border
designs (Plates 78–79, 82, 102–3, 112–13, 126, 180, 182–3, 190, 198 and 201).

Identified examples of overglaze enamel painted Caughley porcelains are very
rare, though, as they are largely unmarked, more specimens probably exist. In
the main they display simple floral motifs often copied from Chinese export
market porcelains. A series of moulded cabbage-leaf design jugs with mask-head
spouts, however, prove an exception, for these may be very finely painted with a
rich variety of designs. Typical examples are to be seen in the Victoria and
Albert Museum and in Colour Plate VIII and Plates 67–71. It is possible, however, that these Caughley jugs were sold in their undecorated state and that they
were ornamented by independent specialists in Worcester (Messrs Chamberlains), or in London by James Giles or others. Also of a special nature are the
scale-blue ground dishes painted with panels of exotic birds, one of which is
shown in Colour Plate IX, but these were probably made especially to order as
replacements to a Worcester service. They must not be regarded as typically
Caughley, and may even have had the enamelled exotic birds and gilding added
by Giles in London, although the underglaze scale-blue ground is obviously
factory work.

In October 1799, Thomas Turner sold the leases of the Caughley porcelain
factory with its coal mine, sagger-making works, etc. to John Rose, Edward
Blakeway and Richard Rose, partners in the nearby Coalport porcelain factory,
by whom the Caughley factory was continued for some fifteen years. The surplus
Caughley porcelain was offered for sale by auction and advertised in Eddowes's
Salopian Journal on October 30th. November 6th and 13th, 1799:

SALE BY AUCTION
CHINA WARE

Being the valuable stock of the Royal Salopian porcelain manufactory,
removed to Shrewsbury for the convenience of sale, the property of Thomas
Turner Esq. (who from his indifferent state of health declines continuing
the said manufactory): which said stock will be sold by auction by Jona-
than Perry, on the premises of Mr Ollier, Pride Hill, Shrewsbury, (the
whole of the house being commodiously prepared for that purpose) on
Thursday the 14th November and five following days (Sunday excepted)
the sale to begin each day at 10 o'clock.

The stock consists of a great number of beautiful tea and coffee equip-
ages of various much approved patterns, in full and short sets, richly

executed in enamel and burnished gold together with a great variety of new and elegant blue and white tea and coffee sets, table and dessert services, muffin plates, butter tubs, etc., mugs, jugs, egg cups and drainers, butter cups, custard cups of different sorts and sizes, pickle shells, eye baths, asparagus servers, toy table and tea sets and candlesticks, etc. in pearl white, with a great variety of other articles, both useful and ornamental, the whole of which is directed to be sold without the least reserve.

To be viewed at the place of sale on Monday, Tuesday and Wednesday preceding the same; and catalogues may be had there, and of the auctioneer.

The amount of porcelain offered would seem to have swamped the market, for in the *Salopian Journal* of November 20th 1799, the last advertised day of the original sale, the following extension notice was published:

'The Sale of the Royal Salopian China on Pride Hill will be continued by J. Perry 'til all is sold, to begin each day precisely at 2 o'clock.'

The fact that the Caughley factory leases were taken over by the Coalport partners in October 1799 has resulted in two sources of information being handed down to us on the extent of the estate, for the Coalport partners were declared bankrupt in 1803 (perhaps due to their banking activities) and their various properties were advertised in the *Salopian Journal* on September 21st and 28th, 1803. The Lots relating to Caughley are set out below:

COALPORT & CAUGHLEY CHINA WORKS
To be sold by auction.

By order of the assignees of Edward Blakeway, John Rose & Robert Winter, bankrupts; at the Lion Inn in Broseley, in the County of Salop, on Friday the 30th Day of Sept. instant . . . at 4 o'clock in the afternoon . . .

Lot II All that other (than Coalport work which comprised Lot I) capital CHINA FACTORY, situate at Caughley, in the County of Salop, and 2 acres of land occupied therewith, with the several warehouses, counting houses, kilns, stove houses, and all the other buildings, necessary for carrying on the manufactory of china to a considerable extent. Also all the machinery, implements, utensils, & tools thereto belonging; together with a considerable stock of china, materials, ingredients, and other articles necessary for carrying on the said works. And also all that COLLIERY or COAL WORK nearby adjoining thereto.

The premises forming this lot are held under an Agreement for a lease, 13 years of which were unexpired at Lady Day last (March 25th, 1803), under the yearly Rent of £500, until certain coals called best coals shall be exhausted, and afterwards the sum of £300 per annum during the residue of the said Term. . . .

5

Lot III All that WATER CORN-MILL called Smithies Mill, situate in the Parishes of Willey and Barrow, in the County of Salop. Also that other MILL near thereto, used for the purpose of grinding materials for the use of the china manufactory at Caughley. Also, two TENEMENTS or DWELLING HOUSES and GARDENS, and several pieces or parcels of land thereto adjoining and belonging, containing together about six acres and a quarter; which premises are held by an indenture of lease for the term of 21 years, 19 were unexpired at Lady Day last (March 25th, 1803), under the yearly Rent of £42'. (This Lease would have been drawn up after Blakeway and Rose had purchased the Caughley works from Thomas Turner).

Lot IV All that BARN, STABLE and COW-HOUSE and 69 acres, 1 rod, 2 perch of Land, therewith occupied situate in the Parish of Broseley in the County of Salop, being part of a farm called Broseley Farm. These premises are held for the residue of a term of 15 years, 12 of which were unexpired at Lady Day last (March 25th, 1803), determinable as therein mentioned under the yearly rent of £55'. (This Lease was also drawn up after Thomas Turner had sold the Caughley factory to Blakeway and John Rose).

Lot V All that water mill called CALCUT MILL, with the wheels, Troughs, Machinery and Appurtences thereto belonging, situate in the Parish of Broseley in the County of Salop. This lot is held by an Indenture of Lease for the residue of a term of 18 years, 12 of which were unexpired on the 24th Day of June last under the yearly rent of £17'. (This Indenture of Lease dates back to the period when Thomas Turner worked the Caughley factory).

Lot VI All that other WATER MILL called the UPPER-CALCUT MILL, adjoining Lot V, with the WHEELS, TROUGHS, MACHINERY and appurtences thereto belonging. This Lot is held by an Indenture of Lease for the residue of a term of 19 years, 12 of which were unexpired on the 24 June last under the yearly Rent of £10.

Mr John Rose of Broseley, aforesaid will shew the whole of the Premises, and further particulars may be had by applying to Mr Bird, Solicitor, Birmingham; Mr Timothy Yates of Madeley, Mr C. Guest, the younger, or Mr Prestwich of Broseley, (the assignee of the Estate and effects of the said Bankrupts) or to Mr Pritchard, Attorney, in Broseley aforesaid.

Further information resulted from an arbitration award dated March 6th, 1804, which rose out of a disagreement between Thomas Turner and John Rose and partners on the interpretation of the 1799 agreement when the Coalport partners took over the Caughley leases. This arbitration award was discovered by Mr Franklin A. Barrett and is printed in full in his book *Caughley & Coalport Porcelain* (1951). Interesting extracts relating to the original agreement are:

... The said Thomas Turner did agree to assign amongst other things all
his interest in a Lease from Mr Browne to him of the several works
buildings and erections called Caughley China Works and also the colliery
then held under lease by him from Mr Browne.... The said Thomas Turner
also agreed to assign ... the unglazed stock of goods (the finished wares
were sold by auction, see Page 4) then in and about the said manufactory
and all the materials, implements, fixtures, moulds, copper plates and
machinery belonging to the said manufactory and colliery. ...

It is regrettable that the date or duration of the Browne-Turner lease is not
given, but it probably dated back to 1754 when a sixty-two year lease was granted,
originally to Ambrose Gallimore, and presumably taken over by Thomas
Turner in the 1770s.

Chapters II to IV deal with the blue and white Caughley porcelains which
constitute about three quarters of the factory's productions. The enamelled
porcelains are discussed in Chapter VI and a check list of the different articles
found in Caughley porcelain is given in Chapter VII, but first it is convenient to
list the marks found on these Caughley, or 'Salopian' (to use the original name)
porcelains.

MARKS

The simplest marks found on Caughley porcelain are the impressed name-marks
SALOPIAN, which exist in two main styles, one with a capital 'S' the rest of
the word being in lower-case letters, and the other having all capital letters, see
reproductions below. These name-marks, which would appear to have been used
during the whole period from *c.* 1775 to the late 1790s, are not common but are
occasionally found on plates, dishes, teapot stands and large objects, and also
occur on the rare black basalt earthenwares, which were made in small quantities at Caughley (Plate 83), but other *earthenwares* bearing the impressed name
'SALOPIAN' were made between *c.* 1882 and *c.* 1912 by the SALOPIAN
ART POTTERY CO. of BENTHALL, near BROSELEY.

Reproductions of typical Caughley impressed name marks.

The rarest mark employed at Caughley occurs on a finely moulded mask-head
jug illustrated in Dr. B. Watney's *English Blue & White Porcelain of the 18th
Century* (1963), this rare mark comprises the names 'Gallimore. Turner'
arranged in a circle, enclosing the word 'Salopian' and probably was used on only
a few special early pieces. I have already explained on Page 2 that Gallimore
was potting at Caughley before Turner came from Worcester to rebuild the   7

earlier Pottery and commence the production of porcelain; it is apparent that
Gallimore and Turner worked in partnership for an initial period.

The most common Caughley underglaze blue mark comprises the initial 'S',
which was sometimes accompanied by a small 'x' or 'o', giving marks such as
'Sx' or 'So', although the extra signs may be above, below or before the 'S'
mark. On printed designs, such as the popular Fisherman pattern, the 'S' mark
is printed in underglaze blue but the added 'x' or 'o' (if present) is painted by
hand, suggesting that these additional devices were the printers' piece-rate signs
(or foremen's checking marks) enabling the individual's daily or weekly output
to be gauged and any faulty application of the printed motifs penalized. Very
rarely are these tally marks found without the 'S' factory mark on printed
examples that are obviously of Caughley manufacture and some pieces with just
the cross or circle, also have the impressed 'SALOPIAN' name-mark.

Underglaze blue 'S' initial marks with additional signs 'o' or 'x'.

Pieces painted by hand in underglaze-blue often bear the 'S' mark but here it
is clearly hand-painted, not printed, and not usually accompanied by the printers'
tally marks 'x' or 'o'. Porcelains of the 1780s and 1790s painted with formal blue
and gold motifs (as Plates 80–81, 96–97, 114, 125, 145, 196, 206 and 207, etc.)
often bear the blue 'S' marks, although patterns of the same period without any
underglaze blue in the design are unmarked.

Blue printed patterns may also be marked with a printed 'C' (see below), a
mark which can at a quick glance, though not on examination, be mistaken for

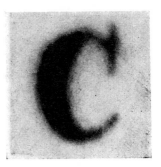

Blue printed Caughley 'C' mark.

a small crescent mark. This mark 'C', which is rather rarer than the standard 'S'
mark and is not accompanied by the 'x' or 'o' tally marks often found with the
latter, is also found on nineteenth century Coalport porcelains decorated with
eighteenth century blue-printed designs, see Page 116 and Plates 220 and 221.

On some early hand-painted blue patterns a 'C'-like *open* crescent (see below) is sometimes found, but this is quite rare (see Plates 48 and 55) and the mark does not appear on the 1780–95 blue and gold designs.

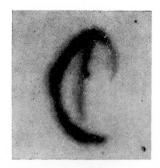

Hand painted C-like open crescent mark rarely found on early Caughley porcelains.

A filled-in, or shaded, crescent is found on much blue printed porcelain *attributed* to the Caughley factory, but this device would appear to have been *very* sparingly (if at all) used at Caughley, and examples bearing the filled-in crescent seem to be of Worcester manufacture (see Page 125). An *open* crescent can occur on *printed* Caughley porcelains as some 'pulls' from the original copper-plates show that this open crescent was engraved on some of these plates (see Page 43). On the other hand Worcester blue-printed porcelains bear a filled-in printed crescent, not an open, unshaded one. The Caughley open crescent also occurs on late Coalport porcelain, which was printed from the original Caughley engraved copper plates (see Page 116 and Plates 218–19).

Worcester shaded crescent mark.

A freely drawn version of the horn-mark of the French Chantilly factory has been attributed to the Caughley factory, but these rare porcelains appear to be of Worcester manufacture and it is noteworthy that the many Caughley examples with the blue Chantilly sprig designs bear the 'S' mark, not the horn device (see Plates 57, 92 and 129).

Caughley plates and dishes decorated with a powder-blue ground, with various reserve panels painted with Chinese-styled landscapes or floral motifs, as shown in Plate 26, sometimes bear mock-Chinese characters, (see below for a typical example). Powder-blue Bow and Worcester specimens may, however, bear similar markings. Some Caughley examples also bear the impressed name mark SALOPIAN, and some pieces bear the 'S' or open crescent marks rather than the Chinese characters.

Underglaze blue Chinese-styled character mark on powder-blue plate
(see Plate 26).

Some fine quality oval baskets are recorded with the impressed or relief moulded mark 'To', a device often associated with the 'repairer' or modeller known as Tebo. (This mark is found also on Bow porcelains *c*. 1750–60, on Worcester porcelains *c*. 1760–9, and on Bristol porcelains *c*. 1770–3. In 1775 he was with Wedgwood's but apparently did not remain there for long). The basket shown in Plate 90 has the relief moulded initials 'IT' which would have been incised into the mould, resulting in the raised letter on the finished article, and may well refer to the same modeller or repairer.

It has been suggested that the rare examples found with the 'To' mark were of Worcester manufacture, decorated at Caughley. This theory seems rather unlikely for, apart from the fact that the baskets are of a later date than Tebo's presumed period at Worcester (*c*. 1760–9), the Caughley decoration is under the glaze, indicating that the *unglazed* baskets must have been sent from Worcester to Caughley and this is a troublesome process. Unglazed as well as overfired, decorated, basket fragments were found on the Caughley site, and it is highly significant that some of the *unglazed* fragments are distorted and must have been made at Caughley, for a distorted, badly-fired example made at Worcester would have been destroyed at Worcester, not shipped up the Severn to Caughley. In my opinion the baskets found with the 'IT' or 'To' marks were made at Caughley, for they differ from the Worcester examples. I also believe that the marks do *not* relate to the mysterious Mr. Tebo, who is mentioned in many books, but rather to a china modeller named John Toulouse. An incised cross also occurs on Caughley baskets of this type, and on other Caughley porcelains, but the device is found on porcelains from several eighteenth century factories.

A further 'repairer's' or workman's mark of an impressed (or incised) star device (see Plate 109) is found occasionally on Caughley porcelains. Strangely this star often appears inside the foot of the small cream-boats shown in Plate

108, but not on any other form of creamer or sauce-boat. An incised 'H' is found on some rare, ornate pieces and this initial is associated with Francois Hardenburg, who was employed at Caughley for an unknown period up to 1788, and then employed at Derby as a modeller.

The marks mentioned previously are not by any means to be found on all Caughley porcelain, for nearly half the total production of the factory was unmarked. With the exception of some rare impressed marked 'SALOPIAN' pieces, all examples decorated *only* with overglaze enamel colours, or only with gilding, are unmarked.

These unmarked specimens can usually be correctly identified by close reference to the shapes and patterns illustrated in this book, which show marked specimens or examples that match factory 'wasters' found on the Caughley site.

Wares bearing the name-mark 'TURNER' or 'TURNER'S PATENT' are of Staffordshire origin and were not made at Caughley.

Some authorities state that Caughley porcelain was sometimes marked with the Worcester 'W' initial mark, but again I believe these pieces are true Worcester porcelains, not Caughley copies.

The various disguised numerals ranging from one to nine decorated with Chinese-styled flourishes are given in all previous ceramic works of reference as Caughley marks but, for the reasons given on Pages 117 to 125, I regard these devices as Worcester marks of the 1770–90 period. I also regard all shaded crescent marks as denoting a Worcester origin, see Pages 125–135.

The important facts leading to the re-attribution to Worcester of a class of porcelains hitherto regarded as of Caughley origin are given separately in Chapter IX, at the end of the Caughley section.

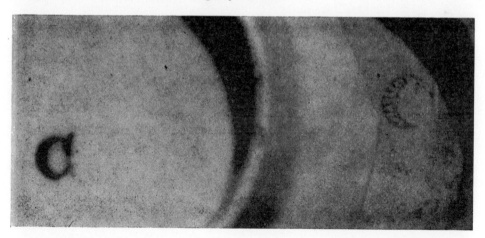

The photographs above show two fragments, one from the Caughley site, showing the typical Caughley printed 'C' mark, the other, unglazed waster is from the Worcester site and shows the blue printed crescent mark with shading, as used on Worcester porcelains but not on Caughley wares. The reader can see that these two marks are not easily confused.

It is convenient to define at this stage, by means of simple outlined drawings, 11

what is meant by the terms 'triangular', 'square' or 'undercut' footrims. The
differing ways in which the footrim was trimmed by the 'turners' can be a great
help in correctly attributing a piece to Caughley, to Worcester or to the Liverpool factories.

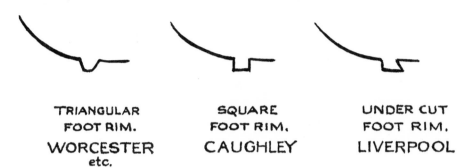

TRIANGULAR FOOT RIM.	SQUARE FOOT RIM.	UNDER CUT FOOT RIM.
WORCESTER etc.	CAUGHLEY	LIVERPOOL

CHAPTER II

CAUGHLEY ORIENTAL-STYLED BLUE PATTERNS

The influence of the imported Chinese blue and white 'Nankin' type porcelain on the Caughley (and Worcester) wares was considerable and, in fact, these imported Oriental patterns probably provided Thomas Turner's main competition, for even though the Chinese porcelains had to be transported half-way across the world they were often cheaper than our native products. In August 1790 Joseph Lygo (see Page 154) wrote:-

> I have been to the Salopian Warehouse to enquire about the wash-hand bason and jugs blue and white, they have got 4 common ones only and the price is 10/6d each, Chamber pots they have none, they have not made any for some time and the reason is foreign Nankin ones are so much cheaper than theirs. . . .

The amount of Chinese porcelain flooding into England (and other European countries) during the second half of the eighteenth century was truly enormous. It was so fashionable at this period, especially for dinner services, that it seems to have been owned by half the middle and upper class families of the period. It was available at a price that Worcester or Caughley could not match, even when the English potters used printed versions of the hand-painted Chinese designs in an effort to reduce costs.

In July 1794 the following dinner service was sold:

> A fine oval Nankin table service of the fine Willow landscape, and dagger border, containing 18 long dishes in 6 sizes, 72 table plates, 24 soup plates, 24 dessert plates, 2 large tureens and dishes, 2 small ditto, 4 sauce boats, 4 stands, 2 large salad vessels and 6 pudding dishes.   £33. 12. 0.

This price works out at just under 4s 3d per unit, and this is higher than many other contemporary references that could be cited. The higher than average price is perhaps accounted for by the quality of the painting, for it seems likely 13 that the 'oval Nankin . . . Willow landscape, and dagger border' design was the same as the Chinese porcelains illustrated in Plate 15. The same design is found printed on Caughley porcelain teawares (Plate 14).

While the English manufacturers could not compete with the Chinese *dinner* services with their large dishes, heavy tureens and numerous plates, they could apparently compete with dessert and tea services, so that, while English blue and white dinner services are extremely rare, teawares comprise well over half the whole output of the Caughley factory. This is not to say that the Chinese potters did not produce tea services, they did, but the Oriental blue and white tea and dessert services are rarer than the English examples.

It now seems probable that Thomas Turner dealt in the inexpensive Chinese Nankin porcelain at Caughley, supplying Oriental porcelain dinner wares and other objects when his own supplies were low or when his customers required the Nankin porcelains. This impression is borne out by the large number of fragments of Nankin blue and white porcelain found on the Caughley factory site, a small selection of which is shown in Plate 9. It is also probable that some of the gilding found on Chinese porcelains, mainly on teawares, was added at Caughley, although some of these gilt enrichments were added at Worcester, Derby and by the London decorators.

It is most certainly true that the imported Chinese porcelains had much influence on those of Caughley and, strangely, it also seems that on occasions the Chinese potters copied the English designs. Several of the printed patterns commonly found on Caughley porcelain and discussed in the following pages are obviously based on hand-painted Chinese blue and white Nankin porcelains, and one of the standard Shropshire teapot forms, shown in Plate 81, derives from a Nankin original. The main features are the relief-moulded spout and handle, the latter with an applied heart at the top and at the lower end (a Chinese part-handle of this design was found on the Caughley site with several Caughley versions of the same design, both glazed and unglazed, together with a plaster of Paris mould for such a handle, see Plate 199).

The Chinese Nankin blue and white teaset shown in Plate 11 is interesting. The teapot shape is the standard Caughley one, even to the ribbing in the body. The same moulded handle appears, reduced, on the coffee cup, and also on the Caughley cups, while the wavy-edged saucers, tea bowls and waste bowl are found on both Caughley and Nankin sets. Colour Plate VI (Page 56) shows a Caughley part teaset following the orental shapes.

For evidence that the Chinese potters also copied some Caughley (or Worcester) patterns and shapes, I would ask the reader to turn to Plate 12, which illustrates a Chinese pierced cress-dish and stand of a typical Worcester and Caughley design, and other Chinese copies include an intricately moulded salad bowl of a pattern found in Caughley (see Plate 167), Lowestoft and Worcester porcelains, and I have seen Chinese copies of these English shapes with a crescent mark. The Oriental potters also made articles of Chantilly shape and standard pattern, these Chinese copies sometimes bearing the French factory's mark—a

hunting horn, showing clearly that the Chinese were working to European prototypes. The explanation of this remarkable situation is simply a matter of economy, for the European retailer could order copies from China that, when imported into France or England, still undersold the original European product.

The Caughley blue and white porcelains bearing patterns with Chinese influence are discussed on subsequent pages in the following order:

(a) Printed scenic designs, pages 16–22.
(b) Hand-painted scenic designs, pages 22–24.
(c) Printed figure patterns, pages 24–26.

In regard to the printed scenic patterns, which comprise a large percentage of the factory's production, the following features should be noted:

(1) All shading is produced by closely engraved parallel lines or crossed lines, except where the foreground has been enlarged to fill gaps shown up by badly placed prints. Washes of colour may appear on *Worcester* porcelains, as shading on the same general type of pattern, see Plates 236, 238–42, 267 and 305.

(2) Each design may occur in its plain state (that is with just the underglaze-blue print) or with gilt borders, handles, knobs, etc. Although some overgilding was undoubtedly added by independent decorators, some was added at the Caughley factory, as gilt 'wasters' found on the site suggest.

(3) All printed Chinese-styled landscape designs listed bear (when marked) clear Salopian printed initial marks, such as 'S', 'Sx' or 'So'. They do not bear crescent or Chinese numeral marks, which denote a Worcester origin (see Chapter IX).

Before proceeding with the list of Chinese-type landscape designs, a word must be said about the Willow pattern. Almost every collector's reference book states that Thomas Turner (or Thomas Minton, while employed at Caughley) introduced the Willow pattern on Caughley porcelain, yet the version so popular during the whole of the nineteenth century and produced by nearly every manufacturer does NOT occur on Caughley porcelain. The salient features of the traditional English 'Willow pattern' design are buildings in the centre or to the right of centre, a prominent Willow tree and two or three figures crossing a bridge to the left, away from the building, two doves being normally placed in the sky above the fleeing lovers! A fence runs across the foreground, and a wide, ornate Chinese-styled border design encloses the whole.

No Caughley blue-printed pattern features a Willow tree *with* figures crossing a bridge away from the buildings. The only Caughley design to feature prominently a Willow tree is the rare pattern shown in Plate 14, but no bridge or fence is shown. The term 'Willow landscape' was used in the eighteenth century (see Page 13), and this probably relates to the Chinese design shown in Plates 10 and 15, which was copied on Caughley porcelains.

The traditional Willow pattern design as it has been known for some one hundred and fifty years, was probably introduced by the Staffordshire potters early in the nineteenth century for the decoration of their earthenwares, which must have undersold the Caughley porcelains. Perhaps the design was indeed first engraved by Thomas Minton, who is said to have been trained as an engraver at Caughley before he established his own engraving business, and later his own pottery. Minton may well have amended standard Caughley designs or taken parts from several to make a whole new pattern.

CHINESE-STYLED WILLOW PATTERN TYPE DESIGNS

Willow-Nankin pattern

The Willow-tree design, shown in Plate 14 and in the 'pull' from the original Caughley engraving, should not be confused with the traditional Willow pattern, for this Caughley one does not include a bridge. It shows an island and buildings

on the right, with a Willow-type tree in the foreground leaning to the left over water, and a small island in the top left corner with two dove-like birds flying above, the uppermost performing a remarkable U-turn!

This printed design is in many respects quite charming and modern. The roofs of the buildings have 'candy stripes' and an unusual 'swiss-roll' type of edging to the small island. The Caughley version has a simple cell outer border, with a *fleur-de-lis*, or dagger, inner border, a pattern which is also found on Chinese Nankin porcelains (Plates 10 and 15). The same basic design is also found on Chinese 'Nankin' porcelains with an ornate 'Fitzhugh'-type border incorporating butterflies (Plate 10) which John Rose copied on his hard-paste porcelain after taking over the Caughley factory in 1799.

16

The Caughley versions normally bear blue-printed 'S', 'Sx' or 'So' marks which are found on teawares and small objects such as custard cups.

A very similar Willow pattern is found, but rarely, on Chinese Nankin-type blue and white porcelain, and a 'pull' from a Caughley copper-plate also depicts

this version with the addition of a boat pulling away from the bank in the left foreground (see above and Plate 10). The pattern is not found on Worcester wares.

Temple Pattern

The pattern name 'Temple' is used many times in the Chamberlain correspondence and accounts, and relates to Caughley blue-printed porcelain. It is probable that it refers to this pattern illustrated below, but it could equally

17

well refer to similar patterns with Temple-like buildings incorporated in the design. Similar contemporary names for these patterns were 'Pagoda' and 'Broseley Nankin'.

The so-called 'Temple' pattern, found almost exclusively on tewares, is illustrated in Plate 16. The main features are two pagoda-type temples with trees between and a figure on horseback crossing a stone-block bridge, with an attendant holding a very long-handled sunshade over the rider. Two figures are standing in a white reserve in the blue shaded foreground.

Porcelains bearing this printed subject normally also bear the printed 'S' mark, sometimes with the workman's 'x' or 'o' added. A close copy of this design is found on Worcester porcelains but here it appears to be hand-painted, not printed (see Plate 261).

Striped Temple Pattern

A very rare Temple pattern includes a Chinese-type Temple on an island, with prominently striped blue and white roofing, and a pot of flame-like foliage standing on a table to the left of the Temple. A garden fence incorporating Swastika-like devices runs down the left side of the island and across the foreground (see Plate 17), a bridge links the main island with a smaller one to the left and two figures are crossing the bridge.

A wide ornate Chinese-style border is associated with this very rare design, not found on Worcester porcelain.

Pagoda Pattern

The 'Pagoda' pattern, normally marked with a printed 'S' and found mainly on tewares, incorporates a series of ornate and tall Chinese styled Pagoda-type

buildings on an island. A small bridge, which two figures are crossing to the right, links the main island with a smaller one on the left (see Plates 18 and 195, also the reproduction of a 'pull' from an original Caughley engraved copperplate of this design, reproduced above). The name 'Pagoda' occurs in the contemporary Chamberlain accounts and probably relates to this design, which is also found on eighteenth century Chinese blue and white 'Nankin' porcelains. A very near copy of it is found on rare early Coalport porcelains but not on Worcester wares.

Fence Pattern

The well-known fence-pattern, as reproduced below from an original Caughley copper-plate, is quite rare on Caughley porcelain, but its Worcester counterpart is relatively common. Examples bearing the printed, shaded crescent mark

are Worcester, and the rarer Caughley version will be found with a clear 'C' or 'S' mark. Many different copper-plates were engraved with this fence-mark so that several slight differences occur (see Pages 132–3,—and Plate 19). The design is also found on Lowestoft porcelains.

Fenced-Garden Pattern

The Fenced-garden design is shown in Plate 20. A tall Chinese-styled building is placed in the centre with a high fence enclosing a garden in front, within which two figures are standing. A low bridge is on the left but no figures are seen on it. The secondary print showing an island to the left of the main one includes a small house raised on high, ladder-like supports, an attractive formal floral border surrounding the complete design.

This printed design is normally marked with the 'S' mark, often with the workman's 'x' or 'o' signs, and it is mainly found on teawares, but not on Worcester specimens.

Fence and House Pattern

The fence and house design differs from the fence pattern found on Worcester porcelains (compare Plate 21 with Plates 262, 263 and 288). The main features, as seen below, are three large rock-like boulders in the foreground, with a large

bamboo-like, four-branched tree spreading from the boulders. A fence runs prominently across the main design with two small houses in the centre under the tree. On saucers, only half the design is shown, so that the boulders, tree and houses are on the right hand side of the design, not in the centre. A smaller version of this main design is found in a circular outline in the centre of bowls.

This pattern is normally found on teawares and is found with the 'S', 'Sx' or 'So' marks. It does not occur on Worcester porcelains.

'Full Nankin' Pattern

A 'pull' from an original Caughley engraved copper-plate is reproduced below, the main design is extremely cramped, comprising a large built-up island on the

left, a smaller one on the right joined by a boulder-work bridge, with two figures crossing.

This ornate, cramped design is found on dessert and dinner wares, not on teawares. The dessert and dinner wares also include sauce-boats, tureens, various dishes and even sandwich sets (see Plates 22, 117–18, 171–76 and 205). This 'Full Nankin' design does not appear on Worcester porcelain, but birds arranged in this V-formation are to be found on many Chinese Nankin-type blue and white porcelains. The original name for this pattern would appear to be 'Full Nankeen' as this description is used in the Chamberlain-Caughley records for dessert services, and this printed design is the only one so far recorded on dessert wares.

Conversation Pattern

The very rare 'Conversation' design (see below) comprises a background of Chinese pagoda-styled buildings with two figures in a white reserve in the dark-blue foreground. The figures, facing each other as if in conversation, do not hold

the normal sunshade and their feet often do not show; in fact, the figures have the general appearance of tadpoles! (Plate 23.)

The design, which occurs on dinner wares and bears the printed 'S' mark, is not found on Worcester porcelains.

Uninhabited Pagoda Pattern

The Chinese-style Temple, or Pagoda, designs previously discussed have featured figures in doorways, windows, or in the foreground. As may be expected the un-inhabited Pagoda design does not show any figures, the windows and doorways being blank, although two figures are depicted crossing a bridge to the left of the main design (see Plate 24). This rare Caughley blue printed design was not employed at Worcester.

Cottage Pattern

The so-called Cottage design, an example of which is seen on a custard cup and cover (Plate 111), is rare and shows two sets of buildings of cottage-type (not as 21 ornate as the pagoda-type buildings seen in other patterns) separated by a tree, with an empty shaped bridge on the left, the whole being enclosed in a simple Chinese-styled cell border. This pattern is not found on Worcester porcelains.

Bandstand Pattern

This rare bandstand design (see below) should not be confused with the Worcester pattern of the same name which normally bears disguised Chinese-styled numeral marks (see Page 120 and Plate 242).

On it a bandstand-like building is shown near the centre with other buildings to the right. One figure can be seen in the bandstand but, unlike the Worcester version, no steps are visible. Two small islands are shown on the left-hand side of the design, connected by a bridge, but having no connection with the larger one containing the 'bandstand'. Examples of this rare pattern have the 'S', 'So' or 'Sx' marks in underglaze blue.

Fitzhugh-Type Border

This wide, ornate border-design (reproduced on Page 23), much used on Chinese porcelains, comprises many interlinked different cell motifs with formal outspread butterflies or moths prominently displayed. This basic border design is found with the 'Pagoda' pattern (see Page 18 and Plate 18) and the 'Fence & House' design (Page 20, Plate 21), and also occurs with the Ironbridge print (Plate 36). This so-called 'Fitzhugh' border can be found on other wares including John Rose's Coalport porcelains and Chinese porcelains.

It occurs now and again on Caughley porcelains merely as a border without any centre design. It is, however, enhanced with a gilt inner border (see Plate 25). I have not noticed this border motif on Worcester porcelains.

Hand-Painted Chinese Styled Designs

Amongst the hand-painted (as opposed to the printed designs discussed previously) Chinese-styled designs are at least two patterns found with a powder-blue ground, as shown in Plate 26. The reserve panels show rather naïvely painted Chinese-styled landscapes. The example shown in Plate 26 bears the impressed name mark 'SALOPIAN' as well as a Chinese-styled blue painted mark (Page 10).

A further class of powder-blue ground Caughley porcelain has a stylized floral centre with eight panels in the normally dark powder-blue ground, examples of which are usually marked with the initial 'S', although the 'C' mark is also found. A slight variation of this design, sometimes bearing a crescent mark seems to be of Worcester origin.

Pull from Caughley copper-plate, showing typical Fitzhugh border designs. See page 22.

One of the most charming of the Caughley Chinese landscape designs is one which occurs on dessert wares, always painted in a bright blue. Although the design has in the past been illustrated as of Derby origin, it occurs only on known Caughley shapes, and many fragments of the pattern were found on the factory site (see Plate 164).

The painting and especially the treatment of the figure in the left foreground, is child-like. The border (shown in Plate 27) is peculiar to this pattern, in which painters' marks such as a cross, lines, or other small devices appear, sometimes inside the footrim. The pattern appears to be restricted to Caughley and Chinese porcelains.

The bridge pattern is a rare, hand-painted Caughley design found on teawares, where a curved bridge links two very small islands, each having a small building set upon it. The reverse, or subsidiary, pattern shows a child-like painting of a windmill between two small buildings, and a simple criss-cross line border completes the design (see Plate 29). It is not found on Worcester porcelains.

A further hand-painted Chinese styled landscape design I have termed the 'Tower', on account of the tall tower-like building seen in the centre of an island (see Plate 28). The pattern is very child-like and three trees appear to grow from

23

a cloud above the tower. Several fragments were found on the Caughley site, some in a finished glazed state, some unglazed, and although the tower pattern is not found on Worcester porcelains, it does occur on post-1799 Caughley-Coalport hard-paste porcelains.

Another child-like, hand-painted design occurs occasionally and uniquely on Caughley porcelains, normally on small thickly potted saucers. A fragment is shown in Plate 29 and complete specimens are in the Victoria and Albert Museum.

Yet another hand-painted Caughley pattern features, within a simple criss-cross border, a very tall, slender tree with two lower ones on the left, all growing from a lower island, and a plough-like object is painted at the extreme left of the island. The pattern is rare and sometimes bears an open crescent mark, but also occurs on Worcester porcelain.

A series of charming miniature, or child's, tea and dinner services (and, of course, odd pieces from such sets) is found with a hand-painted Chinese-like island design. This pattern has a central tree with two small hut-like houses, which are frequently off the island, at each side of the island. Two sailing ships are depicted in the foreground of most pieces, but on some small objects these are not present.

Numerous fragments of these children's teasets were found on the factory site, several pieces in a half-complete state. Typical wares with this design are shown in Colour Plate IV (Page 44) and Plate 30.

The low creamer shown in Plate 107 bears another rare Caughley hand-painted design. Some other hand-painted designs were apparently made, for fragments were found on the factory site, but as yet no complete specimens have been reported.

Chinese-Styled Figure Designs

Having discussed the various Chinese-styled scenic designs, we can now turn to the patterns incorporating Chinese figures. Whereas most of the former are confined to the Caughley factory (and to porcelains of Oriental manufacture) the figure patterns are common to both Worcester and Caughley, the slight differences between the two versions being listed in Chapter IX.

La Pêche

This design depicts a seated lady holding a fishing rod, with a second figure standing behind a gate-like structure (Plate 31 and Page 133).

This design is normally found in conjunction with 'La Promenade Chînoise'.

La Promenade Chînoise

A tall Chinese lady stands holding a sunshade over her left shoulder; a small boy stands against the mother's far side. Ornamental garden structures are seen to right and left (Plate 32). This design is normally found in conjunction with

'La Pêche' (see above and Page 133).

Fisherman design

This well-known design is so important to the study of Caughley porcelain
and occurs on such a variety of shapes that Chapter III is devoted entirely to it.

Bell-toy Pattern

In this pattern a Chinese lady sits by a tub of fruit and a jardinière-like object.
Her child stands on one side of her and holds out a stick-toy comprising four
bells on crossed arms, while a vase of flowers stands on the opposite side. One
cannot write of left or right with this design, for in some versions the design is
reversed, showing the vase on the right instead of the left. This pattern is depicted in Plates 34 and 149.

The subsidiary print found on the reverse of cups, tea bowls and other objects
shows a group of three vases, two of which hold plants. Its border is normally
a simple blue edge line. Caughley examples are often marked with the printed
'S' mark, sometimes with the workman's 'o' or 'x' sign, giving 'Sx' or 'So'.

This design was one of the earliest employed on Caughley porcelain, for it is
found on the mug dated 1776 in the Victoria and Albert Museum (Plate 149).
It also appears on teawares but is one of the rarer Caughley designs, and the
subject was re-used by the Coalport partners on their post-1799 hard-paste
porcelain. The original name of this pattern was probably 'Image', the Chamber-
lain/Caughley accounts contain several references to 'Image' or 'Image-blue
edge' teawares. However, the name could equally well relate to the close version
discussed on the next page.

Mother and Child, or Seated-figure Pattern

This design, normally found on teawares, is basically very similar in the main components to the 'Bell-toy' pattern just discussed, the main difference being that the child, instead of holding aloft a prominent bell-toy, now holds a small clover-leaf shaped hand-fan, which is held close to the body in the crook of his right elbow (see Plate 35).

The subsidiary print found on the reverse of cups and other round objects is very similar to that found on the 'Bell-toy' pattern, depicting three vases (two with plants) and a church-like building (see Plate 255). This pattern also has a simple blue-line border. It is often unmarked but may bear the printed 'S' or 'C' initial marks, although rare examples with a hand-painted open crescent are found. The printed and shaded crescent mark occurs on Worcester versions of this design, which can be distinguished by several small differences in the print (see Page 134).

Apart from the Fisherman pattern to be discussed in Chapter III, only four Caughley patterns feature Chinese figures. However, the engraved copper-plates passed down to the Coalport porcelain company with other Caughley engraved designs included the following:

L'Oiseau Chînois, showing a Chinese standing figure by an elaborate standing bird cage. The print is found on Worcester and Derby porcelain, but I have not seen it applied to Caughley wares. See C. Cook's *The Life and Work of Robert Hancock* (1948) Item 76.

La Dame Chînoise, depicting a very tall Chinese lady preceding an attendant holding a sunshade over her, while a small boy runs in front holding a bird on a stick. The subject was probably engraved by Robert Hancock, and versions are found on Bristol, Derby and Worcester porcelain, but as yet I have not seen the design applied to Caughley porcelain, although the management had available an engraved copper-plate of it. See C. Cook's *The Life and Death of Robert Hancock* (1948) Item 26, and 'Pull' reproduced below.

CHAPTER III

THE FISHERMAN PATTERN

The design (see Colour Plate I) we now know as the 'Fisherman' pattern was originally, in the eighteenth century, called 'Pleasure Boat'. It is of vital importance for the study of Thomas Turner's Caughley porcelain, for it enables us to distinguish between his productions and the similar blue-printed Worcester porcelains. Further, it is found on a wide range of Caughley porcelain, and records of the original prices for many of these articles have been preserved. These are, of course, most interesting and in many instances the prices charged for the popular 'Fisherman' pattern serve as a guide to other standard printed designs.

From the collector's point of view this pattern has the great advantage that, on the one hand, examples (especially of teawares) can be found with little difficulty while on the other, the hope of discovering a rare piece adds zest to his search. An almost complete range of Caughley shapes can be discovered in this one pattern, the objects ranging in size from a miniature jug only 2 inches high to large punch bowls or moulded cabbage-leaf jugs.

The differences between the Caughley and the Worcester versions of this print are explained in Chapter IX, on Page 131, and shown in Plates 229–32. To summarize briefly, it can be stated that all Caughley examples show:

(a) A tight, straight fishing line being used by the seated fisherman who is shown on an island depicted above the main standing fisherman, except on some very small objects, which do not include this seated figure.

(b) The inner *fleur de lis* type border is fully shaded, and does not show parallel lines for shading.

(c) The Caughley standing fisherman is tall and lean, and whereas the fish he is holding is short and fat, the Worcester fish is long and slender.

Many other minor differences can be discovered by the reader by examining a Worcester example alongside a marked Caughley one, or by comparing Plate 229 with Plate 230.

When marked, the Caughley 'Fisherman' designs bear the printed 'S' mark, often with workmen's signs such as 'x' or 'o' painted by hand, resulting in 'Sx' or

'So' marks. The impressed SALOPIAN name mark may occur on plates or large objects. 'Fisherman' decorated porcelains bearing the filled-in crescent mark or any of the fancy disguised numeral marks (see Page 117) are NOT of Caughley origin and, for the reasons given in Chapter IX, they are attributed to Worcester.

The source of the contemporary prices quoted on the following pages is the Chamberlain account books, which record amongst other wares a large range of Caughley porcelain purchased from Thomas Turner for sale in Chamberlain's retail shop in Worcester. While a fuller review of this intertrading between Turner of Caughley and Chamberlain at Worcester is given in Chapter V, in this section we are concerned solely with the 'Fisherman' or 'Pleasure Boat' design. Most examples show only the underglaze-blue design but some rare specimens were embellished with gilt edges and inner borders, which may have been added by Chamberlain at Worcester or by some of the London decorators and gilders.

The following list is arranged in alphabetical order and includes articles mentioned in the Chamberlain accounts, and objects recorded as having this underglaze-blue printed pattern. The list may subsequently prove to be incomplete, if fresh 'Fisherman' articles are reported as a result of the awakening interest in Caughley porcelains.

Artichoke Cups

These cups were made in two sizes, each being sold at 4d, although some references use the term 'Artichoke cups' and others 'artichoke butter cups', it would seem that both descriptions relate to a small covered cup such as is illustrated in Plate 85.

Asparagus Servers

These open-ended objects (Plate 86) are often called knife rests in error. Contemporary accounts show clearly their real use and original name. They were sold at 6d each, the same price as was charged for egg cups, eye baths and other small objects.

The 'Fisherman' print is normally found placed in an upright position but it was occasionally applied in a sideways manner. Asparagus servers were mentioned in the advertisement for the last sale of Caughley stock held in November 1799 (see Page 5).

Baking Dishes

These oval, deep-sided dishes were made in at least eight sizes. Specimens are today very rare, as might be expected with purely utilitarian objects which are discarded as soon as their useful life is finished. An example is shown in Plate 87 and this, like most baking dishes, bears the impressed 'SALOPIAN' name mark.

The Chamberlain accounts record, in most cases, only the prices for 'seconds', that is, slightly faulty examples. The cost of perfect pieces would be about one third higher. The prices for 'seconds' were:

1st size	1/-
2nd ,,	1/-
3rd ,,	1/2d
4th ,,	1/4d
5th ,,	1/8d (price for 'best' 2/6d)
6th ,,	2/- (price for 'best' 3/-)
7th ,,	2/8d
8th ,,	2/8d (price for 'best' 4/-)

The extremely rare, shaped-edged dish shown in Plate 88 may be a baking, or pie, dish as it is much deeper than a normal dessert service dish.

Baskets

The normal form of Caughley or Worcester basket is oval with twig handles at each end—as Plate 90 but I have yet to find one of these with the blue printed 'Fisherman' subject.

An attractive circular basket was, however, made and two examples of differing sizes are shown in Plate 91, where one has been reversed to show the raised flowers applied at the junctions of the pierced design.

Basons

A 'bason' is a small bowl holding up to a pint of liquid. The waste or slop-bowl found with teasets is therefore correctly termed a bason. 'Bowls' on the other hand held upwards of a quart.

Basons were made in three basic sizes, to hold a quarter of a pint, half a pint or a pint. The average diameter of such bowls at the top edge is $4\frac{1}{4}$, 5 and 6 inches, but these sizes may vary according to the depth of the bason. Standard prices for basons bearing the 'Fisherman' print were 5d for the quarter pint size, 8d for the half pint and 1s for the pint bason.

Bowls

As explained under the heading of 'basons', the term 'Bowl' was used only for large vessels containing a quart or more of liquid. The quart size decorated with the 'Fisherman' print was 2s, the three pint size 3s and the three quart (six pint) size 7s 6d.

Candlesticks

The Chamberlain accounts include references to 'Pleasure Boat' alias 'Fisherman' pattern 'hand candlesticks', also known as chamber candlesticks.

The candle holder is in the centre of a low, circular pan with a handle at one side, under which appears a relief moulded head (Plate 95).

The original price was 2s, examples are today extremely rare. The same basic shape was made at Worcester and these examples often have a pierced edge.

Centre-Dish, Centre-Piece

The centre dish issued with Caughley dessert services takes two basic forms. The 29 earliest and rarest, shown in Plate 98, is an enlarged 'melon' shaped dish (a smaller version of which occurs as one of the basic shapes of dessert service side dishes), 12¼ inches by 8¾ inches, and standing 2¼ inches high.

The standard, post-1780, form is 3¼ inches deep and is of shaped oval outline (Plate 99). Specimens measure 12½ inches long by 7¾ inches and sometimes bear the impressed 'SALOPIAN' name mark.

Chocolate Cups

Chocolate cups and saucers (Plate 101) were also decorated with the 'Fisherman' design. The original price of the two-handled cup was 9d, but examples are now very rare.

Coffee Cans

Small straight-sided mugs about 2½ inches high are called coffee cans. They are quite rare and certainly rarer than the shaped sided coffee cups; the handle takes the form of a ribbed loop.

Coffee Cups

The tall, handled coffee-cups (unlike the low, handleless tea bowls) were, of course, part of complete tea and coffee services. The individual price of these cups was surprisingly high at 7d, perhaps owing to the high risk of distortion in the firing due to the pull of the handle.

A straight sided 'coffee can' was also made which has the appearance of a very small mug, see above.

Coffee Pots

One pint Caughley coffee pots were decorated with the 'Fisherman', or 'Pleasure Boat', print, the original price being 3s 6d. The next size, holding one and a half pints, was 4s 6d, and the quart size 5s. Few specimens seem to have survived and they are now extremely rare.

Creamers

The contemporary name for a creamer or cream jug was 'ewer' or 'cream ewer'. The simple sparrow-beak creamer (Plate 141) was that normally included in tea services, and these were made in several sizes, though most of the larger specimens were probably milk jugs rather than cream ewers.

The low relief moulded creamer illustrated in Plate 107 was originally called a 'Chelsea-ewer', which was made in two basic forms, the 'low' and the 'tall'. These were often sold on their own at 8d each, although some were also included in complete tea services. The tall version is extremely rare.

Dessert Services

Caughley 'Fisherman' pattern 'Full' dessert services originally comprised:

    Centre Dish
    2 tureens, covers & stands
    2 ladles to do.

4 square dishes
4 shell shaped dishes
4 heart shaped dishes
4 melon dishes
24 plates.

The basic make-up could of course be amended to suit the customer's individual needs and some large services also included a pair of ice pails. The separate components are treated separately in this alphabetical list.

Dessert Dishes

Caughley dessert services were equipped with side dishes of four basic forms:

(1) 'Square', in which the four sides are of equal length, though deeply curved (see Plates 65, 113, 114 and 115).
(2) 'Shell'. This is the only side dish form to have a handle (Plates 76, 112, 113 and 115). The basic handled shell dish was internationally popular and was much used on the Continent. Its popularity extended into the nineteenth century and these dishes are found on Coalport, Worcester and other porcelains up to about 1820.
(3) 'Heart'. An elongated heart-shaped dessert dish (Colour Plate IX, Plates 112 and 115).
(4) 'Melon' dish—to use the original description—could also be described as an oval or diamond-shaped dish with convex and concave curved outline (Plates 112, 113, 114 and 115).

It should be noted that these basic shapes of dessert service dishes are not confined to the Caughley factory, for they were popular shapes of the period and were used also at Worcester.

Dinner Services

I have not seen Caughley dinner wares bearing the 'Fisherman' pattern although some may have been made. Dinner wares would include large tureens, covered vegetable dishes, large oval dishes, soup plates and large meat plates with a diameter of 10 inches (Page 93).

Egg Cups

'Fisherman' pattern egg cups are distinctly rare. Egg cups or 'egg stands' were priced at 8*d* each in the Chamberlain accounts of 'Goods recd. from Thos. Turner Esq', when decorated with the 'Pleasure Boat' or 'Fisherman' design, or 6*d* in the white undecorated state.

Egg Drainers or Strainers

The small, pierced, circular, handled dishes shown in Plate 119 were egg drainers or strainers (not tea strainers as they are often called today). They were sometimes sold with an egg cup.

Two versions are found, one with a loop twig-like handle, the other has a small, moulded, leaf-like handle. The individual price was 6*d*.

31

Eye Baths

The attractive moulded eye baths found with the 'Pleasure Boat' or 'Fisherman' pattern were originally sold for 6*d* each. Few seem to have survived normal wear and tear or been preserved, so that today they can be classed as one of the desirable rarities. They can occur in two forms, plain (as Plate 122) or with ornamental moulded stem and bowl (as Plate 121), the plain version being even rarer than the moulded design.

Ewers, see Water-Ewers and Wash Basins, Page 37.

Ice-Pails

I have not seen a Caughley ice-pail decorated with the 'Pleasure Boat' pattern, but as dessert services bear this design and as some large services include two ice-pails, examples probably exist and these should be of the shape depicted in Plate 125.

Jugs

The class of Caughley jug most often encountered is the moulded cabbage-leaf variety with a mask-head spout (Colour Plate II, Plate 33, etc.), the original name for which was 'Dutch Jugs'.

The Chamberlain accounts list the following sizes with the 'Fisherman' print:

Gallon size	10/6d
2 quart	6/-
3 pint	4/6d
quart	3/6d

but further sizes may have been made at Caughley and sold to other customers. Specimens often have the blue printed 'S' mark.

A further attractive type of jug was made with a gracefully plain curved body and handle, and the moulded mask-head spout (Plate 136). The quart size with Fisherman print was 2*s* 6*d*, a shilling cheaper than the same size cabbage-leaf jug. Today these plain jugs are very rare and are more expensive than the relatively common moulded cabbage-leaf jug.

Leaf-Dishes

The finely moulded and large sized leaf-dish shown in Plate 137 is a very rare piece, as the leaf-dishes normally found are much smaller and simpler.

Plate 138 shows the standard Caughley version (without the seated Fisherman, as the object is too small to include this feature) with two unglazed fragments from the factory site. One of these 'wasters' is reversed to show the relief moulded veining on the reverse (see also Plate 285). Specimens were made in at least four sizes:

1st	size	5d
2nd	,,	7d
3rd	,,	9d
4th	,,	1/-

These were originally used for pickles, for the Chamberlain records include the description—'6 Vine leaves for Pickles, Pleasure Boat, at 7d. 3/6d'.

A further form of leaf-dish is smaller and deeper, with an applied twig-like handle and three relief moulded leaf-like feet. A mould for such a leaf-dish was found on the factory site with several unglazed fragments (Plate 140). These dishes too were made in several sizes, ranging in length from about $2\frac{3}{4}$ inches to $3\frac{1}{2}$ inches.

Mugs

Two early, pre-1785 Caughley mugs are shown in Plates 148 and 147 respectively, the first is of a graceful bell-shape, very rarely found today, and the second, even rarer, is barrel-shaped.

Most Caughley mugs are cylindrical with, from about 1785, the handle often having an overlapping reinforcement at the top (Plate 151). Three sizes were made with the Fisherman pattern, the pint mug at 1s 9d and the half pint size at 1s 3d. The larger mugs, holding a quart or more, were originally called 'Toast cups' or 'Toast mugs', the quart size Fisherman 'Toast cup' being originally priced at 2s 6d. Some very small, mug-like objects are perhaps straight-sided coffee cups or 'coffee cans', but from 3 inches upwards specimens can be regarded as mugs.

The Caughley mug is normally lower and wider in the body than the standard, tall, slender Worcester mugs (see Plates 258-9). A rare version is low and very wide.

Mustard Pot

Caughley mustard pots decorated with the 'Fisherman' design were originally sold for 8d or 1s, with the attractively moulded spoon. Many must have been sold but seem to have suffered a high accident rate, for specimens are rarely found today.

A typical mustard pot is shown in Plate 156, but it must be noted that the Worcester factory made very similar pots (see Plates 289-90). The Caughley pots normally have floral knobs, as illustrated, but some examples have a plain turned knob.

Plates

The large saucer-shaped plates with a plain edge were originally bread and butter plates in a tea service. A 'Full' tea service would include two such plates, of different sizes, the large plate costing originally 1s 6d, the smaller one 1s 3d.

Other, shaped-edged plates were originally part of dessert services, the commonest, and perhaps the earliest, having a curved outline with twenty-four projections (Plate 158). This basic form was also popular at the Worcester factory.

A rare plate form has six, long, shallow curves with six intervening small projections (Plates 114 and 115). An even rarer pattern is shown in Plate 159, with four large, shallow, convex curves separated by three concave sections, and relief moulded panelling running inward from these projections across the edge of the plate. Dessert plates sometimes bear the impressed name-mark SALO-PIAN, as well as the blue-printed 'S' mark normally associated with the 'Fisherman' pattern. All basic shapes of plates were made in different sizes that could be chosen according to the customer's requirements.

Saffron Pots

The description 'Saffron pots' occurs many times in the Chamberlain accounts relating to Caughley porcelain, where when decorated with the 'Fisherman' pattern, they were priced at 1*s* 3*d*.

It is my personal belief that the objects (Plates 165–6) we now call 'spittoons' were really 'saffron pots', for apart from the facts that I cannot link the description 'Saffron pot' with any other known Caughley shape, and that no spittoons are mentioned in the reasonably full Chamberlain records, the pots, if spittoons, are so small that they would have had to be held to the mouth, in which case one would have expected a handle to be fitted (see also Page 103).

A dictionary definition of saffron reads: 'a plant, variety of crocus, with light purple flowers, long cultivated in the East and later introduced to Europe, the dried orange-red stigmas of which yield a dye, also an aromatic, pungent drug, and flavouring substance.' These pots could well have held such bulbs and the contemporary records clearly show that the Caughley factory made 'Saffron pots', some of which bore the 'Pleasure Boat' or 'Fisherman' print. Examples are now rare.

Salad Dishes

The standard Caughley salad dish, shown in Plate 167, is so ornately moulded as to prevent the use of the large 'Fisherman' design, and so it seems that a simpler salad bowl was used when this popular pattern was required on such a vessel.

Plate 169 shows a low, shaped-edged, sexagonal bowl of extreme rarity that was probably intended to be a salad or cress dish. The diameter of this specimen, which bears the impressed SALOPIAN name mark, is $9\frac{1}{2}$ inches and it stands just over 2 inches high, but smaller examples were made.

A deep salad dish is shown in Plate 168. This form is rare in pre-1799 Caughley porcelain but a slightly larger version of the same basic shape is found with post-1799 John Rose hard-paste porcelains. Apart from the different bodies, the shape of the foot is a useful guide, Turner specimens having a circular foot, while in John Rose examples the foot follows the shape of the top edge, and is therefore square not round.

Sauce-Boats

The large Caughley relief-moulded sauce-boats (as opposed to the smaller 'cream boats') are of two basic models, when decorated with the 'Fisherman' print. The two designs are clearly seen in Plates 172–3 and need not be described. As with other objects, sauce-boats were made in different sizes, but the Chamberlain records unfortunately give only one price, that of 1*s* 3*d* for the second size. A Worcester example is shown in Plate 292.

Shell Dishes

The Chamberlain records include several references to 'Scallop Shells' or 'Oyster Shells' decorated with the 'Fisherman' pattern. These were made in three sizes, $4\frac{1}{4}$, $5\frac{1}{2}$ and $6\frac{1}{4}$ inches long. Examples always seem to bear the 'Fisherman' pattern and some specimens are marked with the standard 'S', 'Sx' or 'So' marks. Examples are shown in Plate 177.

Spoon Trays

The shaped-edged long narrow trays were incorporated in 'full' tea services to hold the hot, wet, spoons (see Page 106 and Plate 181).

When sold singly the original price of 'Fisherman' examples was 1s 3d. The normal mark is the blue-printed initial 'S', and some spoon trays also bear the impressed name mark 'SALOPIAN'.

Spoons or Ladles

Ladles or spoons with circular, instead of spoon-shaped, bowls are very rare. One is shown in Plate 179 with two fragments from the factory site. These spoons or ladles were originally supplied with the two small tureens found with complete dessert services, but naturally few porcelain ladles have survived normal usage.

Sugar Bowls

Covered sugar bowls, or 'sugar boxes' to use the contemporary term, were included in 'full' tea services, the price being originally 1s 3d.

Tart Pan

'Tart pans', as shown in Plate 184, are often now called 'patty pans'. Caughley examples were made in at least three sizes with a top diameter of about $3\frac{1}{2}$, 4 and 5 inches. Prices were 6d, 8d and 1s.

Taster?

The exact purpose of the small wine-taster or scoop shown in Plate 186 is not known. It comprises a deep circular bowl, just over two inches in diameter and an inch high, with a moulded, stubby handle. Examples are very rare but unglazed fragments were found on the site and these show that slight variations of size may occur.

Tea Bowls

Tea bowls are the small, handleless tea cups found with most eighteenth century tea services, and on some occasions sets of cups were sold on their own without the teapot and other expensive articles. Handled cups are discussed under the heading 'coffee cups' (see Page 30).

Tea Caddies

The small, vase-shaped, covered caddies found in complete tea services were originally termed 'tea canisters'; with the passing of the years the small covers have often been lost and now even the bases are rarely found. Different shapes of Caughley 'tea canisters' are shown in Plate 189.

Teapots

Caughley 'Fisherman' teapots are found in two basic shapes, the early standard globular form and the barrel shape (as Plates 197 and 201). Prices originally ranged from about 2*s* to 3*s* according to size.

Teapot Stands

The standard Caughley teapot stand shape, shown in Plate 203, when decorated with the 'Fisherman' or 'Pleasure Boat' design cost 1*s* 3*d*.

Tea Services

A 'full' Caughley teaset in the 'Fisherman' pattern would have comprised:

Teapot and cover
Teapot stand
Spoon tray
Sugar bowl and cover
Tea caddy and cover
Waste bowl
Creamer (sometimes with cover)
2 bread and butter plates (of different sizes)
12 handleless tea bowls
12 handled coffee cups
12 saucers
A coffee pot and cover was included in some services.

The composition of tea services could, of course, be modified to suit the individual customer's needs. The components are treated separately in this alphabetical list.

Tea Services—Toy or Miniature

Charming miniature teasets for children (Plate 193) were made in the 'Fisherman' or 'Pleasure Boat' pattern. These are sometimes quite wrongly regarded as travellers' samples, they were, however, a standard saleable line and are featured in the closing down sale as 'toy table and tea sets'. They are also included in the Chamberlain accounts:

'2 Toy tea setts, Pleasure Boat   4/8d
cup & saucer, toy, Pleasure Boat   3½d'

Complete sets are, of course, now extremely rare, as are all components of such sets, with the exception of the tea bowls and saucers, and these are by no means common. I have seen toy coffee pots, teapots and creamers as well as the tea bowls and saucers. It would appear that teapot stands and spoon trays were not made for these children's services.

Tureens

Small shaped oval tureens and covers, some 5½ to 6 inches long, were originally supplied in dessert services, which would include a pair of tureens and covers, stands and ladles. They were described as sugar and cream tureens and are today quite rare.

I have not found any specimens of dinner wares bearing the 'Fisherman' pattern, but any large tureen that may subsequently be reported will be from such a service.

Water-Ewers and Wash Basins

Some of the rarest of utilitarian objects are the wash-hand basins and ewers which were originally used in wash stands in a bedroom. The bowls are large with a wide flange, so that the bowl sat in the opening at the top of the wash stand (as Plate 211).

The ewer was often of bottle shape, as Plate 209, but some late wash-hand basins had a handled jug, instead of the bottle-shaped ewer, which must have presented difficulties when the hands were wet and soapy (see Page 113 and Plate 210).

CHAPTER IV

EUROPEAN DESIGNS, IN UNDERGLAZE BLUE

In the previous two chapters designs showing Oriental influence have been discussed, but by no means all Caughley patterns reflect the Eastern taste. European scenic and figure patterns were engraved or painted by hand and numerous flower or fruit designs were very popular. A large class of hand-painted floral, sprig patterns were close copies of the popular French porcelains.

In this chapter the scenic and figure patterns will be listed first, followed on Page 40 by the many fruit and flower designs. The first scenic pattern to be discussed must be the printed view of the Ironbridge at Coalbrookdale, the first Ironbridge ever to have been erected, and opened in 1779, which was situated within three miles of the Caughley factory, just upstream from that of Coalport. An imposing view, with shipping on the river, was engraved and may be found on some Caughley cabbage-leaf jugs (Colour Plate II), and occasionally on bowls (Plate 36). The engraved copper-plates were sold by Turner to John Rose and the Coalport partners in 1799, and the design was re-issued on the post-1799 hard-paste porcelains, and pulls from the original Caughley engraved copper-plate are included in the Coalport 'ragbook' of old printed patterns. All pieces bearing this fine print of the local Ironbridge are now very rare and the design occurs only on Shropshire porcelains.

The figure subjects, seated Britannia and a flying figure of Fame, would seem to have been restricted to the very rare moulded mask-head jugs of the shape illustrated in Plate 132.

Another rare underglaze blue print was known as the 'Travellers', and depicts a man on a donkey with a woman and child by his side (Plate 37), the cell and dagger border being similar to that found surrounding the 'Pleasure Boat' or 'Fisherman' pattern. A secondary print of a woman and child in landscape is sometimes found with this design. The design would appear to have been restricted to the Caughley factory.

A class of hand-painted underglaze blue scenic painting, meticulous and quite charming, is found on Caughley porcelains, normally dessert wares, and these patterns were enriched with gilt borders. It is strange that these pieces are so rare and that the distinctive hand is not found on other wares, for at present only six examples are known to me, but many more pieces must await discovery. A fine centre-dish is shown in colour, page 48 and a detail of a tureen stand is illustrated in Plate 38, while two further dishes are in the Victoria and Albert Museum. This style of painting is confined to the Caughley factory and the blue is peculiarly bright. Other subjects may occur on special presentation pieces, such as the milkmaid and the cow painted on the 'Sarah Wenlock. God speed the Dairy' mug in the Victoria and Albert Museum.

Turning to patterns which are found on both Caughley and Worcester porcelains, we find two most attractive designs featuring birds. The first, an attractive blue-printed design was applied to teawares and rarely to jugs, depicts two or more birds perched in the branches of a tree, see Colour Plate III and Plates 39 and 141. Several slightly different versions of the print are found and the pattern was also very popular at the Worcester factory, see Page 134. The Turner engraved copper-plates were re-used by John Rose after he took over the Caughley factory at the end of 1799, and these prints then occur on the new hard-paste porcelains (see Page 114).

The Chamberlain-Turner accounts indicate some contemporary prices for Caughley porcelains decorated with the bird prints. In 1788 we find listed:

2 setts (tea cups and saucers) of Birds, blue	£3.	4.	8.
2 ½ pint basins do.		1.	6.
2 Pint do. do.		2.	4.
2 teapots do.		4.	6.
2 cream jugs do.		1.	6.

Other prices for blue printed 'Bird' wares were:

Pint coffee pot	3.	0.
Pint and a half do.	4.	0.
Low 'Chelsea' ewers		8d

Another very attractive underglaze-blue print depicts a parrot perched on a branch, about to peck at an assortment of fruit conveniently posed below. This complicated print is found on Caughley jugs, both of the moulded cabbage-leaf type (see Plate 40) and of the graceful plain shape, and also found on mugs. Contrary to a statement made by the usually extremely sound authority, Dr Bernard Watney, this print is also found on Worcester porcelains (see Page 121 and Plate 260).

The Chamberlain-Turner accounts give the following contemporary prices for Caughley porcelains bearing the Parrot print in underglaze blue:

Pint sized jugs	2.	0.
2 Pint do.	3.	0.
3 Pint do.	4.	0.
Pint sized mugs	1.	6.
2 Pint do.	2.	0.

To readers who may expect to find in this section mention of the fine sporting prints, the attractive prints of European figures in landscape and the milkmaid subject, I must state that my researches suggest that these appear on Worcester, not Caughley, porcelains. These designs are illustrated in Plates 246–254 and are discussed in Chapter IX.

Fruit Patterns

Some fruit patterns, particularly the so-called pine-cone design (see below and Plate 41), may owe their origin to an Oriental prototype, and several other designs are also found on Worcester porcelains (see Chapter IX). It must be made clear that the Caughley examples do NOT bear the shaded, or filled-in, crescent mark but have the blue-printed 'C' or 'S' initial marks. The position is, however, complicated by the fact that many of the Caughley pieces do not bear any mark at all.

The so-called pine-cone or Mulberry design is found on a representative range of Caughley porcelains, from baskets to water jugs, but not on tewares.

This design was also exceedingly popular at Worcester, and in fact the Worcester examples are more often met with than the Caughley version, although many Worcester pieces have been incorrectly attributed in the past to the Caughley factory (see Chapter IX).

The pine-cone design is sometimes associated with three small groups of fruit—two plums on a twig, a rather misshapen apple and a pear-like fruit.

They appear, with the pine-cone design, on large objects such as salad bowls (Plate 167), where groups of fruit and flowers are also found. These prints, some of which were also re-used on mid-nineteenth century Coalport porcelains, were all engraved on the same copper-plate and a pull from this is reproduced above.

An attractive group of fruit and flowers is shown on the mug illustrated on 41

Plate 150, and on some very rare prints these two flowers are placed to the left of the fruit. This rare version is sometimes found on sauceboats of the shape shown in Plate 173, and a Chamberlain account dated January 27th, 1789 gives the original cost for three sizes of such sauceboats:

Sauce boats, 2nd size, Fruit 1/4d.
     do.   3rd size, do. 1/6d.
     do.   4th size, do. 2/-

The pull from the original Caughley engraved copper-plate, reproduced in Plate 42, also shows a rare subject, an apple, cut to show the core and seeds. Another apple print is shown on the 'saffer-pot' or 'spittoon' in Plate 165.

One of the most attractive Caughley blue-printed patterns, originally known as 'fruit and wreath', depicts fruit within oval or circular panels, enclosed by a most graceful wavy border with running swags of leaves. The same standard

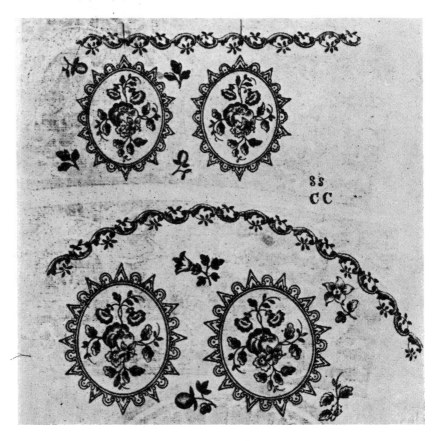

design was also applied to Worcester porcelains (see Page 134), and is more often found on Worcester than it is on Caughley porcelains. It was applied in the main to teawares but can also occur on other objects, such as patty, or tart, pans (Plate 185), and pulls from the original Caughley engraved copper-plates are reproduced above, note 'S' and 'C' marks.

Several small compositions of fruit are associated with this panelled 'fruit and wreath' design, including one of a gooseberry.

Although the above-mentioned fruit patterns were printed, some hand-painted designs do occur, though rarely. The 'S' marked coffee-pot illustrated in Plate 106 is a good example, and a hand-painted gooseberry-like fruit is found on some small objects such as leaf-dishes, Plate 286.

Finally, some fine prints of vegetables, including a bunch of carrots, and a cos lettuce with spring onions, are found on the outside of the ornately moulded salad bowls, as Plate 167.

Flower Patterns

English-styled flower patterns will be discussed first, followed by patterns in the French style. Probably the finest Caughley floral print depicts a large full-blown rose, seen to advantage in Plates 45 and 135, an 'S' marked mug and jug.

A further fine rose print is reproduced below.

This reproduction of a pull taken from the original Caughley engraved copper-plate, is interesting as it shows that two different marks were engraved for use with this pattern, a clear, shaded or filled-in initial 'C', and an *open*, or unshaded, crescent mark. The fact that this crescent is not shaded is of great importance, for although the design also appears on Worcester porcelain, the Worcester crescent was shaded, or filled-in, as was the normal practice on all Worcester *printed* designs. This pattern is probably that referred to many times in the Chamberlain-Caughley accounts as 'Rose'.

Another shared Worcester and Caughley flower print is reproduced below. It is quite often found on crescent marked Worcester porcelains, especially teawares (and mustard pots) but is comparatively rare on Caughley wares. As the pull from the original copper-plates suggests, the Caughley pieces bear the 'C' or 'S' initial marks rather than the Worcester shaded, or filled-in crescent mark.

An impression of a further Caughley floral print is shown in Plate 153. Two other rare designs are illustrated in Mr Franklin Barrett's *Caughley & Coalport Porcelain*, Plate 5, and several small floral prints are found on large pieces, such as cress dishes or salad bowls, being used as secondary prints or 'space-fillers'.

Some flower patterns were also painted by hand, the special presentation jug of 1778 shown in Plate 47, serves as a very good example; a mug of 1776 would appear to be by the same hand (see Plate 48). Formal floral sprays were also painted on very rare inkpots and pounce-pots or 'sanders' within printed cell borders. A small but attractive class of Caughley porcelain is hand painted with simple floral sprays, in a peculiar bright underglaze blue, very similar to that used on the very rare English view designs (see Colour Plate V). A typical 'S' marked tea bowl and saucer and an egg strainer are shown in Plate 50. The dinner service shown in Plate 116 is painted in the same style as is a teapot-stand included in Plate 203.

The site fragments, and tea bowl and saucer, illustrated in Plate 53, are of a hand-painted formal floral design known as 'Lily' pattern. It was probably based on an Oriental design and was made by most English manufacturers from the 1770s. It was very popular on Worcester porcelain, much used at the Dr Wall factory and by succeeding partnerships, the Chamberlain factory also produced this design and it remained in vogue right through the nineteenth century and into the twentieth century. It was chosen by Queen Charlotte when she visited the City of Worcester in 1788, since when this formal blue design (with some gilt and enamel enrichments) has been known as the 'Queen Charlotte' or 'Royal Lily' pattern, the latter term occurring in the Chamberlain-Caughley accounts from 1789. It is quite rare on Caughley porcelain but when present it is normally accompanied by the 'S' initial mark. The similar Worcester porcelains bear the crescent mark, open, not shaded. Examples are sometimes enriched with gilt embellishments.

A fine part tea service in the Victoria and Albert Museum presents several problems. These pieces have a blue ground broken up with irregular darker circles, as if oil-spotted. Shaped white panels are reserved into this ground and underglaze blue floral sprays are painted in these reserve panels. Examples from this service have been illustrated as Caughley and some pieces do bear an open crescent mark with a pronounced 'C'-like appearance. However, the potting details and the shapes point to a Worcester origin and I do not consider that these pieces were made at Caughley, although I am not, in this instance, absolutely certain. The situation might well be clarified when other pieces with this rare design are reported.

French-styled Floral Patterns

Thomas Turner, who visited France in 1787 (see Page 155) and may well have made previous journeys, was influenced to a great extent by the French and Belgian porcelains of Chantilly and Tournay type, which were hand-painted with simple flower patterns. Certain shapes are also in the French style, especially those forms shown in Plates 57, 129, 146 and 170.

Indeed, the popular carnation pattern was probably copied from French and Belgian (Tournay) porcelains, although it is also to be found on other English porcelains, notably Derby and Worcester. This design is sometimes hand-painted (as on the mug, dated 1778, illustrated in Plate 55) but more often printed in underglaze blue. This design, with several variations of border and secondary prints, is found on teawares and dessert wares. On plates and dishes the print is often associated with moulded basket-work borders ('Tournay basket rim') in the Continental style. The Chamberlain-Caughley accounts include such references as '8 Dessert plates, Tournay baskett (border) Carnation (pattern) 3rd size 12/-' (May, 1789). Once again the crescent marked Worcester specimens are more plentiful than the marked ones from Caughley.

The 'Chantilly-sprig' pattern is seen to advantage on the basket-bordered small tureen illustrated in Plate 57, or the very rare jardinière shown in Plate 129, on the fluted salad-bowl shown in Plate 170 and on the monteith, reproduced in Plate 146. Examples, when marked, bear a Caughley 'S' mark not a copy of the Chantilly hunting-horn device. Many fragments of 'Chantilly-sprig' patterned plates were found on the factory site and most specimens of this design have a blue line-edging, they are clean and neat looking.[1] The pattern, however, proved

[1] Blue and white Chantilly porcelains of this type can be seen in room 128, at the Victoria and Albert Museum in London.

45

unpopular with the Chamberlains (see notes related to letter written in September, 1789, on Page 51). Caughley Chantilly-sprig designs were included in a Christie sale held in February, 1780 (see Page 151).

Another hand-painted underglaze blue sprig pattern has a wide, solid, blue border with saw-tooth edge (see cup and saucer in Plate 51) and custard cup (Plate 111) and teapot (Plate 49), a design which does not occur on Worcester porcelain. The teapot painted with swags of flowers (see Plate 200) is a very rare design, perhaps unique, and the most unusual and graceful moulded form and crisply modelled handle suggests the French influence.

It is highly probable that further floral designs exist but those mentioned in the preceding pages are the main, standard, ones.

CHAPTER V

THE CHAMBERLAIN TRADE WITH CAUGHLEY

Robert Chamberlain was apparently the first apprentice taken by the original (so-called Dr Wall) Worcester porcelain factory, who after the termination of his apprenticeship, progressed until he was in charge of the gilding and decorating of all Worcester porcelain, from about 1775 to *c.* 1783, when Thomas Flight purchased the works.

Between 1783 and 1789 Chamberlain may have independently decorated Worcester porcelain for Flights by contract, for the wording of John Flight's diary[1] is obscure. He makes no mention of the Chamberlains (Robert, and his son, Humphrey) leaving Flight's employment but laments the fact that Chamberlain had taken the former Flight retail shop at 33 High Street, Worcester and that he had to hire Mrs Hampton to 'teach us gilding . . .' (as if there were no gilders in the employment of the Worcester factory at this period) and at the same period (May 1789) Flights found it necessary to hire three of Chamberlain's decorators. The loss of the two Chamberlains would seem to have left the Flights not only without two key decorators, but without any employees capable of decorating their porcelain. The relevant diary entry read:

> . . . I was sorry to learn [on returning from a buying trip to France] Chamberlain and his son had taken our old House and intended setting up a retail shop . . . I at last agreed with Mrs Hampton to come down with us and teach us the Gilding . . . I left London to come and reside here in Worcester on Sunday the 7th (of June, 1789). . . . I had been employ'd in building a kiln. We hired 3 of Chamberlain's men who are now with us. . . .

and, of greater importance, the last three lines of the following quotation:

[1] See "John Flight of Worcester", an article by Geoffrey Wills in *The Connoisseur*, July, 1947.

June 21st, 1789:

. . . While my Brother and I were determining upon opening a shop in London [the shop in Coventry Street was opened in February, 1789] Chamberlain was treating about taking our old [retail] House, had I known this then the connection most likely would not have taken place between my Brother and I, and what we could have done had we not met with Mrs Hampton I cannot tell. I see no possible way by which we could have carried on the business. . . .

By at least 1789 the Chamberlains had set up as independent decorators in Worcester, having severed all direct connections with Flights. Chamberlain had apparently already built kilns by June 1789 (and if he had worked independently from 1783 the kilns could date from this period) for on June 28th John Flight was having great trouble firing his decorated porcelains and he wrote in his diary—'We think of trying to erect one (a kiln) on the Plan of Chamberlain's' and on July 12th he wrote—'we sent for the man who built Chamberlain's kiln who gave us every necessary dimension and said he could easily build one for us. . . .'

We learn from Flight's diary that Robert Chamberlain and his son opened their shop at 33 High Street on June 27th, 1789. 'Yesterday, Chamberlain opened his shop, I was rather surprised as I thought they were hardly ready yet, but they talk of making a flaming shew in about 2 months'. [Diary entry, June 28th, 1789]. At this period the Chamberlains were merely decorators and retailers; they did not as yet manufacture their own porcelain. The blank, undecorated, porcelain would hardly have been purchased from Messrs Flights, for keen rivalry was at first experienced, each trying to engage the other's decorators and gilders. The porcelain for Chamberlain's decorating establishment and for the stocking of their retail shop was very largely acquired from Thomas Turner's Caughley porcelain factory, and it would appear that Chamberlains also decorated much Caughley porcelain for Thomas Turner, which was returned either to Caughley by river or forwarded to the London establishment of 'The Salopian China Warehouse' at 5 Portugal Street.

It is a matter of speculation as to how Robert Chamberlain and his son, Humphrey, came suddenly to sever their longstanding connection with the Worcester Porcelain Company, and open, on their own account, the former Worcester retail shop. On the modest wages then paid to porcelain decorators they could not have built up much capital and it seems at least possible that they had for some years a working arrangement to decorate all the Worcester porcelain, perhaps in a separate establishment, so that they would be in a stronger position to start on their own account. It is also evident that the Chamberlains had at least one sleeping partner, Richard Nash was undoubtedly the main backer, for the Chamberlain accounts record over many years the amounts and interest due to Nash. It is very likely, too, that Thomas Turner of Caughley loaned money to the Chamberlains for their new venture, so ensuring a close link between his manufactory and the former decorators of his rival's porcelains (who were to become decorators of his own porcelain and one of his best customers through the Chamberlains' retail shop in High Street, Worcester). The facts behind the above statement are contained in a Chamberlain 'Summary of Accounts, August 17th, 1789 to June, 1792', where balances of fourteen hundred pounds are credited to both Richard Nash and to Thomas Turner. There is also a payment to Turner of fifty pounds for interest, and this very strongly indicates that a formal loan had been made from Thomas Turner to the Chamberlains. This loan from Turner would appear to have been paid off before the 1796 summary of accounts, although payments of interest to Richard Nash were continued for many years.

The importance of the intertrading between Chamberlain of Worcester and Turner of Caughley is that very many of the original Chamberlain order books have been preserved, sometimes with notes on the main contents of letters sent to Thomas Turner at Caughley. These shed much light on the Caughley productions, the standard shapes and patterns, as well as the original prices. It would seem that these entries were brief notes of the main points contained in letters sent by Humphrey Chamberlain to Caughley and it is possible that Robert Chamberlain was at Caughley in 1789 and that Humphrey in Worcester was in fact writing to his father at Caughley. The Chamberlain accounts list several expenses for Mr Chamberlain's journeys to Caughley.

The next section in this chapter mainly comprises extracts from the Chamberlain account books, with bracketed notes or explanations added in some instances to make the original meaning clear. There will be found several references to 'Broseley' in describing Caughley shapes or patterns, a name taken from the nearest township and the normal description (with 'Shropshire') for Caughley porcelains.

The selection of 'orders and remarks' sent from Chamberlain in Worcester to Caughley starts in August 1789,[1] but from the wording 'no more . . .' or 'before ordered' it is obvious that earlier orders were placed.

13 August, 1789. Orders & Remarks

The saucers 2nd [size] new fluted, fine blue borders to the cups sent, are very much wanted.

No more of them very large size teapot stands.

Plain cups & saucers common are much wanted, with pint or ½ pint basons both best & seconds.[2]

4 Dozen pint Dutch jugs [cabbage-leaf, mask head jugs] white.

4 dozen quart   do.

12 three-pint   do.

6 two-Quart   do.

The cups with the large handles before ordered of the Bute shape—very much wanted.

---

[1] Some entries date back to the second half of 1788.
[2] 'Seconds' were slightly faulty wares sold at a reduced rate.

Temple [pattern] best teas wanting next Saturday in complete sets if possible (Must be sent next week).

Teapots of both sizes and pint & ½ pint basons.

Shrewsbury plain ware as above much wanted.

Pleasure Boat etc. etc. different sizes.

Fine Blue Birds-eye [pattern]. Plain Dresden flower & Borders of different shapes & sizes.

Dèjeune of various sorts & plain pint white basons.

No more common chocolate cups old make in blue, rather a few French or Bute shape in white.

The teapots to be most of them Barrel shape of all patterns, plain or fluted.

Wanted immediately 3 or 4 complete [tea] setts of Shropshire [shape].

1st size Plain [shape] with Barrel teapot, 2nd or 3rd size for gilding.

August 20th, 1789. Order & Remarks

Dutch jugs [cabbage-leaf mask head jugs] common, best & seconds—

24 Quart without border
24 3-pint   do.   do.
12 2-Quart   do.   do.
12 Pint   do.   do.
24 Quart mugs, wine measure
24 very small ½ pint

3 or 4 dozen of very small sauce boats, sorted.

A few dozen small Chelsea [shape] ewers in blue at 8d. each.
    do. do. do. gadroon boats   do.   at 6d. each.

A few egg drainers in blue.

Small Chelsea [shape] ewers, white, overcharged 4d. each.

No more mustard pots, note these sent overcharged 4d. each.

August 23rd, 1789. Orders, Remarks

I unpacked three casks yesterday & was much surprised to find such a small quantity of Blue goods—can only say we are every day disobliging our customers & injuring ourselves for want of them—in reality we find more difficulty in getting the goods than we do in selling them, must beg you to forward the Temple [pattern] the quantity particularly wanted is two tea pots 3rd [size] barrel [shape], two slop basons—two ½ pint basons, two milks—no sugar box . . . .

We want at this time fifteen or twenty complete sets of teas Pleasure boat & Shrewsbury plain ware [not fluted] with some Shropshire [shape or pattern].

The teapots to be principally 3rd or 4th [sizes] barrel [shape], if the cups are but a little larger it would be a great advantage in the sale.

A great quantity of the 2/6d. Teas with basons, milk ewers & teapots, best & seconds, if my father can settle the business with Mr Turner.

We sold a great number of the 2nd [size] teas, seconds at 2/8d. with 5 per cent for ready money so that you will easily see our Profit is on the wrong side of the Post—I think unless Mr Turner can allow us fifteen per cent shall not be able to clear ourselves as we certainly must sell on the same terms as our neighbours [Messrs Flights] or not at all.

The handled cups that you have sent us are so much out of date [? word indistinct] that I am sure we shall find great difficulty to sell them at the second price, indeed my opinion is we never shall.

My father to remember respecting the glass.

Believe we have about 6 or 7 basons in the House instead of as many gross. Hardly a pint or quart jug.

Hope I have seen the last of Raddish dishes & centres the last is a most terrible shape to my taste & what is worse have often the mortification to have my opinion confirmed by a general dislike.

No more mustard pots, those that we have, there is no spoons sent to them. Wanted some egg strainers, blue & white and a few Dresden [styled] flower & border do. & [egg] stands do.

Please to stop sending the basket Chantilly [? word indistinct] handled cups & saucers they will not sell here.

36 Coffees Plain, festoon charged 1/4d. each, must certainly be a very wide mistake or a very extravagant charge.

Wanted an assortment of tea and coffee pot covers, Mr Turner promised a basket full.

24 Caudle cups & stands, Shanked bell fluted, white.

The ½ pint Crucibles of the excellent Cobalt promised.

Beg you not send any more 2nd teas Shropshire & Temple they will not do at any rate at 7/- per sett.

Shall be glad to have teapot, [bread & butter] plates etc. etc. to make the Setts complete.

Some Setts complete 1st Plain Shrewsbury.

No more best teas Pleasure Boat 2nd [size] unless they can be sent at 5/6d.

September 4th, 1789.

I am sorry to inform Mr Turner it is now three months since I ordered 8 cups & saucers 2nd long handled Bute shape white. 4 coffee do. & 2 cream ewers with large handles on them & slop basins & sugar do, they are for a lady in Gloucester who I am apprehensive must by this time be greatly offended at our delay. The teapot Barrel shape Temple [pattern] we are likewise in very great want of.

Basons of every sort blue wanted particularly ½ pint Image.

I own myself disappointed upon opening every cask, to find such a large Quantity of those high priced 2nd [size] Teas which we cannot sell & so few of the first size seconds which we can sell. Must request you will not send any more basket Chantilly sprig nor Dresden flower & border, except the saucers to the last 3rd [size] cups.

No more 2nd teas Shropshire & Temple [patterns] to be sent, as 7/- is a charge we cannot sell them at. Wanted teapots, Plates etc. to make those sets we have complete.

No more 2nd teas Pleasure Boat [Fisherman pattern], unless they can be sent at the Worcester Price 5/6d. (See Page 126).

Please to send no more white seconds until further orders as at present we really want room to put them.

Want of teapot stands prevents our making up a complete sett of blue & gold Fly (see Plate 61) the same with respect to the Royal Jasmine & Birds-Eye, of the first No. 1 size Plates, stands and [spoon] tray, the last [Birds-Eye pattern] 2 [size] B & B Plates.

The sorter must be more particular in his attention to the goods when packed, in twenty ewers Temple [pattern] as took of the cask 9 of them were cracked. The 3 large teapot stands Dresden flower & border are every one fled in the shop, therefore must request you will send some less liable to meet the same misfortune. The $\frac{1}{2}$ Pint mug blue & white are all of them considerably too large—shall be glad to have as many as possible of common patterns.

Hope Mr Turner will excuse our sending up some crown glass which we have under an absolute necessity of taking from a very good customer once Flights before we heard it would not be acceptable, shall take care in future. [There is a total lack of punctuation in this sentence, but if a comma is placed after 'Flights' some sense is gained implying that Chamberlain had to take glass from 'a very good' customer who had formerly traded with Messrs Flights].

September 14th

6, 1st [size] Fly Plates, Dessert—all that have hitherto been sent have been charged 2d.

The Caudle cups in the last cask marked as Fly were plain white. No common $\frac{1}{2}$ pint Basons Image yet come those repeatedly sent for.

September 23rd

Particularly wanted the 2/6d. Teas best & 2nd Pint & $\frac{1}{2}$ Pint Basons, all Patterns.

Bread & Butter Plates both sizes Common Patterns wanting very much. Sauce boats common patterns between the smallest size we have of the Chelsea [shape] ewers.

2 flower pots to pattern sent for Lord Courtney.[1]

The order to be made up directly of the tall caudle cups, covers & stands, Royal stripe.

[1] The original order for Lord Viscount Courtney's '2 new shape flower pots' is entered in the shop book on the same date, September 23rd, 1798. On February 8th, 1790, Chamberlains invoiced to Lord Courtney, Roderham Castle, Devon, '2 large flower pots and covers, fine purple ground. Richly gilt. £10.10.0. Send by the Bristol Waggon'. It would seem that these were of Caughley make as they were mentioned in correspondence to Caughley.

October 5th, 1789

We are greatly distressed for want of new fluted white—short of every article but [teapot] stands, [spoon] trays & sugar boxes. Quart Dutch [Cabbage-leaf mask head jugs] jugs & pint do, white, pint & ½ pint mugs white.

2nd plain white plates by the next wherry.

A few wash-hand basons & ewers blue & different sizes as soon as possible —with their prices.

3 Dozen chocolate cups, new fluted white.

The flower pots [wanted? presumably a reminder for Lord Courtney's].

The blue bordered new fluted, shall be glad to have by the first conveyance.

1st [size] B & B [bread & butter] plates & teapot stands. Fly [pattern].

1st [size] Dessert plates, Fly particularly wanted.

A few dozen of different sized tumblers, white.

6 Quart & 6 pint [size] toast mugs, common patterns, particularly want 1 or 2 B & B [bread and butter] plates 2nd [size] Bute shape, broad blue border to the saucers.

Some of these 'orders and remarks' indicate that some trouble was experienced by the Chamberlains in obtaining from Caughley exactly what was required for the Worcester retail shop—that some orders were considerably delayed, and some unordered goods were sent. One copy letter prefaced by the note 'Copy of a letter from Hump. Chamberlain to Mr Thos. Turner, Caughley, being an answer to 2 letters dated 8th & 10th Jany. 93' and dated January, 12th, 1793, confirms this.

Worc. Jany 12. 1793.

Sir.

I received your two letters & in answer to the first respecting the shanked canisters, have to say that the order stood last Xmas settling /92 when both the books was put alike by your Clerks as under.

Blue ribbon Shank'd Canister on order		16
Blue bordered	do.	10
White	do.	30
		56

Received May 31st No 22 (case number?) Shanked Cannister				66
June 14th „ 23	„	„		8
July 13th „ 25	„	„		2
Exclusive of them returned which was				29
			Total	105

I believe they will find a difficulty in producing an order for shanked canisters since the time mentioned above as I well know there has been no alteration in the order given them, except desiring them to send the whole order, while this far I fancy will be found . . . to prove we are not always in the wrong.

The next thing that presents itself is the excuse set up by them as a reason for our not having goods, 'thus we have been continually checking & harrosing them, sometimes under one pretence & at other times on another'. In answer to that we have only to say that if they *will persist* in so unfounded & erroneous excuse we shall not be content with their only saying so, because I really think after we have suffered so very materially for many months past the very attempt to defend on any other ground than unforeseen events is an aggravation of our misfortunes.

With respect to the assertion in your last letter saying you were convinced I meant to deceive you in the quantity of stone & clay coming up, am really astonished, what end it answer harrosing my mind with disbelieving all I can say, particularly when you was in possession of Mrs C (Chamberlains?) two letters which ought to have convinced you. The one I well know mentioned 40 tons by mistake but its really [inconceivable (?) word indistinct] you should take no notice of the other which was solely wrote to contradict the former. . . .

You was pleased to say your rider informed you that we held no incouragement to the country customers by no means expected, for answer I can't form the least idea what be meant—we only known that we [treat] everybody as well as we can which I always concerned due to every good customer, but if your rider is willing to hear & believe every story that will be told by some shopkeepers he will [corner of page torn off] . . . to do but I should like to inform them we do [not intend? page torn] answering every story he may pick up . . .

Shall beg leave to say a few more words to the last part of your letter wherein you desire us immediately to remit you cash—which request will be complied with in a few days, & still further can't help remarking the (2 words indistinct) the letter is wrote with, Have only to repeat once more, that we have never had the least intention of doing anything to the detriment of your manufactory, but on the contrary the whole that has been done, or will be, is to the essential interest of both, even if you will for a moment fancy me the most ungrateful person living still it is impossible to point out as my interest which I would be bound to prove most clearly & which is the wellknown sentiments of the family—that being the case tis very improbable I should be the first to injure myself provided I had not a spark of gratitude.

Have only room to add that I shall always adhere to the above declaration—unless by receiving a kind of treatment we do not deserve, are *forced* to such refuge in a way we have never yet intertained or thought of pursuing.

The family joins me in respects & are happy to hear Mrs Tr. (Turner) surprised you in her recovered health.

   I remain,
    Sir,
     Your Humble Servant,
      H.C.

This copy letter clearly shows that a certain amount of mistrust existed between Turner and one of his most important customers, Chamberlain at Worcester. However, the accounts show that intertrading was carried on after the date of this letter (January 1793) and after the period when Chamberlains had started to manufacture their own porcelain, a necessity which was perhaps forced on them by the difficulty of getting the right kinds of saleable porcelains promptly from Turner at Caughley.

However, from at least the end of 1788 the Chamberlains received a vast quantity of Turner's Caughley porcelain, both for sale on their own account and for gilding and decoration for Turner. Luckily many of the original accounts are preserved in the original Chamberlain records.

One Chamberlain account book which was commenced in 1788 includes detailed lists of Caughley porcelains, enamelled and gilt, by the Chamberlains at Worcester. The completed goods were then either forwarded to London or returned to the Caughley factory. On the first page of this book the standard enamelled and gilt patterns of the period are listed with the piece-rates. The original order of the list has been retained, as it is probable that the first designs were the earliest to be introduced.

New fluted shape

Plymouth	2/8d
Plymouth festoon	1/6d
Royal Fly	1/1d
Royal Jessamine	1/3d
Royal Weel (*sic*) border	no price
Blue & gold festoon	9d
White & gold festoon	1/2d
Blue & Gold Birds-eye	11d
White & gold wreath	11d
Blue & gold chain, bridge border, No. 4	9d

Bute shape

Blue & gold chain with springs	9d
Shrewsbury bridge border	7d
Shrewsbury edge & line	5d
Broseley edge & line	5d
Broseley simple edge	4d
Broseley bridge border	7d
Shropshire edge & line	no price
Temple edge & line[1]	no price
Dagger border, edge & line	5d
Pleasure boat, edge & line[1]	no price

Broseley shape

White & gold sprigs	8d
Gold chain border	11d
Plain (shape)[2] fine blue spots upon the glaze	8d

[1] The 'Temple' and 'Pleasure Boat' designs are standard Caughley under-glaze blue-printed designs. The 'edge & line' will refer to the gilt edge and inner line sometimes added to these patterns.

[2] 'Plain' in all probability means that the shapes were not fluted.

Blue spots		11d
Plain [shape], white & gold sprigs		7d
New fluted [shape] fawn & gold		1/3d
do	white, gold edge	4d
do	white & gold spangles	1/3d
do	jet [black] sprigs	no price
do	Royal Curtain	no price
plain [shape] white & gold wreath		no price
plain [shape] blue edge, gold chain & bridge border		8d
plain [shape] green & gold sprigs		no price
plain [shape] link & gold		no price
Dresden gold edge		4d
Tulip gold edge		4d
Dresden red border		3d
plain [shape] blue & gold festoon		8d
Bell fluted [shape] Iron Bridge (border)		10d
Ladys sprig		9d
Sprig & border		1/6d
New fly festoon		1/2d

The above prices relate to the cost of decorating individual 'pieces' but, as a teapot, for instance, would involve more work than a cup, the following scale of 'piece' charges was used.

Teapot 4th [large size]	$3\frac{1}{2}$
Teapot 3 & 2nd [sizes]	3
Teapot stand	$1\frac{1}{2}$
Spoon tray	$1\frac{1}{2}$
Cream ewer	$1\frac{1}{2}$
milk pot & cover	2
sugar box and cover	$2\frac{1}{2}$
Slop bason, pint	2
do. $\frac{1}{2}$ pint	$1\frac{1}{2}$
tea canister & cover	2
Plate 2nd [large size]	$2\frac{1}{2}$
Plate 1st [size]	2
Saucer	1
Teacup	1
Coffee cup	1

so that, for example, a 'Royal Fly' teapot listed at 1s 1d would cost three and a half times this piece-rate, or 3s 9½d.

Although all these designs are overglaze enamelled and gilt patterns added to Caughley blanks (or porcelains decorated only with underglaze blue), a large proportion of the porcelains listed on the following pages are of standard Caughley blue and white patterns ordered by the Chamberlains for sale in their retail shop, proving that not all items were intended for decoration to be added at Worcester. Numerous extracts from these original Chamberlain accounts are given on the following pages as they show the types of porcelains then being supplied from the Caughley factory, with their prices. Several references to them will be found in other places in the text where articles included in these accounts

56 are illustrated or discussed.

TO GOODS Recd. from Thos. Turner, Esq.

BEST GOODS

					@			
2	Pint Dutch[1] jugs, fine blue edge[2]				@	2/-		4/-
2	Quarts	do	do			3/-		6/-
3	Quarts	do	Flowers			3/-		9/-
1	3 Pint	do	do			4/-		4/-
6	2 Quart	do	do			5/6	£1.	13.-
1	3 Pint	do	Mulberry			4/6		4/6
3	2 Quart	do	do			6/-		18/-
6	3 Pint	do	Pleasure Boat			4/6	£1.	7.-
6	2 Quarts	do	do			6/-	1.	16.-
1	Gallon	do	do			10/6		10. 6.
6	½ pint mugs		Mulberry, common			1/-		6/-
6	¼ do		parrot do			1/-		6/-
12	½ do		Flowers do			1/-		12/-
12	½ do		Fishing			1/-		12/-
12	¼ do		Mulberry bordered			1/3		15/-
12	¼ do		Pleasure Boat, bordered			1/3		15/-
6	Pint mugs		Parrot, common			1/6		9/-
12	do		Flowers do			1/6		18/-
12	do		Fishing do			1/6		18/-
12	do		Mulberry, bordered			1/9	£1.	1.-
12	do		Pleasure Boat do			1/9	£1.	1.-
12	Mustard pots & covers do					1/-		12/-
48	Cups 2nd size, handled, new fluted white[3]					10/- a doz.	£2.	-.-
72	Cups 2nd size, not handled, new fluted white					6/6 a doz.	£1.	19.-
87	Saucers, 2nd size	,,	,,	,,		6/6 a doz.	£2.	7/1½
7	Pint basons	,,	,,	,,		1/3d		8/9
12	Teapots 4th size	,,	,,	,,		3/6d	£2.	2.-
7	Sugar boxes & covers	,,	,,	,,		1/9d		12/3
5	B & B (bread & butter) plates	,,	,,			1/9d		8/9
10	Teapot stands	,,	,,	,,		1/-		10/-
12	upright ewers	,,	,,	,,		1/3		15/-
84	Coffees	,,	,,	,,		9/- a doz.	£3.	3/-
1	Spoon tray	,,	,,	,,		1/-		1/-
2	Sugar boxes & covers, Bute [shape] blue					2/6		5/-
1	ewer		do	do		2/-		2/-
1	[spoon] tray		do	do		1/6		1/6
36	cups 2nd size, new fluted, blue border					1/3	£2.	5/-
2	Pint basons	do	do			3/-		6/-
1	sugar box & cover	do	do			3/-		3/-
1	Teapot 4th size	do	do			4/6		4/6
1	upright ewer	do	do			2/-		2/-
18	Coffees	do	do			1/6	£1.	7/-
2	[tea] canisters	do	do			2/-		4/-
2	Saffer pots, Pleasure Boat					1/3		2/6
2	do	common Nankin				1/-		2/-
2	do	do	Rose			1/-		2/-

[1] Original name for the mask-head spouted cabbage-leaf moulded jugs as Plate 33, etc.

[2] Presumably these 'fine blue edge' jugs were otherwise undecorated and may have been further embellished by Chamberlains (see Colour Plate VIII).

[3] These 'new fluted white' teawares with other white or 'blue bordered' Caughley porcelains must have been decorated or further embellished by the Chamberlain decorating establishment at Worcester and these examples seem to have been accepted as factory decoration.

12	Sauce boats 2nd size, Shoe[1] make, Fruit				1/4	16/-
12	do	3rd size	do	do	1/6	18/-
6	do	4th size	do	do	2/-	12/-
12	do	3rd size		Pleasure Boat	1/6	18/-
6	do	4th size		do	2/-	12/-
6	Dozen asparagus servers[2]			do	6d	£1. 16/-
24	Custard cups, Shanked border				8d	16/-
2	Pint & ½ coffee pots, Pleasure Boat				4/6d	9/-
2	Quart	do		do	6/-	12/-
1	do	do	Temple		6/6d	6/6
1	do	do	Shropshire		6/6d	6/6
8	Teapots 2nd size	Rose			1/9d	14/-
2	Chamber pots, French Chantilly sprig				4/-	8/-

April 22nd, 1789

24	Dessert plates 3rd size, Dresden [pattern] Chantilly make[3]				1/6	£1. 16/-
4	Melon (shaped) dishes 1st size		do		5/-	£1. -.-
4	square	dishes	do	do	5/-	£1. -.-
2	Heart (shaped)	do	do	do	5/-	10/-
4	Shell (shaped)	do		do	4/-	16/-
2	sugar tureens & covers			do	4/6d	9/-
2	stands to do			do	3/-	6/-
2	spoons to do			do	4/6	9/-
12	cups 2nd [size] new fluted. Shrewsbury [pattern]				8d	8/-
12	saucers	do		do	8d	8/-
24	coffees	do		do	1/-	£1. 4/-
3	pint basons	do		do	2/-	6/-
2	½ pint basons	do		do	1/-	2/-
1	spoon tray	do		do	2/-	2/-
2	B & B [bread & butter] 1st [size]	do		do	1/6	3/-
2	do 2nd [size]	do		do	2/-	4/-

May 11th, 1789

2	sauce boats, 2nd size, Pleasure Boat	1/3d	15/-
8	do	do	Full Nankin	2/-	16/-
6	do	3rd size,	do	3/-	18/-

May 16th, 1789

1	Wash Stand bottle & (?) bason, Shrewsbury-Nankin		12/6
8	Dessert plates, Tournay baskett[4] carnation 3rd size		12/-

May 30th, 1789

4	Quart Dutch jugs, white	3/-	12/-
2	sugar tureens, covers & stands & spoons, Full Nankeen	9/-	18/-
4	Melons [shaped dishes] ,, ,,	5/-	£1. -.-
4	Shells [,, ,,] ,, ,,	4/-	16/-
2	Hearts [,, ,,] ,, ,,	5/-	10/-

[1] Abbreviation for Shropshire.
[2] See Page 85 and Plate 86.
[3] This and other references to plates of 'Chantilly make' may well refer to the moulded edge Chantilly *shape* (see Plate 56) rather than to the fact that they were of French manufacture.
[4] The 'Tournay baskett' design plate would refer to the shape with moulded basket work edge, 'Carnation' is the added pattern (see Plate 160).

4 Square Compotiers	Full Nankin	5/-	£1. -.-
16 Dessert plates 3rd	„ „	1/6	£1. 4/-

(Similar dessert wares of 'Dresden flower & border' were priced as these).

July 23rd, 1789

62 French [shaped] shell (dessert dishes) White		2/-	£6. 4/-
45 Heart [„] dishes „		3/-	£6. 15/-
31 Melon [„] „ „		2/6	£3. 17/6
70 Square Compotiers „		2/6	£8. 15.-
3 Centre Pieces „		7/-	£1. 1/-
18 Raddish dishes, leaf-handle „		2/-	£1. 16/-
36 Teapots 4th [size] Broseley [shape] „		4/-	£7. 4/-
73 Cups 1st [size] Broseley [shaped] White		6½	£1. 19. 6½
32 Cups 2nd [size] do „		8d	£1. 1. 6
5 Saucers 2nd [size] do „		8d	3. 4.

July 30th, 1789

8 Setts of teas 1st size, Common Nankin [pattern]			2/6	£1. 0. 0.
3 Setts of do	Rose		2/6	7. 6.
2 Setts of do	Birds		3/-	6. 0.
2 Teapots 2nd [size]	New Landscape		1/9	3. 6.
3 do	2nd	Bridge	1/9	5. 3.
3 do	1st [size]	Image	1/4	4. 0.
3 do	2nd [size]	do	1/9	5. 3.
3 do	2nd [size]	Fruit	1/9	5. 3.
3 do	1st [size]	do	1/4	4. 0.
3 do	2nd [size]	Nankin	1/9	5. 3.
3 do	2nd [size]	Rose	1/9	5. 3.
3 do	1st [size]	Birds	1/4	4. 0.
3 do	2nd [size]	do	1/9	5. 3.
2 do	1st [size]	Nankeen	1/4	2. 8.
17 Milks	1st [size]	Nankeen	6d	8. 6.
17 do	do	Landscape	6d	8. 6.
5 do	do	Bridge	6d	2. 6.
17 do	do	Rose	6d	8. 6.
15 do	do	Image	6d	7. 6.
3 do	do	Fruit	6d	1. 6.
11 do	do	Birds	6d	5. 6.
12 chocolate cups		Pleasure Boat	9d	9. 0.
12 coffee cups		Birds	6d	6. 0.
18 do		Nankeen	6d	9. 0.
18 do		Rose	6d	9. 0.
3 Teapots 1st [size]		Rose	1/4	4. 0.

In August 1789 on some pages the heading reads—'Goods Recd from the Manufactory' but is soon replaced by the former description, 'recd from Thos. Turner Esq.' and as these pages quite clearly run on consecutively it can be seen that at this period the Chamberlain clerks regarded Turner's Caughley factory as 'The Manufactory', from where all their porcelains were acquired.

A very long list is given under the general date 1789 (without any mention of day or month) under the heading:

GOODS RECD. FROM THOS. TURNER ESQ. CAUGHLEY. WITH A COPY OF ALL ORDERS & REMARKS.

This lengthy list, extracts from which are given below, is important as it gives the names of different basic shapes of teaware:

RECEIVED

BROSELEY, WHITE

  6 teapots.
  6 stands.
  6 [spoon] trays.
  6 milks.
  6 sugar boxes.
  6 pint basons.
  6 [tea] canisters.
  6 B. & B. [bread & butter] plates 1st [size].
  6 do   2nd [size].
  6 dozen cups.
  6 dozen saucers.
  36 coffees.

BUTE, WHITE

  (This list gives the same assortment of teawares as is given above under 'Broseley, White').

BUTE (Shape) BROAD BLUE BOARDER

(Here is listed a similar selection of teawares with the addition of '6 ½-Pint Mugs, blue border top & bottom').

NEW FLUTED SHREWSBURY

(Here is listed a similar selection of teawares).

COMMON MAKE WITH BARREL TEAPOT. FLEUR DE LIS.

(Here is listed a similar selection of teawares).

NEW FLUTED BROAD BLUE BORDER

(Here is listed a similar selection of teawares).

NEW FLUTED FESTOON FOR GILDING

(Here is listed a similar selection of teawares to make 48 sets).

NEW FLUTED FLY (Pattern)

(Here is listed a similar selection of teawares to make 48 sets).

NEW FLUTED PLYMOUTH (Pattern)

(Here is listed a similar selection of teawares to make 58 sets).

ROYAL STRIPE

2 complete sets, new fluted (with a larger cup).

ROYAL JESSAMINE

12 Complete sets, new fluted.

BIRDS-EYE (Pattern) NEW FLUTED

 6 Complete sets, no handles [to tea cups]
 12 Dessert plates, Tournay basket rimmed
 6 pint mugs, new mug pattern [shape?]
 6 ½ pint mugs,   do.

HANDLED BASKET (MOULDED BORDER) CHAN (Chantilly) Sg (Sprig).
(A selection of teawares are given under this heading).

1 DESSERT SERVICE AS UNDER FINE FULL NANKEEN

4 Square dishes
4 Melon [shaped dishes]
4 Shell [do]
2 Heart [do]
2 Sugar Tureens & Covers, stands & spoons
1 Centrepiece
24 Dessert plates.

1 DESSERT SERVICE DRESDEN FLOWERS & BORDER

(Here follows a list of dessert wares as listed under 'Full Nankeen' above).

The 1789 list also gives a good idea of other Caughley objects and patterns supplied to Chamberlain, a selection of which is set out below:

Great Quantity [4 gross received] of cups & saucers—Vaughn's turning.
24 Quart Dutch jugs [the mask head cabbage-leaf moulded jugs as Plates 67–71].
       White.
24 Pint   do
24 Pint mugs with a good handle, broad & narrow, full pints principally.
24 ½ Pint   do.
12 Caudle cups, covers & stands, with two handles.
12 Caudle cups & strainers, no covers.
36 Egg cups & strainers, white.
6 Quart mugs with a good handle, not to be too thick.
24 Egg cups, Pleasure Boat.
4 short complete sets Toys [miniature wares], larger.
4 short complete sets Toys painted, larger.
   Quart bowls, Pleasure Boat.
3 Pint   do   do
2 Quart   do   do
3 Quart   do   do
   Gallon   do   do
12 ½ pint mugs, full measure, thin blue border top & bottom but not so wide in border.
6 Quart jugs blue bordered top & bottom but narrow.
6 butter tubs & covers, round with stands.
4 dozen Lambs, white [probably not of Caughley make see Page 70].
6 Ink stands double nankeen border.
2 Radish dishes, full nankeen.
6 Candlesticks, Pleasure Boat.
6   do   White.
6 Caudle cups & covers with stands, Derby make, white.
12   do   do 2 handled, Bell fluted, Shrewsbury.
12   do   do   do Bell fluted, White.
6   do   do   do Dresden flowers & border.
120 Milks, all sizes to match teas.
6 Saffer pots, 1/3d.
   A few custard cups [12 received].
   A few coffee pots, all sizes.
   Dutch jugs, all sizes.
   A few mustard pots at 1/- [12 received].
4 Wash hand bottles & basons.
   Very few Chamber pots.
6 sauce boats every size & pattern.

61

6 Salad dishes different sorts.
1 Table [Dinner] service.
6 Pickle leaves.
6 Artichoke cups.
9 Egg stands, white.
6   do   & drainers, Pleasure Boat.
  An assortment new ribbed Nankeen & sprig, etc.
12 ice cups & covers, different patterns.
12 Tumblers.
12 Chamber candlesticks.
12 [candle] extinguishers.
72 Asparagus servers at 6d.
24 eye baths.
6 deep salad dishes.
  The toy china is too small but send a few.
2 Morters each size [perhaps not of Caughley make].
1 Gallon Dutch jug, Pleasure Boat.
1 Pint   do   Nankeen
2 Baking dishes.
4 ½ pint mugs, round handle, broad blue border.

Ordered June 30th (1789)

24 Dessert plates 1st [size] Fly [pattern].
24   do   do 4th [size] do.
  with proportional dishes & centrepiece, not the shape centre we have of yours.
  margin date 'July 1st' (1789).
24 Dessert plates, 1st [size] Royal Lily [pattern, see Plates 53 & 54].
24   do   do 2nd do   do   do
24   do   do 3rd do   do   do
24   do   do 4th do   do   do
2 Ice Pails & covers   do   do
  with proportional [requirements of dishes, etc.]
6 Pint jugs   do   do
12 caudle cups, covers & stands   do
  with a handsome top [handle] to the cover.
12 common   do 2 handles,   do
       without covers.
12   do   do 1 handle do   do
6 ½ pint mugs   do   do
24 chocolate cups & stands do   do
24 large Breakfast cups &
     saucers   do   do
24 pint mugs Plymouth [pattern], the painters to put 6 stripes.
24 ½ pints   do   let the blue be as strong as possible.
6 caudle cups & stands, Plymouth, with handsome cover.
6   do   do   do   without covers.
6 of those tall caudle cups you have Derby make.
24 Quarter pint Basons with 1 handle, plain white.
24 stands
24 blue bordered do.
6 2 quart jugs, plain white.
2   do   do   with blue border.
6 of the tall caudle cups, Royal Stripe, with covers.
6 of the old shape   do   do   do
6 ½ pint mugs.   do

The above were 'Best Goods', but other items supplied to the Chamberlains
62 were 'seconds', or slightly faulty wares. The following is a list of 'seconds'

entered in the Chamberlain books on July 30th, 1789, under the heading 'Goods received from Thomas Turner Esq'.

SECONDS

6	Coffee [cups], Broseley White			4½d		2/3d
2	B & B [bread & butter] plates 1st [size] white			7½d		1/3d
5	do	2nd [size] do		9½d		4/4½
29	[tea] Cannisters		do	9d	£1.	1/9
3	coffee pots		do	2/6d		7/6
48	Dessert Plates, Full Nankeen			1/-	2.	8/-
4	Setts of teas 1st [size] Broseley Nankeen			5/-	1.	-.-
6	Setts of do 2nd [size] New fluted Shrewsbury			5/4	1.	12/-
14	Setts of teas 2nd [size] Image, blue edge			2/8	1.	17/4
5	Quart mugs		white	1/-		5/-
1	Teapot 1st [size] plain		do	8d		8d
1	do 2nd [size] do		do	10½d		10½d
6	Pint basons	do	do	5d		
13	Milks 1st [size]	do	do	3d		
24	Coffees	do	do	3d		
1	Quart Jug		do	1/6d		1/6d
4	Low Chelsea ewers		do	4d		1/4d
2	Coach pots, Full Nankeen			1/4d		

It will be observed that the Chamberlain purchases from the Caughley factory fall into two categories—underglaze blue (mainly printed) designs, and white (undecorated) porcelains. This is because the Chamberlains were decorators and gilders—they had no need to buy enamelled patterns. The underglaze-blue printed designs were very good inexpensive selling lines, and, although the application of the blue prints to the body before glazing meant that the Chamberlains could not themselves produce these wares, they probably added gilt lines and gold ornamentation to handles and knobs of the Caughley blue printed porcelains.

The white, undecorated Caughley porcelains purchased by Chamberlains were, of course, decorated at Worcester by Chamberlain's gilders and painters. Some of these were intended for sale in their own retail shop but others painted for Thomas Turner, were returned to Caughley or forwarded to Turner's London warehouse, the 'Salopian China Warehouse' at 5 Portugal Street, Lincolns Inn Fields, London.

Many of the designs added by the Chamberlains at Worcester are shown in the Turner-Chamberlain accounts set out in two separate columns, the first apparently being the price of the undecorated Caughley object (which had already been charged to Chamberlain, the second giving the cost of decorating the object. One half page is particularly interesting in that the heading reads:

'GOODS RETURNED NOT FIT FOR GILDING'.

The following list therefore shows the Caughley goods in the state that they were received from Caughley, some of which were apparently partly decorated with blue-printed designs, or with the underglaze-blue portions of patterns, combining blue with overglaze gilding. Patterns such as 'Nankeen border', 'Temple', 'Shropshire Nankeen', 'Birds-eye', 'Fly' are mentioned and were only sent to the

Chamberlains for gilt borders and other enrichments to be added. In the following list (dated July 15th 1790) of returned goods, the normal second column of gilding charges is, of course, not given.

10	Milks & covers, Broseley Nankeen border	£1. 5. 0.
2	Ewers, Birds-eye	5. 0.
6	Cups do	6. 3.
5	Saucers do	5. 2½
2	Coffees do	2. 8.
1	[tea] canister & cover, Birds-Eye	2. 6.
3	coffees, Fly	4. 0.
4	do new fluted white	3. 0.
1	do plain, Festoon	10.
2	do Shropshire Nankeen	1. 8.
1	Sugar box & cover do	1. 9.
1	Teapot stand	2. 0.
1	Saucer dagger border	5.
1	Cup Broseley Nankeen border	10.
12	Sugar boxes to have lids	18. 0.

The goods, incidentally were apparently packed in hay, for some later lists of returned goods were 'broke in Cartage, no Hay between'.

The following selections from the original Chamberlain records show Caughley porcelains decorated by the Chamberlains at Worcester. They are given to show not only the relative cost of the basic white porcelain (first column) and the added decoration (given in the second column), but also the types of pattern decorated and gilt by the Chamberlains. These lists appear under the page headings 'THOS TURNER ESQR. TO CHAMBERLAIN & SON' in the Chamberlain records:

July 22nd 1789   *decoration*

1	complete set of Broseley Bridge border	£2. 2. 6.	£1. 7. 0.
1	cup & saucer[1] Jett [black enamel] festoons	1. 1.	1. 10.
1	do with gold star	1. 1.	1. 10.
1	do Blue & gold birds-eye	2. 1.	1. 10.
1	do Royal Jessamine	2. 1.	1. 10.
1	do Jett [black enamel] flowers	1. 1.	1. 1.
1	do Black Segg [first letter indistinct]	1. 1.	1. 2.
1	do Green & gold Royal Wheel- [word indistinct]-border	1. 1.	3. 0.
1	do Purple & gold	2. 1.	2. 6.
1	do white & gold sprigs	5d	1. 2.
1	do fine blue & gold sprigs	5d	1. 4.
1	do Tulip with gold edge	5d	1. 8.
1	do Green & gold sprigs	5d	9d
10	Setts of teas [cups & saucers] red bordered	£1. 5. 0.	£1. 10. 0.
24	Dessert plates, Dresden flowers, gold edge & Ring [centre?]	£1. 16. 0.	£1. 5. 0.
1	Centrepiece do	10. 6.	4. 1.
2	Sauce tureens, do complete	18. 0.	8. 4.
4	Richmond [shape name] shells, Dresden flowers	16. 0.	8. 0.
10	Dishes do	£2. 0. 0.	£1. 5. 0.

[1] These cups and saucers of different designs appear to be pattern pieces, see accounts under October 27th, 1789. The undecorated cups and saucers at 1s 1d each were white blanks, those at 2s 1d having some underglaze blue portions (Plates 60, 61, 80 and 81).

Oct. 8th 1789

1	Complete set of Royal star	£2. 17. 0.	£2. 14. 0.	
1	do Birds-Eye	£2. 17. 0.	£2. 6. 0.	
1	Pint mug with J. BRODHURST CHERTON in gold	1. 6.⎫		7. 0.
1	½ Pint do do	1. 0.⎭		

Oct. 20th 1789

1	Complete set of Broseley Bridge border	£2. 2. 0.	£1. 7. 0.
6	coffees plain Temple gilt edge & ring	5. 0.	2. 0.
1	complete white & gold Pomegranate (2 coffees short).	17. 7.	£1. 6. 10.
12	Saucers Broseley white & gold for sprigs— the set before sent.	8. 0.	8. 0.

Oct. 27th 1789

1	complete set of white & gold Festoon (4 coffee extra, except canisters)	£1. 13. 3.	£3. 0. 4.
1	complete set Blue & gold Festoon	£2 17. 0.	£1. 18. 0.

Patterns sent[1]

1	cup & saucer Royal Star	2. 1.	2. 2.
1	do Birds-eye	2. 1.	1. 10.
1	do Royal Jessamine	2. 1.	2. 6.
1	do white & gold festoon	1. 1.	2. 4.
1	do blue & gold do	2. 1.	1. 6.
1	do white & gold wreath	1. 1.	1. 10.
1	do fawn & gold do	1. 1.	2. 4.
1	do 1st [size] blue & gold sprig	5d	1. 4.
1	do do white & gold sprig	5d	1. 2.

Jan. 28th 1790

TO CAUGHLEY

1	Complete sett of Royal Star	£2. 17. 0.	£2. 14. 0.
1	do new fluted gold festoon	£1. 11. 9.	£2. 18. 0.
6	coffees do do	4. 6.	7. 0.
1	B & B plate 1st [size] new fluted gold festoon	1. 3.	2. 4.
1	do 2nd [size] do do	1. 9.	2. 11.
1	Teapot stand do	1. 0.	1. 9.
1	[spoon] tray do	1. 0.	1. 9.
1	[tea] cannister do	1. 6.	2. 4.
12	cups & saucers, new fluted, Blue & gold	£1. 5. 0.	18. 0.
1	Slop Bason do	2. 6.	1. 6.
1	sugar box & cover do	2. 6.	1. 10½
1	Teapot 4th (size) do	3. 6.	2. 7½
1	Ewer do	2. 6.	1. 1½
1	complete set, Dagger border edge & line	£1. 14. 0.	£1. 1. 0.
1	do new fluted festoon in colours	£1. 11. 9.	£4. 0. 0.

May 22nd 1790

6	Melons [shaped dessert dishes] Royal Lily [see Plates 53 and 54]	£1. 10. 0.	18. 0.
2	Squares [shaped dessert dishes] do	10. 0.	6. 0.
1	Tureen & stand do	2. 6.	2. 0.
6	Dessert Plates 3rd [size] do	9. 0.	7. 6.

[1] The patterns show standard Caughley-Chamberlain designs of the period with the relative cost of the different styles of decoration. The cups costed at 2s 1d (before decoration by Chamberlain) have underglaze blue in the design (as Plates 60, 61, 80 and 81). This was applied at Caughley and these cups and saucers are therefore more expensive than the plain ones at 1s 1d without underglaze blue.

1	Coffee pot Broseley [shape] Nankeen edge & line	7. 6.	2. 6.
2	do new fluted Birds-eye	15. 0.	11. 0.
1	Complete [tea] sett plain 1st [size] white & gold sprigs, Princess Amelia's border.	18. 10.	£1. 18. 0.

Although this Chamberlain account book, giving details of goods decorated for Thomas Turner of Caughley, consists of 213 pages, listing many thousands of articles, I have space to quote from only four of these pages. The book, however, ends with a personal note which is worth repeating and is an amusing break between the lists of goods given in this Chapter:

'When prizing [sic] the above bill [dated May 25th 1791] we had word sent [that] a large company of strangers were coming. I therefore hasten'd to send off your account and left one side of ours unfinished—by which means there is a difference on the china side of 2/5. Mr Turner knowledge how I am situated in a retail shop will I hope plead some excuse for this or any other similar mistake I may undesigningly have made.'

Another old Chamberlain book has written on the outside of the cover, 'Mr Turner's Order Book April 9th 1791' and clearly follows on from a similar earlier book, as the first few entries are 'orders from the Old Book'. In the main this book lists teawares that were to be gilt or enamelled by the Chamberlains at Worcester, the amount of porcelain listed being very large, totalling many thousands of articles. One half page lists the following pieces to be enamelled with 'French sprigs' and as there are 163 pages in this one book, the total is very considerable.

468 Cups. 1st size
472 Saucers   „
 32 Cups 2nd size
 34 saucers.   „
 35 Pint Basons
 36 Sugar Boxes
 28 Teapots
 34 Teapot stands
 37 Spoon trays
 19 Ewers
232 coffee cups
 72 plates
 27 tea cannisters
 12 half pint basons
  7 quarter pint basons
  6 low Ewers

The main designs added to these Caughley porcelains by Chamberlains during the period, April 1791 to May 1793, covered by this book are:

Birds-Eye border[1] (normally enamelled on 'new fluted shapes')
Blue border, No. 4.
Blue & gold festoon
Blue & gold sprigs
Blue & green sprig and border
Broseley edge and line

[1] Notes regarding slight changes from the normal version of the bird's eye design are noted against some entries—'Stars on the outside instead of sprigs and between the stars small rose buds in gold' or '1 cup with the star in the bottom but no circle of gold round'.

Broseley, edge border
Broseley gold edge
Broseley gold sprigs
Broseley Nankeen chain border
Brown edge
Dagger border
Dresden gold edge
Foreign wreath, enamelled
French sprigs
Gilt edge and ring
Hoppole pattern
Lady's sprigs (Plate 64)
Pink border
Plymouth, gilt festoon
Royal Fly
Royal Jesamine
Royal Star

While the vast majority of entries refer to tea services or parts of such sets, there are a few entries which relate to other wares. These in particular occur under the name of Mr Ferguson, who would appear to have had a retail, or wholesale, shop in Holland for, apart from references to 'Dutch sets' and the components of such Dutch services, there is an entry, 'pattern will be sent from Holland'. Mr Ferguson required in August 1792 several unusual and interesting articles:

A pattern of all the different things done in crests, Coats of Arms etc. etc. which may be broken or cracked.
1 pattern of china bottle and stand, round, pint and quart size.
6 half pint mugs made wide and painted in round panel with Hope, Virtue, Landscape etc.
1 cup and saucer with Prince of Orange Coat of Arms.
A pattern of Table (dinner) service.
A   do   of dessert.
Some patterns of Buttons and Knife handles.
1 Complete set blue and gold Birds-Eye, but star, instead of the blue sprigs in the outside and between each star put a small rose bud in gold. The fluted cups to be the same size of our sets. The star at the bottom to be the same as the Birds Eye.
1 complete set new fluted with fine blue border under the glaze with a running wreath in gold and the same small sprig on the outside as the pattern called Amitie. Stars at the bottom of the cups, etc. . . . . .

In addition to the porcelains that were sent from Caughley with underglaze-blue decoration, and which were gilt by the Chamberlains at Worcester, Chamberlain also purchased a very large amount of white, completely undecorated porcelain. This was of standard Caughley shapes and would have been decorated with overglaze enamel patterns or with gilding. Some of it may have been completed to Turner's order, but much must have been destined for Chamberlain's own retail shop in Worcester. Many pages could be filled with descriptions of Caughley white porcelain listed in the Chamberlain accounts, but a few items selected at random, all of 1789 date, give an idea of the range of these. Apart from the many components of tea and dessert services, the wares include:

15	dożen small gadroon boats, white		6d	£4.	10.	0.
7	Dolphin ewers	,,	6d		3.	6.
35	small milks, common	,,	6d		17.	6.

67

2	Saffer pots	White	1/-		2.	0.
2	ice cups & covers	,,	1/-		2.	0.
20	complete setts of toys (child's teasets)	,,	3/6	£3.	10.	0.
26	Raddish dishes	,,	2/-	£2.	12.	0.
2	Quart Jugs	,,	5/6		11.	0.
6	caudle cups and covers, 2 handles	,,	2/-		12.	0.
13	Stands to do	,,	1/-		13.	0.
24	Paint stands, white to pattern		3d		6.	0.
5	candlesticks	,,	2/-		10.	0.
14	egg drainers	,,	4d		4.	8.
1	Ice pail, pan and cover	,,	18/-		18.	0.
13	¼ Pint mugs	,,	6d		6.	6.
11	½ Pint mugs	,,	1/-		11.	0.
14	Pint mugs	,,	1/6	£1.	1.	0.
11	Quart mugs	,,	2/-	£1.	2.	0.
27	Quart Dutch jugs	,,	3/-	£4.	1.	0.
29	Tumblers, 1st size, horn shape	,,	4d		9.	8.
37	Tumblers, 2nd size, horn shape	,,	6d		18.	6.
19	Pint Dutch jugs	,,	2/-	£1.	18.	0.
2	Quart do	,,	3/-		6.	0.
19	egg stands	,,	6d		9.	6.
10	Pint mugs	,,	1/6		15.	0.
15	Quart mugs	,,	2/-	£1.	10.	0.
18	Raddish dishes, leaf handled	,,	2/-	£1.	16.	0.

The amount of Caughley porcelain purchased by Messrs Chamberlains at Worcester, or decorated by the Chamberlains and sold back to Thomas Turner at Caughley, was very large, and the transactions took place over several years, from 1788, continuing after the Chamberlains had started to make their own porcelains. The cost totals for this intertrading during the years 1792 and 1793 are set out in the Chamberlain accounts.

1792

Bot. of Thos. Turner Esq. Salop

To China as per 49 invoices from December 21st (*sic*) 1791 to December 31st 1792.		£2,053.	6.	7½
To Undercharges, etc.		7.	6.	6.
To Damaged china gilt		25.	14.	1.
		£2,086.	10.	1½
By Overcharges, etc.			9.	18. 7½
		£2,076.	11.	6.
By Discount 25 per cent		519.	2.	10½
		£1,557.	8.	7½
To Gilding	£20. 3. 7½			
By Discount 5 per cent	1. 0. 2½		19.	3. 5.
		£1,576.	12.	0½
fwd		£1,576.	12.	0½
To Packages, nett			13.	11. 4.
		£1,590.	3.	4½

Sold Thos. Turner Esq. Salop

From December 12th 1791 to December 31st 1792.	
China, Best	£839. 11. 11½
Undercharges, etc.	11. 17. 10½
	£851. 9. 10.
To overcharges, etc.	3. 7. 3½
	£848. 2. 6½
To Discount 25 per cent	212. 0. 7½
	£636. 1. 11.

By Gilding	£572. 18. 9½	
Discount 5 per cent	28. 12. 11.	544. 5. 10½
		£1180. 7. 9½
Clear goods	10. 7. 6.	
Undercharges etc.	23. 9. 8¼	33. 17. 2¼
		£1214. 4. 11¾
Clear goods, overcharged		2. 2. 11½
		£1212. 2. 0¼

1793

Bot. of Thos. Turner Esq. Salop

For china nett amount from December 31st 1792 up to 23rd November 1793.	£1054. 13. 0¾

Sold Thos. Turner Esq. Salop

By China, Gilding etc. nett from 31st December 1792 to 20th November 1793.	£843. 17. 0½

However, by no means all Caughley porcelain decorated by Chamberlain at Worcester was carried out for Turner, as Chamberlain himself sold much of it. The following typical entry in the Chamberlain sales books will illustrate this point, the porcelains referred to being, apparently, standard, well-known, blue-printed Caughley wares.

February 28th 1791.
  Mr Willm. Taylor. Warrington, Lancashire.

2	Setts of teas, Rose			4/6d
2	Setts	Nankin		4/6
2	Setts	Image		4/6d
2	Setts	Birds, blue edge		5/4d
2	Setts	New Temple		6/-
2	Setts	circled landscape		7/-
2	pint bason		@ 1/1	2/2d
2	½ pint do		@ 8½	1/5d
2	milks do		@ 8½	1/5d
2	Pint basons, Temple			1/10d
2	½ pint do	do	@ 7d	1/2d
2	milks	do	@ 7d	1/2d
6	Pint basons	Rose, Image & Nankeen	@ 9d	4/6d
6	½ pint do	do	@ 5½	2/9d
6	Milks do	do	@ 5½	2/9d

The Chamberlain accounts pose one intriguing problem, for they include several references to figures and groups, as well as to animal models. In the Chamberlain-Turner order book under February 2nd, 1791, the following note was entered:

'Wanted for the Manufactory.
A few enamelled figures & doggs of all
sorts immediately'.

It is probable that the 'manufactory' was the Caughley works, and another book, where Chamberlain's decorating and gilding charges for enhancing Turner's Caughley porcelain are listed, gives at the same period:

		Ware	Decorating Cost
6	Single figures, Dancing	15/-	6/-
4	do do , Gardners	10/-	4/-
2	do , with child	5/-	2/-
10	pair single figures, Enamel'd	£2. 10. 0.	£1. 0. 0.
7	double do do	£1. 8. 0.	8/2
2	Women with a child each	5/-	2/-
2	pair single figures, Dancing	5/-	4/-
2	Greyhounds, killing the Hare	3/-	1/6

and in April and May 1791 there was listed:

		Ware	Decorating Cost
40	Pointer Dogs, Enaml'd	£1. 10. 0.	£1. 0. 0.
1	Double figure	4/-	1/2
6	pair of single figures	£1. 10. 0.	12/-
130	Pointer dogs Enamel'd	£4. 17. 6.	£3. 5. 0.
12	dogs a fiteing (sic), Enamel'd	2/3	9/-
3	French Terriers do	2/3	1/6
12	Foxes do	9/-	6/-
12	Catts at Play do	12/-	9/-
12	double figures do	£2. 8. 0.	14/-
14	Men do with a child each Enamel'd	£1. 15. 0.	14/-
8	Women figures with a child each, enamel'd	£1. 0. 0.	8/-
6	do do single do	15/-	6/-
6	men do do do	15/-	6/-
15	Houses Enall'd to pattern (pattern returned)	£1. 2. 6.	£1. 2. 6.

It would seem that these undecorated figures and animals were sent from Caughley for decoration at Worcester, and then returned to Turner, but it is most unlikely that they were of Caughley manufacture, for no figures or animals with Caughley characteristics are at present known. The most likely explanation is that Turner purchased these undecorated figures from the Derby factory to meet a market for which he did not cater himself.

In support of this theory there is the fact that two fragments of typical Derby bisque (unglazed) white groups were found on the Caughley site, and that models matching some of these descriptions are to be found in the published lists of Derby models. Other Derby-type figures were sold by Chamberlain at his retail shop in High Street, Worcester between 1789 and 1792, or are included in the 1792 stock list, for example:

'Turks' @ 4/-
'1 Group of biscuit [unglazed] figures' 15/-
'1 Group of Figures, large white' 14/-
'Pair of Lambs' 1/6d
'3 Pointers & partridges' 9/-
'1 Greyhound & hare' 1/6d
'23 sheep, plain white' 7/8d

The fact that some at least of these figures came from Turner at Caughley (but were not necessarily made there) is shown by the Chamberlain records of 'goods received from Thos. Turner Esq. Caughley', which included in 1789:

A Group of Shepperd & Shepperdess etc.
4 doz. Lambs, white.
75 pair of Dogs, white, per pair 1/6
17 pair of fancy figures, white, a child, each 5/-
20 small Lambs, white @ 4d with note '20 lambs overcharged 1d each, price fixed by Mr Turner.
3 dozen ditto.
1 pair of Biscuit Single Figures @ 18/6
1 group   do.   15/-
2 Pair of Figures, damaged   15/-
note 'This Figure gave to Mrs C' and 15/- deducted.

and in 1790:

42 Gardners, white. £5.5.0
10 pair of Fancy figures with a child @ 5/- each
5 pair of   do   do   less size @ 5/-
17 small Fancy figures, each 2/6

It is, of course, possible but most unlikely that these models were made at Caughley, but if they were in fact originally of Derby origin, then it is apparent that some Derby models were decorated by Chamberlain at Worcester, a fact hitherto unknown to historians of this subject. It is apparent from these Chamberlain records, that Turner of Caughley dealt in Derby wares, for in a list of "Goods Recd. from Thos. Turner Esq. Caughley . . ." we find "6 Caudle cups & covers with stands, Derby make, white" and "6 of those tall Caudle cups you have Derby make" (see Pages 61 & 62).

In this chapter we have learned that some Caughley blue and white designs were enhanced, by Chamberlains' gilders, with gilt edges and border designs. This contemporary treatment should not be confused with 'clobbering', in which blue and white porcelains of various types—Chinese Nankin porcelain, Worcester as well as Caughley, were enriched with overglaze enamels, normally green, red and gold, resulting in a most unhappy heavy appearance. Some of this 'clobbering' would appear to have been added in the nineteenth century by persons seeking to make more desirable the then unfashionable blue and white wares.

CHAPTER VI

DESIGNS OTHER THAN BLUE AND WHITE

In this chapter we have to deal with the overglaze designs, both enamelled and gilt, found on Caughley porcelain, and also with the rare, black, basalt-bodied wares.

I believe that the Caughley factory was concerned in the main with producing relatively inexpensive porcelains, decorated in underglaze blue, and that very little overglaze enamel painting was carried out there. The enamelled and gilt Caughley porcelains would appear to belong, in the main, to the last ten years of the factory's existence, when Chamberlain at Worcester was decorating Caughley porcelains for Turner and for his own retail shop in Worcester. Enamelled porcelains illustrated in previous books as Caughley are, in several cases, Worcester, like the teapot and stand shown in Plate 307.

In July 1775, Robert Hancock 'now engaged in the Salopian China Manufactory', advertised that he had 'an ample assortment of the blue & white, and will with all possible expedition proceed in the enamelled . . . china . . ' (see Page 3) but there is no evidence to show that enamelled porcelain was in fact decorated at Caughley. There is a glaring shortage of enamel pieces amongst the thousands of blue and white 'wasters' found on the factory site and, while it must be admitted that enamelled designs always have far fewer failings, owing to the relatively low firing temperature they experienced, the fact remains that many enamelled 'wasters' were found of the post-1799 John Rose porcelains made at the same factory.

Some Caughley porcelains, seemingly of the 1775–85 period are found with enamelled designs which, however, could have been added by independent decorators, such as Giles of London, whose account books record transactions with Thomas Turner while at Worcester and at Caughley (see Page 78).

The teawares shown in Plates 58 and 59 are, on the evidence of form, of the 1775–85 period, and the slight floral sprays may be factory decoration, but most

Caughley overglaze decoration is of the post-1789 period, when Chamberlain was actively engaged in decorating Caughley porcelains, so that this chapter is closely linked with the preceding one. Some of this Caughley porcelain was supplied to Chamberlain in the white state, without any decoration, but much bore underglaze blue decoration such as flowers, blue borders, or lines, and examples of these part-decorated wares are included in the factory wasters shown in Plate 8.

On occasions, the Chamberlains requested variations in these standard blue bordered wares—

12 ½ pint mugs, . . thin blue border top & bottom but not so wide in border. (see Page 61).
24 pint mugs Plymouth (pattern), the painters to put 6 stripes.
24 ½ pints do let the blue be as strong as possible. (see Page 62.)

These partly decorated blue designs were finished with gilt edges and gold enrichments, sometimes over the underglaze blue stripes, or borders. Examples of finished designs are shown in Colour Plate VII and Plates 60, 61, 80, 81, 96, 97, etc, and the names for some of the very popular and attractive blue and gold patterns, according to the contemporary accounts, were: Birds-Eye, Dresden Flowers, Royal Fly, Royal Stripe, Royal Jessamine, and others listed in Chapter V. These and similar designs are illustrated in Plates 60 and 61.

Chamberlains were apparently not the only decorators to finish partly decorated porcelains. Joseph Lygo, the manager of the London shop of the Derby porcelain factory, reported back to William Duesbury in September, 1786:

. . . they [the retailers] all of them go to the Worcester & Salopian Warehouses and buy goods unfinished, and then have them gilt, which most makes it impossible to do any business with them, . . . there is still more and more of the goods made, laid with the blue only. . . .

It is interesting to see from this contemporary reference from a knowledgeable source that the Worcester warehouse was also selling blue decorated porcelains which needed to be finished with added gilding.

Although several London dealers and decorators must have been capable of gilding these Caughley and other porcelains, today we know of very few of these decorators and dealers. In the 1790s William Hewson of 86 Aldgate Without, London, purchased quantities of white porcelain from the Chamberlains, presumably subsequently decorated by Hewson. It is also possible that the famous Baxter decorating studio painted Caughley porcelains in the late 1790s, as it certainly purchased large quantities of Coalport porcelain (made at Caughley after 1799), and it is likely that this was a natural continuation of earlier trade with the Caughley factory under Thomas Turner.

To return to the main decorators of Caughley porcelain, Messrs Chamberlain of Worcester (apart from the porcelains incorporating both underglaze blue, added during manufacture, and overglaze gilding), must have decorated a further range of Caughley porcelain with overglaze enamelled patterns, for they purchased vast quantities of white Caughley porcelain. It would be impossible to list all the undecorated wares shown in the Chamberlain account books, but sample entries from 1789 include:

> Cabbage-leaf, mask-head jugs, in all sizes [see Plates 67 to 71] both in white and with blue borders added.
> Mugs, all sizes, both white and with blue borders.
> Caudle cups and saucers.
> Dessert wares.
> Raddish dishes, leaf handle
> Egg cups & strainers.
> Candlesticks.
> Bowls.
> Toy teasets.
> Tumblers.

with other articles listed on Pages 67–8, and hundreds of articles of teaware.

These wholly undecorated Caughley porcelains sent to the Chamberlains were, of course, decorated with purely overglaze enamel and gilt motifs, some of the enamelled designs listed in the Chamberlain accounts being described as— Foreign Wreath—enamelled; French Sprigs; Lady's Sprigs; Pink Border; Gilt Edge and Ring.

In some instances the Chamberlain account books list many single cups and saucers decorated with different designs. It is extremely likely that these were painted as pattern samples, and in at least one instance a list of such different items is headed 'Patterns sent'. Overglaze designs painted on Caughley porcelain by the Chamberlain decorators in 1789 include the following, listed with the decorating charge for one cup and saucer.

Jett [black] festoons	[cost of decoration]	1/10d.
Jett [black] festoons	,,	1/1d.
Gold star	,,	1/10d.
Green & gold Royal Wheel border	,,	3/-
White & gold festoon	,,	2/4d.
White & gold sprigs	,,	1/2d.
White & gold sprigs—chain border	,,	1/10d.
Green & gold sprigs	,,	9d.
Tulip with gold edge	,,	1/8d.
Fine blue & gold edge	,,	1/4d.
White & gold wreath	,,	1/10d.
Fawn & gold wreath	,,	2/4d.

There are many further references to other wares enamelled by Chamberlains to Turner's order but, in most cases, little information is entered in the account books, such entries as '12 low Ewers Enamel'd Different' being unhelpful in identifying the designs today.

In contrast to the rather slight patterns listed above, more ornate designs are sometimes found on marked Caughley porcelains, for example, the covered tureen and stand shown in Plate 66, which is a very good example of the colourful 'Japan' or Oriental inspired designs. It bears the impressed 'SALOPIAN' name mark but was found with other unmarked pieces of a matching dessert service which appeared to be of Worcester make. This mixed service was perhaps one supplied by the Chamberlains to 'Mrs Squire at Lady Knollizic, Soho Square, London' in August 1789:

```
1 Centrepiece, scarllet [sic] & gold Japan
2 heart [shaped] dishes        do.
4 mellon [shaped] dishes       do.
2 cream tureens, complete      do.
10 Plates                      do.
         Sent per Smiths Waggon, Aug. 27th, 1789.
```

Another very colourful 'Japan' pattern occasionally found on Caughley porcelain is known as the 'Bishop Sumner' or 'Bengal Tiger' design (Plate 65). It is found on Chinese porcelain, on Dr Wall Worcester porcelain, on Caughley porcelain, as well as on later Chamberlain Worcester and Coalport porcelain. In fact it was so popular that it is to be found on the wares of nearly every porcelain manufacturer. It is mentioned many times in the Chamberlain accounts as 'Draggon', and from 1795 was entered in Chamberlain's own pattern book under the number '75', so that from this period Chamberlain's own porcelains painted with this design normally bear the painted pattern number '75'. The earlier versions painted on Caughley porcelain do not bear any pattern number as they were decorated before the practice of pattern numbering was commenced.

Much of the white Caughley porcelain sold to Chamberlain at Worcester was subsequently bought back by Turner in its finished, decorated state. In December 1789, the following decorated porcelains were ordered from Chamberlains for 'Thos. Turner, Esq. at the Salopian China Warehouse, No. 5, Portugall Street, Lincoln Inn Fields, London':

```
1 complete sett Broseley White & gold Festoon
1        do.     Gold Wreath
1        do.     Bird-Eye
1        do.     Blue & gold Festoon
1        do.     White & gold Festoon
2        do.     New Royal Festoon
1 Sett of Patterns
1 Dessert service, Full Nankin, (gilt) Edge & line
```

Subsequent orders in the same Chamberlain-Turner order book include the following notes:

```
Jany. 23rd, 1790. 'Orders & Remarks from T. Turner Esq.
4 dessert services—Fleur de lis
1 dessert service, blue & gold Birds Eye
The colour'd setts much wanted, before ordered'.

April 23rd, 1790.
6 Quart Jugs, enamel'd different patterns, not as Rich as those before sent.
6 Pint    do.      do.
6 Quart Mugs       do.
```

Some of the finest overglaze painting on Caughley porcelain is to be found on the moulded Cabbage-leaf jugs, a good range of which can be seen at the Victoria and Albert Museum, some being reproduced in Colour Plate VIII and Plates

67–71. I wish that I could accept this as factory decoration but it seems apparent that they were decorated for Turner of Caughley by Chamberlain at Worcester, whose account books record many purchases of white cabbage-leaf jugs, and also specimens with only the underglaze blue border at top and bottom (as Colour Plate VIII). The 1790 note from Turner's London warehouse addressed to Chamberlain requesting jugs 'enamel'd different patterns, not as Rich as those before sent . . .', provides yet more evidence that Chamberlain was painting these jugs for Turner.

Some of these Caughley cabbage-leaf moulded jugs were, however, decorated for Chamberlain's own retail shop in Worcester, the specimen shown in Plate 67 having been probably prepared for the local market, as the central panel shows a view of the City of Worcester. The style of decoration, with gilt sprays of flowers at the sides and small sprigs scattered about the body, is repeated on several other jugs of this type (see Plates 69 and 70).

One of the finest Caughley cabbage-leaf moulded jugs is shown in Colour Plate VIII. This specimen, now in the Victoria and Albert Museum, is painted with birds in landscapes and the same painter's hand can be recognized on marked Chamberlain porcelain over a long period. The artist was, in fact, George Davis, who from at least July, 1793, was Chamberlain's highest paid artist and was also presumably the foreman, as on several occasions all the decorator's wages were recorded as being given to Davis 'for the men'. Typical entries for Davis' painting on later Chamberlain porcelain include:

1	Quart jug, Davis's birds.	£1. 1. 0.
6	Chocolates & saucers, Davis' birds.	£4. 4. 0.
1	can & saucer, blue border, Davis's birds in the front of the cup & bottom of saucer, yellow between.	£1. 11. 6.

Apart from colourful bird compositions, Davis also painted fruit and flowers and some of the fine quality flower painting on the Caughley cabbage-leaf jugs may well be by his hand, and at least one superb Caughley jug, which bears on the front a typical Davis bird composition, has on the sides finely enamelled fruit and floral compositions by the same hand. The central gilt border, seen on the Davis bird painted jug shown in Colour Plate VIII, is to be found on other jugs of the same type with different painted motifs, indicating a common source of decoration (see Plates 68 and 69). The use of *overglaze* blue enamel in the borders is noteworthy, and again helps to identify specimens from one decorating establishment, probably Chamberlains.

One of the finest specimens of a gilt cabbage-leaf jug is shown in Plate 71. It is decorated with the crowned Royal Garter and motto (the badge of King George IV, as Prince of Wales) within an elaborate panel, and the gilt floral sprays each side of it are of the very finest quality. This jug, with matching tea-ware (Plate 74), was sold at Messrs Sotheby's London salerooms in 1967; another is in the Victoria and Albert Museum.

Other Caughley porcelains with Royal subjects were certainly decorated by Chamberlain's enamellers and gilders, as is shown by entries in the Chamberlain account books, where records of seemingly ornate goods decorated with the Prince of Wales' feather crest were sent to Turner's London warehouse:

2 Quart Dutch Jugs, fine blue border, richly gilt,
Princes Feathers, etc. etc.   £2. 2. 0.
                                                        (charge for gilding)
(January 24th, 1790)

On April 9th more articles decorated with the Prince's Feathers were sent by Chamberlain to Turner's London premises. They are listed below with the *decorating charges*, which are extremely high, indicating a very ornate design, for in general these charges are some four times higher than that recorded for standard patterns.

2	Teapots, Princes Feather		£3. 0. 0.
2	Stands to do.	do.	£1. 6. 0.
2	Sugar Boxes & covers	do.	£2. 4. 0.
2	Pint Basons	do.	£1. 16. 0.
2	Ewers, new shape	do.	£1. 6. 0.
2	B & B plates 1st [size]	do.	£1. 16. 0.
2	do. 2nd [size]	do.	£2. 4. 0.
11	Caudle Cups	do.	£7. 16. 0.
1	Stands to do.	do.	£7. 16. 0.
11	Chocolates	do.	£6. 12. 0.
1	Stands to do.	do.	£6. 12. 0.

A cup painted with the Prince of Wales' feather crest is shown in Plate 73.

In October, 1790, similarly very expensively decorated porcelains were painted or gilt with the Duke of York's bearings, a few sample prices being:—

1	Teapot,	Duke of York	3/6 (cost of undecorated ware)				£1. 10. 0.	
							(decoration)	
7	Chocolate cups	do.	7/-	,,	,,	,,	£3. 15. 10	,,
12	,, stands	do.	9/-	,,	,,	,,	£6. 10. 0.	,,

A very tasteful design sometimes found on Caughley porcelain is called 'Amitie', basically consisting of a central, circular panel in which are painted two doves, with the inscription 'L'Amitie' written on a scroll above them. Typical teawares painted with this pattern are shown in Plate 75. This pattern, which is rare, may not have been introduced before June, 1791, when an entry in the cash book records the payment of eight pence for the receipt of a parcel sent from Birmingham with the 'design Amitie'. Subsequent Chamberlain sales records show sales of this design, often with the abbreviation 'Brosy' for Broseley, the nearest township to the Caughley factory and a description often used by the Chamberlain clerks to denote porcelains of Caughley origin. Sets were listed at both seven and six guineas:

1	complete set. Brosy. New Amitie			£7. 7. 0.
6	coffee cups	do.	extra	£1. 0. 0.
				(January 10th, 1792)
2	complete setts, 2nd [size] Nf'd (new fluted form) Doves L'Amitie			£12. 12. 0.
				(August 6th, 1792)

Slight variations of this pattern occur, the central 'L'Amitie' motif remaining constant, but different borders being employed. The same basic design was also painted on Chamberlain's own porcelains, which are of different forms from the Caughley ones shown in Plate 75.

The very rare and perhaps unique oval deep dish or bowl (Plate 77) with yellow border and finely painted wreath of flowers, was almost certainly decorated outside the factory, perhaps at a London decorating establishment. The handled dish shown in Plate 76 was probably originally part of a handsome dessert service and again the decoration could have been added in London, perhaps at the workshop of an independent London decorator, Giles, for the gilt chains of husks, fruit and insect painting are reminiscent of the decoration favoured by him.

The London account books of James Giles, who, having died in 1780, can have decorated only early Caughley porcelain, show that between 1771 and 1776 he purchased from the main, so-called 'Dr Wall' Worcester factory, goods to the value of £1,370. 14. 0, but only £174. 16. 2d. worth of porcelain from Thomas Turner, and most of this was Worcester porcelain rather than Caughley wares. Up to June 24th 1775, the Turner entries in Giles' account books were put under the heading, 'Mr Thos. Turner at Worcester'. A new set of entries later in the book is headed 'Mr Thomas Turner of Caughley Hall' and commences with a cross-reference to the last Worcester entry—'June 24th, 1775. bot. forward from folio 39. £9. 3. 9½d.' These Giles' entries show that Worcester porcelain was sent by Giles to Hussey, the London agent for the Salopian warehouse. They also show that Turner had supplied Giles with 'Worcester china', on sale or return, up to May, 1775, and the sole reference to Caughley, or 'Salopian', porcelain appears under the date, November 17th, 1775:

To a parcel sent with Salopian white, errors excepted. £6. 2. 6d.

Unfortunately, the only surviving Giles' account book does not continue long after this date, and it may be that Giles did not continue his decorating trade up to his death in 1780, for in a five day sale of his Stock in Trade in March 1774, the catalogue announced that, 'Mr James Giles, Chinaman and enameller' was 'quitting that business'. However, the situation is complicated by the fact that the account book continues to 1776, in that year a further sale of his 'elegant and valuable stock' being held, and also Giles advertised that he 'continues to paint and enamel all sorts of china . . .' Some of this porcelain may have been of Caughley make but the quantity must have been small, and pre-1780 in date. The finely gilt cup and saucer shown in Plate 82 is very much in the style attributed to Giles' London decorating studio.

It has been suggested that Thomas Baxter gilded, or otherwise decorated, some Caughley porcelains at his London decorating establishment but, as the first record of this establishment is the sewer-rate of the Michaelmas quarter of 1797, it follows that Baxter could have decorated little Caughley porcelain in the two years between 1797 and October 1799 when Turner sold the factory.

It must be pointed out that the stock of Caughley porcelain advertised in the closing down sale held in November 1799, included porcelains 'richly executed in enamel and burnished gold . . .', but we have no proof that this was Caughley decoration; it could well have been Chamberlain decorated goods returned to Caughley for distribution and sale.

If readers should find damaged, or otherwise faulty, specimens of enamelled porcelain, it might be of interest to know that such articles were sold by Chamberlain in bulk to certain dealers at very low rates. In October 1792, Thomas Cumson, a very regular purchaser, took:

880 pieces damaged Enamel	£22.	
620 pieces damaged goods	£15. 10. 0.	

Some of the most attractive Caughley porcelains are those decorated with gilding only; for example, the designs shown in Plates 78, 79, 112, 198 and 201 are particularly pleasing and even modern in style.

It is difficult to know if this gilding is factory or outside work, but the Chamberlain gilders were most certainly responsible for some of these designs, for many white and gold patterns are listed in the contemporary account books showing the cost of decorating wares for Turner at Caughley. A few sample entries for gilt designs are given below with Chamberlain's charges to Turner for gilding these designs:

1	Complete set of white & gold festoons	£2. 18. 0.	(gilding charges)
1	complete set of white & gold Pomegranate	£1. 8. 2.	,,
1	complete set of white & gold wreath	£2. 6. 0.	,,
1	complete set of white & gold Broseley gold sprigs	£1. 13. 4.	,,
6	coffee plain Shropshire gold edge	1. 6.	,,
1	complete set of Toys (teaware) white & gold sprigs	4. 6.	,,
12	cups, gilt with crest	£2. 8. 0.	,,
1	complete sett, white & gold sprigs, Prince Amelia's border	£1. 18. 0.	,,
1	do. do. Toys do. do. do.	4. 6.	,,

Some of the 'Thomas Turner—Chamberlain & Son' accounts include special designs gilt to a pattern, a fact that suggests that at this period, *c.* 1789–92, Turner at Caughley did not have his own enamellers or gilders, otherwise he would have had no need to send patterns to Worcester for extra pieces to be decorated. In some cases the record of postage paid on letters received by Chamberlain from Turner at Caughley gives an indication of their content, and notes such as 'letter, with crest from Caughley' suggest that special designs were sent to Chamberlain to be enamelled on to Turner's Caughley porcelain for Turner's own customers. Other Caughley items decorated by Chamberlains 'to pattern' include:

1	Pint bason, rose colour flowers, gold edge, to pattern	1/2d.
1	sugar box do.	1/5½d.
8	coffees gilt arch. leaf border to pattern	5/4d.
	(June 14th, 1789)	
2	Saucers Broseley white & gold edge and line to pattern	10d.
	(November 19th, 1789)	

5   Saucers Broseley antique border and purple sprigs to
    pattern   5/-
                        (January 28th, 1790)
4   cups & saucers white & gold to Derby Pattern   9/4d.
                        (September 6th, 1790)

These and similar entries for goods decorated to pattern and sent to Caughley suggest strongly that the Chamberlain decorating establishment at Worcester was Thomas Turner's only means of decorating his own Caughley porcelain with overglaze enamel colours and gilding, for the patterns do not appear to be intricate ones, and if Turner had had any gilders or enamellers they should have been capable of decorating these wares on the site, without the need to send the objects to Worcester.

On the other hand, it is possible that Turner employed at least some gilders at Caughley at one period, for a few fragments of white and gold designs were discovered on the factory site. One is shown in Plate 113, with part of a matching dessert service. Other fragments found on the Caughley factory site show gilt borders added to standard blue printed patterns. The existence of rare gilt fragments on the factory site does not finally prove that the articles were gilt there, for they could represent Chamberlain decorated porcelains returned to the factory and damaged in transit as we have abundant proof that this movement of decorated porcelain was practised.

There is the further point that the gilt fragments found at Caughley had been fired, and the gilding subsequently burnished and, as the burnishing is the last decorating process, it is obvious that when the pieces reached this stage they had been checked for previous faults, either in the porcelain itself or in the subsequent decoration, and should have been without any fault that would have necessitated the article being discarded.

Several Caughley pieces bearing gilt enrichments also show the gilder's number or piece-rate tally mark on the inside of the footrim. Apart from numbers (which reached as high as 55) initials are also found in this position, 'T' and 'M' being relatively common, and in one instance (Colour Plate IV)[1] the name 'MORRIS' is found on the teapot and teapot stand of a service which bears the initial 'M' on the smaller pieces, so that the gilder's initial 'M' can be linked with the name 'MORRIS'. Similar gilt numbers or initials are found on blue and white Chinese Nankin-type porcelains bearing gilt borders, added in England. Chinese porcelains of this type are shown in Plates 11 and 13, and the total amount enhanced in this way must have been very considerable, for today, some 175 years later, specimens are by no means rare.

The gilding of Chinese blue and white porcelain was probably centred in London, where many decorators and gilders practised their craft, and if we can accept that the Chinese porcelains bearing English gilders' *number* tally marks are London decorated, then it seems probable that the similarly decorated and marked Caughley porcelains were also enhanced by London decorators. It is rather unlikely that these pieces were decorated at Chamberlain's Worcester

[1] See page 56.

establishment, as no such tally marks are found on Chamberlain's own porcelains made and decorated at the same period (or within about five years) of the probable date of these Caughley and Chinese porcelains, *i.e.* about 1780–95.

The gilt Caughley porcelains bearing gilders' *initial* marks may have been decorated at the factory, as at least five site fragments bear such initials, but this is not conclusive, as much research remains to be carried out on the source of the gilding found on Caughley and Chinese Nankin-type porcelains.

Even if it is subsequently shown that some overglaze enamel decoration was added by Caughley artists, it will probably be impossible to differentiate between factory decoration and that added by Chamberlains at Worcester, but as much of this Worcester decoration was added expressly on Turner's orders, and was subsequently either returned to the Caughley factory in Shropshire or to the Caughley factory's London establishment, it is convenient to regard all Caughley porcelains as such, and not to call them Chamberlain-Worcester.

It should be made clear that the Caughley porcelains decorated by Chamberlain at Worcester do not appear to have been marked with Chamberlain's name. The use of the various written 'Chamberlain Warranted' marks would seem to have been confined to Chamberlain's own porcelain, which he started to produce in the early 1790s, although he continued to decorate Caughley porcelains for several years after establishing his own factory. No overglaze mark therefore occurs on Caughley enamelled or gilt wares, the impressed name mark 'SALO-PIAN' found on some specimens having been added during manufacture as was the underglaze blue initial 'S', which may be found on porcelains bearing some underglaze blue, such as blue borders. The crescent and 'C' marks are not found on wholly enamelled or gilt Caughley wares and the wares do not bear pattern numbers.

Very little is known about the Caughley workmen, especially the painters (that is if any were employed, apart from the underglaze blue painters). Llewellyn Jewitt, writing in the *Art Journal* of March, 1862, states:

> Of the painters employed at Caughley, it will be sufficient to say that amongst those employed there, were John Parker, Thomas Fennell, and Henry Boden, famous for their skill in flowers; and that of Muss, Silk and others, excelled in landscapes and figures—some sepia landscapes for their fine artistic treatment; while among the gilders, a most important art, and one to which special attention has always been directed at these works, were men of the name of Rutland, March and Randall, who were considered proficients. Of the latter, a nephew . . . (John Randall) is still employed at the works, principally on birds.

While subsequent writers have copied Jewitt in attributing these artists to the Caughley factory, it would seem most likely that he really was referring to the Coalport works in its early days, not to the Caughley factory, for his wording '. . . special attention has always been [rather than 'was'] directed . . .' and 'a nephew is still employed at the works' indicates that he had the existing Coalport factory in mind. Jewitt also continued in the next paragraph to list the then present day COALPORT artists. This would also explain the mention of 'sepia landscapes being remarkable' and the inclusion of three painters 'famous for their skill in flowers', for it is difficult to link these descriptions with Caughley porcelain. In passing it should be mentioned that Jewitt associated Silk's name with landscapes and figures and yet the only signed example known to me is a superb flower painting. He was probably correct in attributing landscape subjects to Muss, for he painted a view, not significantly of the Caughley works, but of the Coalport factory which is reproduced (in line engraving) by Jewitt.

Of the true Caughley workmen we know only of:

(a) Richard Hicks (born 1765) who was apparently apprenticed to Thomas Turner at Caughley where he learned the art of copper-plate engraving with Thomas Minton. Hicks later went to Staffordshire where he was a partner in the important firm of Hicks, Meigh & Johnson (1822–35). He died in 1844.

(b) John Lawrence, who was employed at Caughley in about 1790, wrote to his former employer William Duesbury of the Derby factory—'I am now in the employ of Mr Turner the Salop China Manufactory . . .'(letter dated April 11th, 1790). Llewellyn Jewitt (*The Ceramic Art of Great Britain*, 1878) wrote of Lawrence as a 'repairer', a description normally applied to one who assembles and finishes porcelain figures and groups. Jewitt states that Lawrence absconded from Derby in 1772 while under articles of agreement.

(c) Vaughan, whose name is mentioned twice in the Chamberlain-Turner accounts and orders. In 1789 the Chamberlains ordered from Turner at Caughley:

'4 gross of cup and saucr.   Vaugh'n's turning'

and on March 6th, 1790, the Chamberlains paid Vaughan 'for Mr Turner' two guineas. It would therefore appear that Vaughan was well known both at Worcester and at Caughley, and that he had special skill in turning as his work was especially requested. Perhaps he was responsible for some of the fluted shapes, although these are normally moulded, not turned on the wheel.

(d) Thomas Blase. Llewellyn Jewitt stated that Thomas Blase was Turner's manager at the Caughley factory in 1795 and apparently Jewitt had a letter dated February 20th, 1795, from Blase to Duesbury (of the Derby porcelain factory) concerning a Derby painter named Withers.

(e) Withers. This painter, presumably Edward Withers, the flower painter, was taken on by Duesbury of the Derby works for a term of three years from September 27th, 1789, at 3s 6d a day, having come up to Derby from London. According to Jewitt, Withers was at Caughley in February, 1795, when letters were exchanged concerning this Derby painter. It is not known if, or for how long, Withers was employed at Caughley but he apparently returned to Derby where his name is included in the factory pattern books.

Local Church registers have not yielded very much information on the Caughley workpeople. The Barrow registers record the burial on March 20th,

1784 of 'Elizabeth Mountford, China Works' who must have been employed at Caughley as it was then the only local china or porcelain factory.

(*f*) There can be no such certainty about 'William Sherratt (Poter)' who in August, 1774, was married to Lydia Steel, as a 'Poter' could have worked at any of the small potteries in the neighbourhood. Nor do the following entries in the Benthall registers:

> Edward Yearsley, Potter, married Elizabeth Garbett in September, 1782.
> Edward Ward, Potter, married Ann Fieldhouse in July, 1793.

provide evidence that Yearsley and Ward were employed at Caughley. Again, even the marriage entry of December 18th, 1794:

> Hiram Hartshorne (of Brosley), Gilder, and Dorothy Glass,

though the description 'Gilder' indicates a porcelain trade rather than a country Pottery, proves nothing, for at this period it is possible that Hartshorne worked at Coalport not at Caughley.

The Caughley site has yielded three scraps of information on the workmen employed there. One of these takes the form of half of an unglazed porcelain turning tool, such as would have been used to finish articles turned on the wheel. The owner has incised his name into the porcelain tool before firing but unfortunately half of this is missing while the remaining part reads:

> Chr. . . .
> Sin. . . .
> his. . . .
> 1783

The second scrap is also a fragment of a potting tool which has the owner's initials 'S.W.' incised, with the date 1782, but we have no name to link with these initials.

The third, named, factory waster takes the form of an oval rough slab of porcelain, painted in underglaze blue, showing two sprays of flowers with the name 'Williams' above and 'No. 19' below. This is clearly a trial—perhaps of a new tone of underglaze blue and the name Williams could relate either to the colour mixer or to a blue painter.

One cannot close this section without mention of *overglaze* printing. Several authorities have stated that Worcester-type *overglaze* printing (normally in black) was practised at Caughley, but I believe that this is an error resulting from the fact that Worcester porcelains of the 1770–90 period have, in the past, been regarded as Caughley. No fragment with such decoration was found on the factory site and, with one exception, all specimens that I have seen were on Worcester forms. The exception is an interesting teapot in Lady Benthall's collection which bears a very fine, non-Worcester, black print and is otherwise completely devoid of decoration. The cover is plain white and there is no gilt line border. It would appear that this was sold in the white and that the print was applied outside the factory, perhaps by Giles, or even by Robert Hancock.

This teapot, or a similar one, is illustrated in the *Transactions of the English Ceramic Circle*, Vol 6, Part I, p. 32.

Basalt Wares

In contrast to the translucent Caughley porcelains, Thomas Turner produced a limited quantity of black, matt-surfaced earthenware of the type known as basalt, a type of body extensively produced at the Wedgwood pottery, and by most late eighteenth century potters.

Caughley examples were marked occasionally with the impressed factory mark 'SALOPIAN', the fine teapot illustrated in Plate 83 being an example. Several factory wasters which display fine engine-turned designs in the Wedgwood style were found on the site. It is probable that some Caughley basalt wares were unmarked, for marked specimens are distinctly rare and the small number of fragments found on the site suggests that these wares were produced only for a limited scale, or for a short period.

Earthenwares

Numerous examples of blue printed opaque earthenware will be found with patterns very similar to those of Caughley or Worcester pieces. Some bear copies of the crescent mark[1] or, rarely, of 'C' or 'S' marks, and although some collectors regard them as of Caughley origin, in no case known to me do the Caughley-type printed subjects found on these pieces exactly match the similar designs on marked Caughley porcelain or impressions taken from the original engraved copper-plates. Furthermore, the earthenware shapes do not correspond with the Caughley porcelain forms. In fact, with the exception of the basalt pieces mentioned above, I do not believe that Thomas Turner made any earthenwares at Caughley between 1775 and the sale of the factory in 1799.

I think that these earthenwares were made by several different potters, in Staffordshire and other ceramic centres, in an effort to undersell the popular Caughley and Worcester porcelains by imitating their wares in the cheaper earthenware body. As there was no copyright law, different manufacturers appear to have copied each other's patterns at will and, of course, Chinese-style Willow-type designs were internationally popular. The Swansea factory, for example, produced numerous Willow-type blue prints on its earthenware. The Caughley-type blue designs on earthenwares often appear later in date than the porcelains they imitate and it is interesting to see mention of 'Salopian pattern' in sales of Swansea earthenwares held in 1808:

A parcel of cups and saucers etc, Salopian pattern	£1.	1.	0.
A breakfast & coffee set, Salopian pattern, complete	£1.	7.	0.

[1] See Plate 84.

CHAPTER VII

CHECK-LIST OF ARTICLES MADE AT CAUGHLEY

This section is arranged in alphabetical order and lists the many articles made at the Caughley factory, several of which are linked with entries found in the Chamberlain-Turner accounts or correspondence, or with fragments recently discovered on the Caughley factory site.

From Plate 85 to 211 the illustrations are also arranged in alphabetical order of the object, to correspond with this list.

This check-list is not complete, for many small unglazed wasters found on the site do not match *known* Caughley objects, so the collector may have the chance of discovering hitherto unidentified Caughley porcelains.

Artichoke Cups

The small covered bowl shown in Plate 85 is probably the article referred to in the Chamberlain-Turner accounts as 'artichoke cups'. Although most entries confine the description to these two words, two entries relating to sales by Chamberlains use the description 'Artichoke Butter cups', decorated to a pattern, at $4\frac{1}{2}d$ or 6*d* for the larger size. Unglazed fragments, with their scalloped edges and angled flange to the cover, were found on the Caughley site. Specimens are now very rare. See also 'Ice-cups', Page 96.

Asparagus servers

These wedge-shaped objects with upright sides (Plate 86) are often referred to, in error, as knife-rests, but the contemporary Chamberlain-Turner accounts make their original purpose quite clear.

They were made in two sizes, the normal, small size having an average length of $2\frac{9}{16}$ inches. Specimens of these interesting objects often bear the blue-printed Fisherman design, and were sold at 6*s* per dozen, or 6*d* each. The Fisherman print was normally applied so that the fisherman was standing upright with his head towards the narrow end, but in some rare cases the print is applied across the body, so that the head is towards a side.

The larger ones measure approximately 3¾ inches in length and were sold for about 9d each, depending on the pattern, some of them being decorated with the various tasteful blue and gold designs. Many fragments were found on the factory site in all stages of manufacture, and it would appear that they were made till the end of the Turner period in 1799. Similar objects were produced at several other factories and are also found in earthenware.

Baking Dishes

These oval dishes, similar to pie dishes (Plate 87) were made, according to the original Chamberlain-Turner account records, in eight different sizes. They appear to have been decorated only with the blue printed Fisherman design and very rarely with the hand painted Chinese landscape design illustrated in Plate 27; these oval baking dishes do not appear to have been made at other English porcelain factories, although similar shaped oval dishes are found in the contemporary Chinese blue and white porcelains.

These utilitarian objects were rarely preserved and specimens are distinctly rare today. Numerous fragments were found on the Caughley factory site, a fact which suggests that very many baking dishes were originally made at that factory.

The deep dish shown in Plate 88 may be a baking or pie dish. The shape is different from the standard dessert dish form and, at 1¾ in. is relatively deep.

Baskets

The rarest and most ornate form of Caughley basket is the so-called Chestnut basket shown in Plate 89, which closely follows a Worcester model. The Caughley examples are rather thicker in the potting, and are therefore also heavier and, while blue and white Worcester Chestnut baskets normally bear a crescent (open or shaded) mark, the Caughley ones should bear the 'S' or 'C' initial device.

The openwork basket shown in Plate 90 is also found in Worcester and in Lowestoft porcelain, and the pine-cone design is found on all versions. Many fragments of such baskets, both glazed and unglazed, were found on the Caughley site, but complete specimens are now rare and the Worcester versions are rather more plentiful. Apart from the slight differences in the added prints, the Caughley baskets, as in the case of the Chestnut types, are rather heavier than the Worcester ones, which are slightly thinner. The Worcester baskets, again, normally bear an open or a shaded crescent, whereas the Caughley ones, when marked, display an 'S' or 'C' mark. Different sizes were made, the normal length being 8¾ in.

The small, circular baskets, shown in Plate 91, are again found in both Worcester and in Caughley porcelain. Apart from the differences in design, such as the clear Salopian version of the Fisherman pattern shown in Plate 91, and the Caughley 'S' or 'C' initial marks, the Worcester specimens can as usual be distinguished by their lighter weight and thinner potting. These baskets were made in several different sizes.

Bottle-stand

One of the rarest articles to be found in Caughley porcelain is a bottle-stand (Plate 92), with two upright pierced holders for bottles, probably to contain oil and vinegar.

Bowls (or basons)

Small bowls, which were included in teasets to hold the slops, are more correctly termed 'basons' as these had a capacity of $\frac{1}{4}$ pint, $\frac{1}{2}$ pint and one pint. Larger vessels of this type holding upwards of a pint are correctly termed bowls and are quite rare, the standard sizes ranging from the quart size to the gallon, but larger ones may have been made to special order.

The prices for undecorated bowls supplied to Chamberlains were:

Quart	1/9d.
3 Pint	2/9d.
2 Quart	3/9d.
Gallon	9/-

The cost of the finished article naturally varied according to the style of decoration but, as the cost of a quart bowl with the blue printed Fisherman design was 5s, it may be assumed that all blue printed designs were of similar price, some three times as expensive as the undecorated bowls.

Bowls were, of course, made by all porcelain manufacturers and in particular the Worcester and the Caughley can be very similar. The slight differences found in shared designs are explained in Chapter IX. In general, the Caughley examples are thicker and therefore heavier, and the top edge of Worcester bowls is often chamfered to form a slight facet.

Small bowls with moulded ribbed sides and of slightly flared shape are very occasionally found with a simple blue-cell border; these, it is thought, may have been part of the fittings of a wash-stand.

Breakfast Services—See 'Sandwich sets', Page 105.

Butter Boats

The Chamberlain-Turner accounts list several 'boats' or 'butter boats'. These were probably the small boat-shaped objects which are normally called creamers and are discussed under the heading '*Cream Boats*' on Page 91.

Butter pots

A Caughley circular butter pot and stand similar to that shown in Plate 263 probably matches the description, 'Round butter tub', found in the Chamberlain-Turner accounts. The basic shape is found in Worcester and in Lowestoft porcelains. These are normally decorated with the fence pattern and the differences found in the individual versions help to distinguish the Worcester specimens from the much rarer Caughley examples. The Worcester specimens normally bear the open, or the shaded, crescent device, whereas the Caughley tubs have the 'S' or 'C' marks.

The oval covered tureen and stand shown in Plate 93 was probably intended to hold butter. Once again these are normally found with the fence pattern and the Worcester, Caughley and Lowestoft factories all produced similar articles. Caughley examples bear the 'C' mark not the crescent, and examples are today rarely found in their complete and perfect state.

Buttons

Caughley buttons must now be the rarest object a collector can hope to find, for I do not know of any existing complete specimen. They were undoubtedly made, for several half-finished or faulty examples have been found on the factory site (Plate 94) and dozens are listed in the Chamberlain-Turner accounts. It would seem that many were gilt or otherwise decorated by Chamberlain at Worcester and, of course, the Caughley site wasters do not bear this added decoration.

Contemporary references to these Caughley buttons include:

'58 Buttons different sizes to gild'
'72 Coat Buttons, ribbed   1/6d. a dozen'
'24   do.   plain, middle
                        size 1/6d. a dozen'
'72 small brest buttons, plain, white   9d. a dozen'

and in April, 1790, the following buttons were forwarded to Mr Cristall in Birmingham:

12 buttons 1st (size) gilt, sorted   9d.
18   do.   2nd (size)   do.   1/6d.
18   do.   3rd (size)   do.   1/10½d.
18   do.   4th (size)   do.   2/3d.

Buttons were also apparently made at the Worcester factory, for two with early overglaze printed specimens are illustrated in Cyril Cook's *Supplement to, The Life and Work of Robert Hancock* (1955) Item 128, and examples have recently been found on the Worcester site.

Cabbage-leaf Jugs—see Jugs, Page 98.

Candlesticks

It is doubtful if the Caughley factory made the tall table candlesticks, although low, handled 'chamber candlesticks' were certainly made, as factory wasters and the Chamberlain-Turner accounts prove. The one illustrated in Plate 95 shows the Caughley version of the Fisherman pattern and the basic shape. Overglaze decorated examples should exist, as white examples were supplied to Chamberlains (at 2s) but all these are now extremely scarce and represents one of the most desirable objects for any collector.

Fine Worcester examples were also made, sometimes with a pierced openwork edge, and they are sometimes very ornately decorated in traditional Worcester styles.

Caudle Cups

Caudle cups were normally fitted with covers and, while most examples have two handles, some were only supplied with one. They do not appear to have been decorated with the standard underglaze blue printed designs, but some bore the blue and gold formal patterns seen on the examples illustrated in Plates 96 and 97. These designs were probably gilt at Chamberlains and some must have been wholly decorated at this Worcester establishment, for undecorated examples were sent to Chamberlains:

4	Caudle cups, 1 handle, Bell fluted, white	@ 2/-	8/-	
7	stands to do.	@ 1/-	7/-	

(June, 1790)

Prices of completed specimens were:

4	Caudle cups & covers, Royal stripe @ 5/-	£1.	0. 0.
1	Caudle cup & cover, Bell plain, Fleur de lis		3/6
2	Caudle cups, 2 handle, Royal Lily @ 3/-		6/-
2	do. stands do. @ 3/-		6/-

Specimens bearing some underglaze blue, added at the factory, should show the 'S' mark, but those having only overglaze enamel decoration, or gilding, are unmarked. They were made with and without fluting but all specimens are, today, rare.

Centre-dish

The 'Centre' or centre-dish was the main component of a dessert service and was intended to contain the centre arrangement of fruit. The centre-dish was oval, and should not be confused with the circular salad bowl which formed part of a dinner service.

The first pattern, which was relatively shallow with a depth of only $2\frac{1}{4}$ inches, was probably an enlarged version of a side dish (Plate 98). The illustrated example of this rare form bears the impressed mark 'SALOPIAN' in capital letters. Similar dishes are found with Worcester services, but the Worcester examples are thinner in the potting and have triangular footrims, without the ninety degree inner angle found on Caughley pieces.

The most common Caughley dessert centre is shown in Colour Plate V and in Plates 99 and 100, and this is probably the one listed in the Chamberlain accounts in October, 1789, as 'oval centre-piece, new model, Fly [pattern] 10/6d.' It is relatively narrow and deep, measuring $7\frac{3}{4} \times 12\frac{1}{2}$ inches with a height of $3\frac{1}{4}$ inches. Some of these bear the impressed name mark 'Salopian', but this is not of great importance, for the shape would appear to be confined to Caughley, except for some rare Chinese hard-paste porcelain examples.

Chamber Pots

Like most utilitarian objects, Caughley (or any eighteenth century) chamber pots are rarely found today as they were discarded when new designs came into favour. In fact, although evidence exists to show that the factory made such objects, I have yet to trace a complete specimen.

The evidence comprises one unglazed factory waster with a turned-over curved edge, and the Chamberlain accounts, where chamber pots (decorated with French Chantilly sprigs) are included at 4*s*, but we also have evidence in the form of a letter quoted on Page 13, which shows that in 1790 the production of these articles had been discontinued as the Chinese 'Nankeen ones are so much cheaper. . . .'

Related 'Coach pots' were also made, as two are featured in the Chamberlain accounts of July, 1789,—'2 coach pots, Full Nankin @ 1/4d. 2/8d. (Page 63).' The 'Full Nankin' pattern is discussed on Page 20.

Chocolate Cups

The large cups and saucers shown in Plates 101 and 102, are chocolate cups. They are rarely found decorated with underglaze-blue prints of Willow pattern type. An account of August, 1789, probably refers to the design shown in Plate 101:

24 Chocolate cups, Temple, @ 1/3d.	£1. 10. 0.
24 saucers do. @ 7d.	14. 0.

Other examples are decorated overglaze in various styles with enamelled and gilt designs (Plate 102) and, being unmarked, have been mistaken for Worcester wares. The distinguishing differences between the two makes are shown in Plate 273. Chocolate cups are rare, especially in the blue and white.

Coffee Cups

Coffee cups were, of course, included in the standard teasets, along with the handleless tea bowls. They were turned by hand, not moulded, so several slight variations of form are to be found. In general the Caughley coffee cups are thicker in the turning than Worcester examples and the Shropshire ones have a high rectangular footrim. The added moulded handle shown in Plates 16, 64 and 195, is confined to Caughley and Chinese porcelains.

Coffee cups cannot be classed as rare, but they are somewhat rarer than the matching tea bowl, perhaps because the handle was liable to suffer damage.

Small, straight-sided mugs under 3 inches high were called 'coffee cans', as opposed to coffee cups, and are rare.

Coffee Pots

Caughley coffee pots are quite rare, though the very similar Worcester ones are *relatively* common. The standard Shropshire coffee pot shape is seen in Plates 103 and 104, where the upward turn at the bottom of the handle, with a slight swelling at this point, can be seen. The handle is also ribbed with a thicker central section. A very rare form of ribbed coffee pot has Chinese-styled ornately moulded handle and spout (Plate 105) matching those found on teapots as illustrated in Plates 198 and 199.

While most coffee pots have a floral knob, a rare variation has a hollow, flame-like knob (Plate 106). This knob would appear to be confined to Caughley examples but the stud-like knob would seem to be unique to Worcester (Plates 238, 242 and 267).

A very rare coffee pot shape of the 1790s is shown in Colour Plate VII with a matching service.

All shapes of coffee pot were made in different sizes, and sometimes in plain or fluted form:

Quart coffee pot, plain, white	5/-
Quart coffee pot, New fluted, white	6/-
(April, 1790)	

Caughley coffee pots were made in the standard blue-printed designs up to at least 1790, for in May, 1790, we find the following pots listed as being received from Caughley by Chamberlain of Worcester:

Pint coffee pot, Bird	3/-
Pint & ½ do. do.	4/-
Pint & ½ do. Fruit	4/-
Pint & ½ do. Image	4/-

Other coffee pots were decorated with overglaze enamelled designs as well as gilt patterns probably added at Worcester by Chamberlain's artists. Quart coffee pots with blue and gold designs, such as the one shown in Colour Plate VII, were originally listed by Chamberlains at 7s 6d each.

Cream Boats

Creamers were small, and generally described in contemporary records as 'boats' or 'ewers'.

The most common moulded cream-ewer is shown in Plate 107, and this was termed 'Chelsea ewer', generally made in the 'low' form but very occasionally in the 'tall' version. The standard price for the blue-printed 'low Chelsea ewers' was 8d each. In February, 1790, for example, Chamberlain received from Caughley:

24 Low Chelsea ewers, fruit blue edge		@ 8d.	16/-
24	do.	Rose	@ 8d.	16/-
24	do.	Nankin	@ 8d.	16/-
24	do.	Image	@ 8d.	16/-
12	do.	Birds	@ 8d.	8/-

Other 'Chelsea ewers' were decorated with hand-painted underglaze blue designs, and with overglaze enamelled and gilt designs. They were extremely popular, and the basic shape was made at most English porcelain factories of the 1760–90 period, and even re-introduced when John Rose took over the Caughley factory in 1799 (see Plate 216 and Page 115). The Caughley examples have the same form of handle as the chocolate cups, (see Plates 101, 102 and 273).

Apart from the many references to Chelsea ewers in the Chamberlain-Turner accounts, there are also numerous mentions of 'gadroon boats', those attractive little creamers that are illustrated in Plates 108 and 109, which were made in two sizes, each selling at 6d:

23 gadroon boats, Image blue edge		@ 6d.	11/6d.
15	do.	fruit do.	@ 6d.	7/6d.
15	do.	Rose do.	@ 6d.	7/6d.
3	do.	Nankin	@ 6d.	1/6d.
21 small	do.	do.	@ 6d.	10/6d.

One peculiarity of the 'gadroon boats' is that these very often have an impressed star inside the footrim (Plate 109), and one example in my collection has three short lines impressed in the same position. These appear to be workmen's piece-rate tally marks, but it is very curious that they appear only on these small cream boats. The 'gadroon boats' were also made at Worcester (Plate 270) and all examples, whether Caughley or Worcester, are most attractive and rather rare.

A very pleasing form of Caughley cream boat, basically of dolphin shape, is shown in Plate 110. White, undecorated 'Dolphin ewers' of this kind were sent from Caughley to Chamberlain in 1789, and were then priced at 6d each. Fragments were found on the Caughley site, but completed specimens are now extremely rare. The same shape was also made at other eighteenth century factories, including Worcester.

Cress Dishes

Pierced, shaped edged, shallow bowls, such as that illustrated in Plate 271, are often called cress dishes, although they could equally have been used for any salad, vegetable or fruit that required draining. These should have a matching under-dish.

They have often been called Caughley, but all examples that I have seen bear the Worcester, filled-in crescent mark, and Worcester versions of standard underglaze blue prints. Similar pierced bowls and under-dishes may have been made at Caughley, and should bear the impressed 'S A L O P I A N' name mark, the blue printed 'S' or 'C' initial marks, or Caughley versions of the standard designs favoured at both Worcester and Caughley. These pierced dishes and stands were also made at the Lowestoft factory.

Cups

In this check list specific cups are discussed under their full title: Caudle cups, Chocolate cups, Coffee cups, Custard cups, Tea cups.

Custard Cups

Custard cups illustrated in Plate 111, are of small size, standing about 3 inches high with the cover. A particularly rare version has an intricately moulded handle.

Decanters

One of the rarest Caughley articles is surely the decanter, the sole reference that I have been able to trace occurring in the Chamberlain accounts on August 7th, 1789, under the heading—'To goods Recd from Thos. Turner Esq.'

    6   Quart Decanters, Parrot, @ 2/-   12/-

The 'Parrot' design is one of the standard Caughley blue-printed patterns (see Plate 40).

Dessert Services

Caughley dessert services (Plates 112–15) normally comprised the following units, which are listed with the prices for the white, undecorated pieces:

1	Centrepiece	@ 7/- or 7/6d.
2	Sugar tureens & covers	@ 3/-
2	Stands to do.	@ 2/-
2	spoons to do.	@ 1/-
4	melon-shaped dishes	@ 2/6d.
4	shell-shaped dishes	@ 2/-
4	square dishes	@ 2/6d.
2	heart-shaped dishes	@ 3/-

Plates (sets were normally sold with 12, 18 or 24 plates, the number and size depending on the customer's requirements).

Some expensive dessert services also had one or two ice-pails (see Page 97). These units are discussed under the separate headings but all shaped side dishes are listed under 'Dessert Service Dishes' below.

The fact that white, undecorated dessert wares were supplied to Chamberlain at Worcester suggests most strongly that some Caughley dessert wares were enamelled at Worcester.

Some Caughley dessert sets were decorated with the elaborate blue-printed Willow-type pattern known as 'Full Nankin', (Plate 115). Dishes with this design were sold in 1789 at about twice the price of the undecorated examples and other patterns were supplied at the same period with the blue and gold designs termed 'Fly', 'Birds Eye', etc. Fully gilt or enamelled designs were probably added by Chamberlain (see Chapter V).

Dessert Service Dishes

The side dishes originally sold with dessert services were of four different shapes. In order of cost (see above) these dessert dishes were:

Heart-shaped (see Colour Plate IX and Plates 112 and 115)
Melon-shaped (see Plates 112–15)
Square-shaped (see Plates 65, 113–15)
Shell-shaped (see Plates 76, 112, 113 and 115).

These dishes, many of which are today separated from the service and may be found as individual pieces, are to be discovered in very many different patterns, most of the overglaze decoration being added at Chamberlain's decorating establishment at Worcester.

The blue and white specimens normally bear standard Caughley initial marks 'C' or 'S', and some dishes of whatever style of decoration bear the impressed name mark 'SALOPIAN'. These very similarly shaped dessert dishes that were made at the Worcester factory, do not, of course, bear the Caughley marks, and in general the Worcester examples are thinly potted and are lighter in weight.

Dinner Services

Caughley dinner services are very rare in anything like a complete state, although dinner plates are relatively common. The services would have included the following units:

2 large tureens, covers & stands
2 (or 4) smaller tureens, covers & stands

4 covered vegetable dishes (probably only in post-1790 services)
Large meat dishes in at least six different sizes
Salad bowl
Sauce boats (in some services)
Meat Plates
Soup plates
Cheese & side plates

These different units are discussed under their separate headings—tureens, salad bowls, plates, etc.

It would appear that only two blue-printed patterns were applied to Caughley dinner services, the best known being the elaborate 'Full Nankin' pattern, seen in Plates 115 and 117–18, in which the price of octagonal meat plates was 1s 9d each. Another, very rare blue-printed design dinner service pattern is depicted in Plate 23. Hand-painted underglaze blue patterns were also applied to dinner services (Plate 116), and some services were decorated with blue and gilt designs, such as 'Dresden flowers'. Tureens of this pattern were priced at £1. 1s but the very large meat platters were the most expensive item, the sixth being priced at £1. 16s, probably on account of the large area that had to be decorated. Two Caughley 'Table' or dinner services are listed in Appendix I, on Page 151. I have seen portions of a finely gilt dinner service of the same shape as that shown in Plate 116.

Dinner services are so rare that it is difficult to state definitely what forms were made. Two basic dish shapes were octagonal and shaped oval (Plates 117 and 118), but other forms may come to light. The reason why very few Caughley (or Worcester) dinner services were made was that the Oriental services were so inexpensive and could be sold at a price with which the English porcelain manufacturers could not compete.

Dinner Service Dishes

Large dishes, oval or octagonal, were supplied in graduating sizes with dinner services, but specimens, especially of the largest ones over 12 in. long, are now very rare. These meat dishes, or platters, were made in at least six sizes, of which sample prices for the blue and gold Dresden flower pattern were:

1st size	6/-
2nd size	9/-
3rd size	12/-
4th size	18/-
5th size	30/-
6th size	36/-

The price of the white, undecorated dishes was approximately one third less than the prices listed above.

Of the standard shapes shown in Plates 117 and 118, one very large octagonal dish from a dinner service of the 'Full Nankin' blue-printed design is no less than 20 in. long and must have presented great difficulties in the firing. One service, sold in 1782, contained twenty dishes (see Page 152).

An unglazed fragment of a large dish (or tureen stand) was found on the factory site, with moulded panels around the edge of a basket or trellis design. As yet no complete specimen has been reported to match this factory 'waster'.

Egg-Cups

Caughley egg-cups, now very rarely found, were made in two basic types, high at 6d in the undecorated state, and low at 4d. When decorated with the Fisherman or Pleasure Boat design, the price was 8d for the high egg-'stand', to use the original description. Many fragments of both the high and the low egg cups were found on the factory site. The 'Low' cup is very elegant, standing less than 1¾ in. high, with a delicately turned rim.

The graceful, handled small object illustrated in Plate 120 is probably an egg-cup and may well be influenced by a French model, the underglaze blue design certainly reflecting this style. The size is admittedly rather large for a normal hen's egg, but it would suit a duck's egg, though it is possible that this pot may have been intended as a custard-cup. The shape is extremely rare and I have seen only one set of six, which has now been split amongst different collectors.

Egg-Drainers or Strainers

Small handled, circular, egg-drainers, or 'egg-strainers', are illustrated in Plate 119. They are sometimes called tea-strainers but the eighteenth century Chamberlain-Turner accounts clearly show their original use, as they were frequently sold with matching egg cups, e.g. '6 egg cups, Pleasure Boat @ 8d. 6 egg drainers, Pleasure Boat @ 6d.'

The egg-drainers, several fragments of which were found on the factory site, were equipped with two types of handle, that most often found having a moulded leaf-like one, while that of the rare variation is looped and twig-like. The original prices were 4d each in the undecorated state, and the most commonly found underglaze blue design, the popular Fisherman or Pleasure Boat pattern, were sold for 6d each. Other designs are found, but very rarely.

It could be that these strainers were also used for other purposes, for some Chamberlain-Caughley accounts list 'Caudle cups & strainers', and yet these egg-drainers are the only pierced strainer-like objects at present known to collectors.

Ewers and Basins, see Water Ewer and Wash Basin, Page 113.

Extinguishers

The Chamberlain records include the one-word description 'Extinguishers', priced at 6d in the undecorated state. These were probably hollow, conical, hat-shaped articles with a small handle at one side. They are found in silver, pewter, earthenware, etc, and were used to snuff out or extinguish the candle. They were often sold with the handled, low 'Chamber' candlesticks but I have not traced a Caughley specimen.

Eye-Baths

The Caughley factory produced at least two varieties of eye-bath, the first being most attractive, with moulded base, stem and bowl (Plate 121). When decorated with the underglaze blue Fisherman pattern the cost was 6d and blue and gold examples were sold for 10d in 1792.

A simpler form of eye-bath was also made, and this is even rarer than the moulded version (Plate 122).

Finger-Bowls

The charmingly simple and finely potted bowl illustrated in Plate 123 would appear to be a finger bowl as it is so similar to the relatively common finger-bowls made in glass. These small bowls were placed on the table so that diners could rinse their sticky fingers. I have been unable to trace contemporary references to Caughley finger-bowls and that illustrated is the only example known to me.

Porcelain finger-bowls were also made at the Worcester factory with stands, or under-dishes and the Worcester examples, too, are exceedingly rare.

Flasks

The small, flattish porcelain flask illustrated in Plate 124 is possibly of Caughley manufacture, and is dated 1777. The attribution is open to some doubt and the discovery of a similar flask with a known Caughley print will provide proof of Shropshire origin.

Flower Pots

As blue and white flower pots of the conventional shape, with straight, slightly angled sides, were made at Worcester, they may well have been made also at Caughley.

However, the only reference to them in the Chamberlain-Turner accounts occurs on November 30th, 1789, when Caughley case number 42 is listed as containing:

> 3 Flower pots, with covers pierced,
> fine blue ground, on feet

No price is given and this may represent a special order rather than a stock line (see also Page 52).

Ice-Cups

The Chamberlain-Turner accounts include several references to covered ice-cups, for instance, in Caughley case number 31, invoiced on September 26th, 1789, there were included:

				@	
12 Ice-cups & covers, Scallop top, white				@ 1/-	12/-
1	do.	do.	do.	Pine pattern	1/6d.

Judging by the price these must have been quite small articles and the description 'scallop top' might suggest that the covered cup shown in Plate 85 as an artichoke cup could, in fact, be an ice-cup.

Ice-Pails

Three-piece containers for ice were included in some of the more expensive dessert services, and today perfect and complete examples are deservedly highly priced. The three pieces were—the main body, a separate pan-like liner and the cover (Plates 125 and 126).

Ice-pails decorated with underglaze blue designs are even more rare than those examples bearing blue and gold designs or purely overglaze enamelled and gilt patterns. In their undecorated state they were priced at 18*s* each.

The first shape of Caughley ice-pail is shown in Plate 125, and in Plate 126 is shown a rare, later version of the 1790s, whose basic shape was also continued into the nineteenth century by John Rose of Coalport. These nineteenth century examples, however, are of hard paste and being thickly potted are very heavy.

Ink Pots

Small circular ink pots with small apertures for pens were made at Caughley, as is evidenced by fragments found on the factory site. The standard shape and underglaze blue design is shown in Plate 127, but examples are now very rare. The repeated, or double Chinese-cell type border found on these rare ink pots would appear to have been called 'Nankeen border', for the description—'ink stands, double nankeen border' is given in the 1789 list of Caughley porcelains supplied to Chamberlains.

The different form illustrated in Plate 128 is quite rare and was made in different sizes.

Jardinière

The jardinière illustrated in Plate 129 represents one of the rarest Caughley specimens—in fact this example was discovered only after the manuscript of this book had, as I then thought, been completed. This fact underlines the point that such jardinieres are of extreme rarity, and also that hitherto unknown objects can still be found to add to the list of shapes made by Thomas Turner at the Caughley factory.

This jardinière very closely resembles a form favoured in France and made at the Sèvres and Chantilly factories. It was apparently made in other sizes, for a base of a larger example was found on the factory site, having a base diameter of $5\frac{1}{2}$ in., against the 4 in. of my specimen.

The underglaze blue decoration of French Chantilly type flower sprays with a blue line border is similar to designs illustrated in Plates 56, 57, 92, 120 and 146. Even though the shape and the added design were copied from French porcelains, this example bears the 'S' mark of the Caughley or 'Salopian' factory, and so underlines the point made on Page 9, that Turner did not copy the marks of other factories.

This rare jardinière, of a type, incidentally, not made at Worcester, is a most pleasing and finely potted example which was offered for sale as French. One wonders how many other French-style, Caughley porcelains of this general type await discovery.

Jugs

The best known type of Caughley jug has a body moulded with cabbage-leaves and a mask-head spout (Colour Plate II and Plates 67–71 and 131). They were originally known as 'Dutch Jugs', and were very popular, versions being made at nearly every English porcelain factory during the 1770–1800 period. The main differences between the Worcester and the Caughley jugs are explained on Pages 138–9.

The Caughley cabbage-leaf jugs were made in several sizes and are found with a variety of underglaze blue and white patterns, although it would appear that overglaze enamelled specimens were decorated by Chamberlain's staff at Worcester.

A selection of 'Dutch' or cabbage-leaf jugs is shown in Colour Plate II, Page 32. Slight variations occur in the form of moulded handle.

A very rare 'S' marked variation of the well-known cabbage-leaf mask-head jug is shown in Plate 132. The outline of the body is similar, although the moulded cabbage-leaf design is replaced with one of basket work, the mask-head spout is retained, and the handle is reminiscent of that found on the 'Dutch' jugs. A rather similar example in a private collection has the rare and interesting underglaze blue mark 'Gallimore Turner' (arranged in a circle, without punctuation, so that either name can be read first), inside which is the description 'SALOPIAN'.[1]

A simple but most attractive form of mask-head jug was also made at Caughley (and at Worcester, see Page 139), typical specimens of which are shown in Colour Plate III and Plates 134–6. This form is normally found with underglaze enamel patterns, and in general these graceful utensils are earlier than most of the 'Dutch' or cabbage-leaf variety. Typical contemporary prices for blue-printed jugs of this type are shown by the Chamberlain-Turner accounts:

Pint jugs, Parrot, no border			2/-
Quart do.	do.	do.	3/-
3 Pint do.	do.	do.	4/-

These Chamberlain-Turner accounts also include a further type of jug described as 'Punch jugs and covers', which, in 1789, were listed at 1s each for undecorated 'seconds', i.e. slightly faulty specimens.

A very rare, or perhaps unique, puzzle jug dated 1778, in the Watney Collection, is illustrated in Plate 133.

Knife and Fork Handles

The Caughley factory site yielded several fragments of cylindrical, handle-like objects which were pierced as if to take a metal prong. Most fragments of these were quite crude, and I took them to be hand-made implements made by the workmen to hold trimming tools. However, Mr David Holgate found a complete

98   [1] See *English Blue & White Porcelain of the 18th Century* by Dr Bernard Watney, fig. 87A.

but unglazed specimen on the site, which would appear to be a knife, or fork handle, a theory supported by the fact that he also found a glazed 'waster' with traces of underglaze blue decoration (Plate 213).

The factory 'wasters' show mould marks indicating that many were made as a commercial line, handles made to hold worker's tools would probably have been hand-made and the wasters also indicate that they were made in several different sizes. The shape, as shown in Plate 213, is quite distinctive and it is likely that complete, decorated specimens will be discovered by collectors to prove that these objects represent an additional Caughley 'line'.

In 1792, a Mr Ferguson ordered some patterns of knife handles, see Page 67.

Ladles, see Spoons

Leaf-Dishes

Several forms of leaf-shaped dishes were made at Caughley as well as at other factories. The fine large, handled leaf-dish illustrated in Plate 137 is extremely rare, far rarer than the similar Worcester leaf-dishes, the form of which is shown in Plate 283.

The smaller leaf-shaped dishes sometimes described in accounts as 'Pickle-leaves' are relatively common, especially when decorated with the Pleasure Boat or Fisherman design, but are rarely found with other decoration. Several different sizes were made up to about 6½ in. long, and similar dishes were made at most factories, including Worcester (see Page 139 and Plate 285).

A rarer form of leaf-dish is small and deep, with three moulded leaf-like feet (Plate 140). A plaster mould for such a dish and several fragments were found on the factory site, but again, the basic shape was made at several other factories.

An unglazed fragment from the Caughley factory site has leaf-veining on the upper surface, and the size and thickness of the fragment indicates that it was part of a large leaf-moulded dish, of a model not yet discovered.

Milk Jugs

Milk jugs, as opposed to cream jugs which are low and of general boat-shape, have an upright general appearance.

The first type of Caughley porcelain milk jug is of the well-known sparrow-beak variety as shown in Plate 141, the earliest examples of which have a simple, grooved, looped handle. A slightly later type, however, often decorated with Chinese-style blue-printed landscape designs, may have a fluted body and be equipped with an ornately moulded, Chinese-styled handle (Plate 142). They were made in different sizes and some were originally fitted with covers. The early, simple form was made at several other factories, including Worcester, and the reader is referred to Chapter IX, Page 140, whereas later variation, with moulded Chinese-style handle, would appear to be unique to the Caughley factory.

A rare form of Caughley milk jug is in the shape of a little barrel, with a small upturned spout and a loop handle placed rather high on the body (Plate 143).

Another rather rare and attractive type has a graceful shaped body, the upper part of which is fluted and leads into a generous wide pouring lip. It has a good, moulded, double curved handle (Plate 143) and would appear to be confined to the Caughley factory, being issued with the teaware shapes shown in Plate 195.

A tall milk jug of simple but graceful shape is shown in Plate 143, with a wide pouring lip and a moulded, reeded loop handle. While not common, this shape also occurs in other makes, including Worcester (see Plate 287). An enlarged version of this shape was issued as a water jug, see Plate 210. A very rare and attractive fluted creamer is shown in Plate 144.

A slightly later form of bucket shape, with the addition of a small pouring lip and a loop handle, appears to be confined to the Caughley factory, although close copies of a slightly later version, discussed below, were made at Worcester.

Whereas the shapes listed above are normally (but not exclusively) found with underglaze blue designs, the next, which normally accompanies the tea-wares shown in Plate 196, is associated with overglaze enamelled or gilt designs or with the blue and gold formal floral designs. This post-1785 type is again basically of bucket shape but the body is normally fluted and has a most graceful moulded handle, with an upward thumb rest at the top and curled returns at the two junctions of the body and handle.

Monteiths

The purpose of a monteith or 'verrière' was to cool wine glasses. It is normally of oval form with a deeply waved edge, from which the glasses hung by their stems, so that the bowls were immersed in the cold water inside the vessel. A very fine one is to be seen in the Caughley cabinet at the Victoria and Albert Museum (Plate 146).

These articles were made in French porcelain and are well-known in silver, but the example in the Victoria and Albert Museum is the only Caughley specimen known and exemplifies Thomas Turner's interest in the French style. It has the initial 'H' incised under the base (with the blue 'S' factory mark) and this mark could very well relate to a French modeller named Francois Hardenburg, who was said to have been brought over to Caughley by Turner in about 1780. He left Caughley in about 1788, and L. Jewitt,[1] writing in 1878, said that Hardenburg subsequently worked in London.

Mugs

Most Caughley mugs or tankards seem to be of cylindrical shape, with straight sides. The early bell-shaped mugs, as well as the barrel-shaped examples illustrated in Plates 147 and 148, are extremely rare.

Cylindrical mugs offer little guidance for correct attribution and one should study the handle rather than the body. On small mugs, standing up to about $4\frac{1}{2}$ in. high, the handle normally takes the form of a concave loop. Worcester mugs normally have a thicker version of this handle with a more pronounced concave

[1] *The Ceramic Art of Great Britain* (1878), Vol. II, Page 110.

recess and this handle is found on all sizes of Worcester mugs, not only on the small ones as is the case with Caughley.

On large Caughley mugs the handle section is convex with two slight indentations at each side near the edge (see Page 141), but Worcester mugs sometimes have a similar handle, rather more slender than the Caughley version. A variation of this handle has an extra strap-like reinforcement at the top (Plates 31, 32, 151 and 152), which later appears to be unique to Caughley, although after 1800 Chamberlain handles may be similar. A rare form of Caughley tankard is very wide and relatively shallow, so that its diameter is slightly greater than its height (Plate 155).

A form of Caughley mug handle which is very rare has a fine scroll thumb grip and a scroll-return at the bottom (Plate 154). Yet another rare form is intricately moulded after a Chinese original, with two heart-shaped panels, one near its top, the other near the bottom (Plate 153), and this was also employed by John Rose after 1799, but his examples are in the characteristic, heavy, hard-paste body. This Caughley handle is also found on teapots and cups but it does not appear to have been employed at Worcester.

Caughley mugs are very often mistaken for Worcester and *vice-versa*, and the reader is referred to Chapter IX, Page 141. Apart from the general differences in shape and potting, the different patterns employed by the two factories are a very useful guide to the true origin of these pieces.

Mugs, like other objects, are found in different sizes, and most standard Caughley blue-printed designs are found on these articles. Some contemporary prices were:

½ Pint mugs.	Flowers	1/-
Pint do.	do.	1/6d.
Quart do.	do.	2/-

The same prices ruled for the Fishing, or 'La Pêche' pattern (Plates 31 and 258) and for the Parrot design. The Mulberry and Pleasure Boat patterns were slightly more expensive at:

½ Pint size	1/3d.
Pint size	1/9d.
Quart size	2/6d.

Mustard Pots

A Caughley wet-mustard pot with spoon is shown in Plate 156 (see Plate 290 for a very similar Worcester example, and Page 141 for the differing details). The Caughley mustard pots are quite rare but occur with the standard underglaze blue-printed designs, such as the Rose, Fence and Pleasure Boat patterns. Strangely, some examples do not have an open notch in the cover for the spoon handle. The standard size is about 3¾ inches high, but rare examples are larger. Most examples have a modelled floral knob, a simple, turned, knob is rarely found.

Dry-mustard pots are of vase, or sugar-sifter, shape with a simple dome cover, as illustrated in Plate 157. These are of extreme rarity. Unglazed fragments of both types were found on the Caughley factory site.

Paint Stands

In 1789 Chamberlain received from Caughley '24 Paint-stands, white to pattern' at 3d each. These are of oblong slab form, normally with three circular depressions and a long trough, and although the Caughley site has yielded many pieces of such paint stands, which were probably intended for amateur artists, few, if any, can have survived.

Patty Pans, see Tart Pans, Page 107.

Pestles and Mortars

Several Pestles and Mortars were included in the Chamberlain-Turner accounts, and were made in different sizes:

Pint Pestle & Mortar	4/-
Quart do. do.	5/-

but there is no proof that these were made at Caughley for, although a broken example has been found on the site, this could have been one used by the workmen. Several potteries are known to have made Pestles and Mortars, and Wedgwood's examples were famous.

Plates

Caughley plates are of three main types—bread and butter plates, two of which were issued with each complete teaset, Dessert plates, and Dinner plates.

The bread and butter plates are of enlarged saucer-shape, without any condiment flange. Most are quite plain in form but some are slightly fluted and have a shaped edge; the latter were issued with moulded tea services of the types shown in Plate 195. Bread and butter plates were of different sizes, each service having a large and a smaller one. The intricately moulded plate shown in Plate 161 represents one of the finest Caughley teaware designs, although this moulded floral pattern was also used at Worcester.

Plates found with dessert services range from about 7 to $8\frac{1}{2}$ inches in diameter, four different sizes being available for individual choice. Most of them had a scalloped edge, as shown in Plate 158, but some with octagonal and moulded edges were also made, both at Caughley and at Worcester. The basket edged ones termed 'Chantilly', after the French prototypes, were very popular in the 1785–95 period (Plates 159 and 160). The plate with irregularly shaped edges and concave and convex curves is particularly rare.

Dinner plates were larger than those found in dessert services—the meat plates ranging from about 9 to $10\frac{1}{2}$ inches in diameter, with the matching soup plates, of course, being of greater depth. The now quite rare, small, side and cheese plates from dinner services can be mistaken for dessert plates, but most have a diameter of less than 7 in. and these can be regarded as dinner service plates.

Pounce-Pots

Pounce-pots, or 'sanders', for sprinkling a drying agent on wet ink, are very rarely found in porcelain, yet three different shapes were made at Caughley. These are shown in Plates 162 and 163 and each is extremely rare. The strange 'diablo' shape enables the articles to be firmly held while shaking, and the recessed top allows the pot to be filled without spilling, because there is no aperture in the base, such as is found in modern sifters.

Radish Dishes

Radish dishes are mentioned in the Chamberlain-Turner accounts, where they are listed in their white or undecorated state at 2s each, a price that suggests such a dish was a largish container, rather than a small leaf-dish.

The oval dish illustrated in Plate 164, with Chinese-styled underglaze blue scenic design, is probably a radish dish, and is shown with part of a matching unglazed handle from the factory site. Specimens are very rare.

Rouge Pots

The Chamberlain accounts include many references to 'Rouge Pots' in the 1790s, but we cannot be certain that these are of Caughley make, for at this period Chamberlain had started to produce his own porcelains. Small conical pots, which could be rouge (or patch) pots, were certainly made at Caughley after 1799 when John Rose succeeded, as several hard-paste examples were found on the site. A sample reference to rouge pots supplied in various styles of decoration is given below, but their origin is open to some doubt:

March 5th, 1792.
    Mr Jones, No. 5 Apple Tree Yard, York Street, St. James's.

102	Rouge pots, white @ 8d.	£3.	8.	0.
42	do. Royal Stripe	£2.	3.	4.
35	do. French (sprig pattern or make?)	£3.	15.	11.
48	do. Gold Sprigs	£2.	16.	0.

Saffer-Pots

The Chamberlain-Turner accounts include several references to 'saffer pots', decorated with a range of typical underglaze blue printed patterns. The original cost of these was 1s each for the standard floral designs, and 1s 3d when decorated with popular 'Pleasure Boat' or Fisherman design.

I believe the saffer-pots were what are now termed spittoons (see Plates 165 and 166) for very many were sold, yet I have been unable to link the patterns listed, or the cost, with any other class of object and, while what we now call spittoons exist in fair numbers, they are not featured in the goods sent down from Caughley to Chamberlain. This opinion is purely personal and is not shared by some other collectors who point out that spittoons were made in other materials, such as pewter, and are of the same shape and were almost certainly intended as a spittoon—probably to be held in the hand.

If the 'saffer pot' was not what we now call a spittoon, it could have been intended to hold saffron bulbs, which are a variety of crocus with light purple flowers, the orange-red stigmas of which yield a flavouring substance, and also a dye. One variety is termed 'Safflower' which, when abbreviated, could give the name Saffer, as found in the Chamberlain-Turner accounts.

Whether these were bulb-pots or spittoons, they were made in slightly different shapes, probably as they were thrown individually on the potter's wheel, not formed repetitively in a mould, and in different sizes, the diameter at the top ranging from $4\frac{1}{2}$ to $5\frac{1}{2}$ in. Two different varieties are shown in Plates 165 and 166, and a Worcester version is shown in Plate 295. All specimens are quite rare.

Salts

It is not known if the Caughley factory made, as a stock line, porcelain salt-cellars, but six 'salts to pattern' were supplied to Chamberlain in July, 1790, and were charged at 2s the six in an undecorated state. As these were made to pattern it can be assumed that they were for a special order. As yet no Caughley salts have been reported.

Salad Bowl

It is difficult to decide which of several shapes of Caughley bowl was originally intended to hold salad, but because of the underglaze blue prints of vegetables found on the outside of the finely moulded, shallow bowls illustrated in Plate 167, it is reasonable to regard these as salad bowls, although sprays of fruit are depicted inside.

These moulded bowls were also made at Worcester (as well as at Lowestoft and by the Chinese potters) and the Worcester examples outnumber those of Caughley. The distinguishing differences are explained on Page 142.

The Chamberlain accounts include several references to 'square sallad vessels' which were priced at 7s 6d each with the blue-printed 'Full Nankin' pattern, (an example of which is in the Victoria and Albert Museum) and 10s 6d when painted with the blue and gold 'Dresden' flower design. The shape of the 'square sallad vessel' is shown in Plate 168. The same basic form, but with a square, instead of a round, foot is found in the post-1799 hard-paste body, and many pieces of such John Rose salad bowls were found on the Caughley site. Completed examples are found, also, with post-1799 dinner services and were a standard component. The shallow bowl shown in Plate 169 is probably a salad bowl, but the basic shape is also found in smaller sizes.

The circular, fluted bowl illustrated in Plate 170, is undoubtedly a salad bowl and a rather similar, shaped-edge, but not fluted, example is shown in Plate 116, with part of a matching dinner service. These Caughley salad bowls are all rare and the forms do not seem to have been produced at the Worcester factory.

Sandwich services comprise a set of four segment dishes which form into an oval, or circular, whole. An oval, or circular, covered bowl fitted into the centre and the set was normally enclosed on a wooden tray, with upright rim and carrying handles. These are normally called breakfast, or supper, sets, but all available eighteenth century and early nineteenth century records use the term SAND-WICH SERVICE.

They are well-known in early nineteenth century pottery and porcelain, but are of extreme rarity in the eighteenth century porcelain. The single segment or fan-shaped dish illustrated in Plate 22, and the set of four shown in Plate 171, with the blue-printed 'Full Nankin' pattern, show that such Sandwich Services were made at the Caughley factory, and contemporary Chamberlain accounts include 'Fann Dishes' but these must be extremely rare and, in fact, I know of only one set of four dishes.

The nineteenth century sandwich services made at Worcester, and in the Staffordshire Potteries, have recessed rims to take the covers to these fan-shaped dishes, but the eighteenth century Caughley dishes lack a definite recess and it is doubtful if they were furnished with covers.

A fan-shape Caughley sandwich dish in the Watney collection is decorated with the hand-painted underglaze-blue pattern, shown in Plate 27.

Sauce-Boats

Caughley sauce-boats were made in four basic moulded shapes, each of the first three listed being produced in four different sizes, and decorated with several different underglaze-blue patterns. They were originally sold in pairs or sets of four or included in dinner services (see Page 94).

The attractively moulded sauce-boat design shown in Plate 172, several un-glazed pieces of which were found on the factory site, is quite rare, and normally bears the 'Pleasure Boat' or Fisherman design.

The half-fluted design illustrated in Plate 173 does not appear to have been used at Worcester. At Caughley two varieties were employed, one, which is very rare, with a moulded basket-work border as seen in Plate 174.

The third shape of Caughley sauce-boat is shown in Plate 176, and is shallow, the main part of the body having broad flutes. The example illustrated bears the 'Full Nankin' design found on so much marked Caughley porcelain. The same basic shallow form of sauce-boat was made at other factories, notably Worcester, Derby and Lowestoft.

A very rare form of fluted sauce-boat is illustrated in Plate 175; one of this pair bears the blue-printed 'C' mark. In addition to these, another form must exist, for a superb, unglazed example of a double-handled sauce-boat was found on the site (Plate 212), but as yet no completed and decorated specimen has been reported. The form suggests that a French-styled pattern might have been added to this graceful shape.

Sauce Tureens, see Tureens, Page 111.

Shell-Shaped Dishes

The 'scallop-shell' dishes, a typical example of which is illustrated in Plate 177, were made in differing sizes and normally bear the popular 'Pleasure Boat' or Fisherman print in underglaze blue. Several fragments were found on the Caughley factory site, and the shape does not appear to have been made at Worcester, although the form was copied in earthenware by several Staffordshire potters.

Larger dishes of shell-shape (as Plate 76) formed part of dessert services (see Page 93).

Spittoons, see Saffer-Pots, Page 103.

Spoons

All Caughley spoons are very rare, partly because few were made and partly because porcelain spoons are so fragile that few have survived. The two small tureens originally sold with dessert services were intended to hold cream and sugar, and were originally equipped with spoons or ladles of the shape shown in Plate 179.

Attractive moulded spoons were also sold with wet-mustard pots (see Plate 290) but these are now very seldom found. A graceful and simple unglazed handle of a small mustard, or salt, spoon was found on the factory site (see Plate 214) but I have not as yet traced a complete, finished specimen.

The small egg-spoon, or possibly caddy-spoon for ladling out tea, illustrated in Plate 178, is again very rare, although several matching fragments were found on the Caughley factory site.

Spoon-Trays

Spoon-trays were included in most pre-1795 tea services, and as the name suggests they were intended to hold the wet tea-spoons. The handleless tea bowl was raised to the mouth on the saucer and the spoon, if left on the saucer, would slip off or swing into the drinker's face, hence the need for a porcelain spoon-tray to hold the discarded, wet, spoon and protect the table.

Caughley spoon-trays were issued in two different shapes, both illustrated in Plate 181, the size and, of course, the added design varying considerably. In general, the shape shown in Plate 181, right, was in use during the 1785–95 period. Similar articles were made at Worcester (and at all other eighteenth century English porcelain factories) and the Worcester examples are illustrated in Plate 296 and discussed on Page 144.

Studs

We have already seen that Thomas Turner made porcelain buttons at the Caughley factory, and it would seem that small porcelain studs were also made, for the factory site has yielded two, fired but unglazed, examples of a stud-like object (Plate 94).

These objects cannot have been knobs, such as are found on Worcester teapots, etc. (Plates 238, 239, 241, 242, 244 and 267), for these would have been affixed to the cover before firing, not after, and the shape is also slightly different. It is probable that no complete, glazed studs have survived and that these factory wasters are the only evidence that studs were in fact made in porcelain.

Sucriers, Sugar Bowls or 'Sugar Boxes'

'Sugar boxes and covers', to use the contemporary term, were part of every complete tea service and the basic shape varied to match the teapot and other pieces.

The earliest shape, to match the circular globular teapot as shown in Plate 197, was of simple circular form with either a simple knob (Plates 58 and 59) or an open flower knob. They are very similar to the contemporary Worcester examples, which are, in fact, far more common than the Caughley specimens. The same shape is also found with the child's miniature tea services.

The moulded 'sugar box' shown in Plate 182, with irregularly spaced ribbing blending into the body towards the base, is found with teasets of the Oriental shapes shown in Plate 195. As with other basic shapes, it is found with a complete range of designs, both underglaze blue, and also with overglazed enamelled or gilt patterns.

The graceful covered 'sugar box' shown in Plate 183, with regular fluting around the body, is normally found with the teasets of the forms shown in Plate 196.

Another form is shown in Plate 78, the body being plain without any fluting and the knob of the mushroom shape, which was the nearest the Caughley factory came to the stud-like knobs favoured by the Worcester management.

Supper Sets, see Sandwich Sets, Page 105.

Tankards, see Mugs, Page 100.

Tart-Pans

Small, shallow, circular dishes are often referred to as 'patty-pans', but the Chamberlain and Turner clerks used the term 'tart-pans'. These were made in several graduating sizes at several English factories, including Worcester.

However, the shape of the Caughley 'tart-pans' would appear to be unique to this Shropshire factory, for these have a reinforced, curved edge, instead of the turned-over, flat flange found on Worcester and Lowestoft pans (Plates 184 and 185).

These Caughley tart-pans are found with standard underglaze-blue designs, including the 'Pleasure Boat' (or Fisherman) design, the 'Fence' and fruit prints, but all examples are now very rare.

Taster?

A very small wine-taster, or scoop, is shown in Plate 186, but the exact purpose of this rare object is not known.

Tea-Bowls

Most early Caughley tea services included handleless tea-bowls and saucers, unlike the handled cups we know today. Apart from the added pattern there is little to distinguish between Caughley and Worcester tea-bowls, except for the rectangular Caughley footrim and the rather thicker potting.

While most tea-bowls are plain, others have ribbing or fluting (see Plates 195 and 196). It would appear that some tea-bowls had their outer surface decorated with a finely moulded floral pattern, but these pieces are of the utmost rarity.

A rare form of tea-bowl and saucer (and related teawares) has a reinforced rim, that is, the rim is thicker than the main part of the article, see Plate 188.

Tea Canisters, Tea Caddies or 'Tea Vases'

Small vase-shaped tea canisters are today the rarest item of teaware, especially if the cover is still with the canister. The standard Caughley forms are illustrated in Plate 189 and with matching teasets in Plates 195 and 196. That shown in Plate 190, with a most delicately moulded open flower knob, is extremely rare.

Many gilt or overglaze caddies were decorated by the Chamberlains at Worcester, for they were sent down from the Caughley factory in the undecorated state, at 1s each.

The tea must have been tipped or poured from the 'tea-vase', for many have a very small opening that will not readily permit the tea leaves to be taken out by a spoon.

Tea Cups

Handled tea cups may be distinguished from coffee cups by their general proportion, coffee cups having a tall and slender appearance, whereas the tea cups are wide and shallow.

Some Caughley cups have moulded 'S'-shaped handles, with a relief-moulded heart-shaped projection at the top of the handle (Plate 191), while others have a handle of double convex curved outline; this handle is also found on cups of fluted or plain shape (Plate 51). A very rare cup with moulded basketwork border and intricate moulded handle is illustrated in Plate 51.

The commonest Caughley tea cup form, found in most teasets of the 1785–99 period, is shown in Plate 192. The deeply inswept 'kick' in the handle is noteworthy and distinguishes these Caughley teacups from the very similar Worcester ones of the same period (Plate 274).

Tea Services

A 'full' or complete Caughley tea service included the following articles:

Teapot and cover
Teapot stand
Spoon-tray
Tea canister
Sugar bowl and cover

Creamer or milk pot
Slop bowl
2 Bread and butter plates of different sizes
12 tea cups (or handleless tea bowls)
12 coffee cups
12 saucers

In addition, some services included a matching coffee pot, but this was normally regarded as an optional extra. On the other hand, some services, especially of the plain shapes with simple designs (such as those illustrated in Plates 58 and 59), were issued as 'short sets', without the teapot stand, spoon-tray or tea canister, and in all cases the customer could vary his order according to his requirement.

The standard tea service shapes are shown in Plates 64, 75, 195 and 196, the fluted forms illustrated in Plates 75 and 195 being of the 1780s and 1790s.

Miniature, or 'Toy', teasets were also made and are sometimes referred to as travellers' samples, a description not borne out by the numerous references to 'Toy' services in the Chamberlain records. These miniature sets bear two under-glaze-blue designs (see Plates 193 and 194) and some overglaze patterns may have been added to Caughley blanks by Chamberlain's artists at Worcester.

Teapots

The earliest form of Caughley teapot is of plain globular shape (see Plates 44 and 197), a form common to several contemporary factories. It is, in fact, called 'Common' in the Chamberlain-Turner records, perhaps as it was a well-known shape shared by many factories, or perhaps because it was simple and inexpensive, and the standard, or 'common', shape.

In the Chamberlain records the 'common' shape is distinguished from the barrel shape:

6 teapots 1st [size] common make, plain white,		1/4d.		8/-
6	do. 2nd [size]	do.	do.	1/9d.	10/6d.
6	do. 2nd [size] barrell	do.	2/-	12/-
6	do. 3rd [size]	do.	do.	2/6d.	15/-.

(September 30th, 1788)

The common globular teapot was made in several sizes and has two types of knob, one of simple mushroom shape and the other depicting an open flower. While the simple mushroom knob distinguishes the Caughley pots from the Worcester specimens, the ones with the flower knob are very similar to those produced at the other factory (see Page 144).

These 'common' globular pots were found with the standard blue-printed patterns, and patterns and prices listed in 1789 include:

Image	1st [size]	1/4d.
do.	2nd [size]	1/9d.
Fruit	1st [size]	1/4d.
do.	2nd [size]	1/9d.
Rose	1st [size]	1/4d.
do.	2nd [size]	1/9d.

Birds	1st [size]	1/4d.
do.	2nd [size]	1/9d.
Nankin	1st [size]	1/4d.
do.	2nd [size]	1/9d.
Pleasure Boat	1st [size]	1/4d.
[Fisherman design]	2nd [size]	2/-

Another form of globular teapot has a completely different moulded handle and spout, the latter being short, and stubby, and relief moulded after an Oriental prototype. The handle form also occurs on Chinese export-market porcelains and has a relief moulded heart at the top and near the bottom (Plate 198). The simple, unfluted shape is seen in Plate 81, and is much rarer than the one with double fluting on the body (Plate 198).

A very rare form of Caughley teapot with a unique, Continental styled handle is illustrated in Plate 200.

The barrel-shaped teapot was introduced about 1780, and continued in favour for the whole of the Turner period up to 1799. The basic barrel shape has three variations. One has a plain, unfluted body, with the standard, double curved handle, the moulded spout having flutes running its whole length of the spout with a shaped pouring aperture, similar to a Worcester form (Plate 49). A second has a similar, unfluted barrel shape, but with a short, stubby spout, fluted for only half its length (see Plate 62) instead of the graceful, slender, fluted one.

The third and most popular, form of Caughley teapot is a fluted version of the second, with the indented double-curved handle, short half-fluted spout and a small moulded mushroom-like knob. This standard teapot shape, which can be seen in Plates 196 and 201, was in general use from about 1780 to the late 1790s; it may be embellished with blue-printed patterns of Temple-type, together with the blue and gold formal patterns and the attractive designs in gold.

The oval teapot and cover illustrated in Plate 202 is extremely rare, and is the only example of this shape known to me, but numerous matching fragments were found on the factory site. It is, however, not known if this teapot is the last shape to have been made at Caughley under Thomas Turner before October, 1799, or if this is the first shape made under the new management in the style of the old designs, and retaining the old, short, half-fluted spout. The potting characteristics relate to the Caughley porcelains, with glaze shrinkage inside the footrim, but the porcelain itself is of the new, hard-paste variety. It therefore seems likely that this style of teapot was a transitional one made by former Turner workmen on the Caughley site, of the new paste introduced by the Coalport partners.

Teapot-Stands

Caughley teapot-stands are of two different shapes, both of which are shown in Plate 203, varying slightly in size to match the different sizes of teapot which stood on them. Slight variations of the standard shapes are found, such as the type with moulded basketwork edges.

The teapot-stand with six, slightly pointed projections (Plate 203, top) would appear to be unique to this factory, but similar shapes to the sexagonal stand were made at other factories, including Worcester (see Page 146).

The purpose of these stands was, of course, to protect the table from the hot teapot and from any drips from the spout.

Toast-Cups

The description 'toast-cup' is used in the Chamberlain-Caughley records, where two sizes are recorded, the quart and the pint size, at 2s, and 1s 6d. These objects were probably a form of tankard.

Trays

Most small dishes, or trays, are really spoon-trays, teapot stands or stands for tureens (see Plates 66, 181 and 203).

The shaped-edged and attractively gilt tray illustrated in Plate 180, is, however, of a different class and its original purpose is not known.

A fragment of a very thickly potted tray, or pen-tray, was found on the factory site. It has an underglaze blue line-edge and sprays of flowers (Plate 214), but as yet no complete specimen has been found to indicate the size or purpose of the complete object.

Tumblers

Caughley tumblers are very rare, though the Chamberlain-Caughley accounts in 1789 include two sizes of 'Tumblers, Horn-shape' at 6d and 4d, for white undecorated examples. In May, 1791, the Chamberlains returned to Turner ten tumblers which had been damaged, presumably in transit from Caughley, but as yet I have been unable to trace a tumbler which is unquestionably of Caughley make, although they were undoubtedly produced.

The blue-printed tumbler illustrated by Dr B. Watney in his *English Blue & White Porcelain of the 18th.Century* as Plate 88a, could be of Worcester origin.

Tureens

Tureens fall into three catagories: large tureens from dinner services, smaller sauce-tureens which were scaled-down versions of the large tureen, and small tureens found in dessert services.

All Caughley dinner wares are rare, tureens especially so. The earliest type of Caughley tureen was probably oblong and octagonal, following in general shape the large meat dish shown in Plate 117, but as yet no large tureen of this form has been recorded. Another untraced shape probably is of oval, lobed form following the form of the large meat dish depicted in Plate 118. These will probably bear the same blue-printed, 'Full Nankin' pattern.

Yet another undiscovered tureen shape is represented by two unglazed part covers, discovered on the Caughley factory site (Plate 204), which are extremely crisply moulded and finished, and the complete tureen must be one of the finest articles the factory can have made.

The tureen, cover and stand, also illustrated in Plate 204, with site wasters, 111 accompanied the dinner service shapes shown in Plate 116, and must represent one of the standard Caughley tureen shapes of the 1780–95 period, although this is the only specimen known to me.

Dinner services normally included one or two of these tureens, with matching covers and under-dishes, and the same service would also have contained two, or four, smaller sauce-tureens, covers and dishes, which were normally-scaled-down counterparts of the large tureens.

Dessert services also included two covered tureens, often referred to as sauce-tureens, although contemporary records describe them as cream and sugar tureens, probably for use with the dessert fruits. A spoon or ladle was originally sold with these tureens, and an aperture is normally let into the edge of the cover for the handle.

The earliest and rarest form of Caughley cream or sugar tureen is shown in Plate 314 with a Worcester tureen of *very* similar form. Unglazed fragments of these, including the characteristic shell-handle, were also found on the Caughley factory site.

Another very rare form of Caughley cream or sugar tureen is shown in Plate 206, a finely gilt and underglaze blue example in the Victoria and Albert Museum. The same double twig handle is found on the standard Caughley dessert tureen form, as shown in Plate 207. A rare variation has a moulded basketwork border (Plate 57). These tureens originally stood on under-dishes that follow the general plan form of the tureen (Plate 66). A further very rare shape of Caughley tureen is illustrated in Plate 205, and is of a form favoured by the French potters. This particular example bears the blue-printed 'Full Nankin' design (see Page 20), but the salient feature is the continuation of the handle design in relief down the cover and into the body. It is probable that this shape may have been made in the large soup-tureen size. These Caughley tureens do not appear to have been copied at other factories, with the exception of that depicted in Plate 314.

Vases

Vases are included in the Chamberlain-Turner records, but it is not certain if these were of Caughley manufacture. On December 24th, 1789, Chamberlain received in case number 49 '3 pr. vasses (*sic*) and covers, White, per pair 10/6d. £1. 11. 6' but the attribution to Caughley is made doubtful by the fact that the other contents of the case do not appear to have been of Turner's own make, but were perhaps Derby porcelain, in which Turner traded. These other goods were: '75 pairs of Dogs, white, per pair 1/6d. £5. 12. 6' and 17 pair of fancy figures at 5s per pair.

However, when, within three weeks, more vases were sent from Caughley to Worcester, they were packed with other obviously Caughley articles of teaware. These articles were:

3 pr. Vasses (*sic*) & covers, white		10/-	£1. 10. 0.
3 pair do. & do. blue bottom top			
& bottom (at)		14/-	
(January 11th, 1790)			

Other vases were listed on September 26th, 1789, but in this case no price is given and the reason for this is not now clear:

3	Jars & cov^{rs}.	Dresden Flowers
3	do. less-size	do.
1	do.	do.
1	Beaker	do.
1	do.	do.
1	do.	do.
1	Jar & 2 Beakers, fruit & N bord^r.	

The Dresden flower design consists of underglaze blue flowers with gilt enrichments, as is seen in Plates 60 and 114. Caughley vases and flare-topped beakers probably exist and should bear 'S' or 'C' initial marks. Indeed, since writing this sentence one 'C' marked beaker-vase has been reported, and is shown in Plate 208, decorated with a standard Caughley underglaze blue print. This small vase was one of a set of three or one of a set of five vases and most probably relates to the entry given above: '1 Jar & 2 Beakers, fruit & N bord^r.'.

Water Ewer (or Jug) & Wash-Basin

Chamberlain-Turner references to these utilitarian, but graceful objects include the following:

3	water ewers & basons, Shrewsbury, at 12/6d. (December 11th, 1789)	£1. 17. 6.
3	wash-hand basons & Ewers, Full Nankeen, at 12/- (November 23rd, 1791)	£1. 16. 0.
1	Bason & Water ewer, Shrews^y Nankin, 12/- (August 14th, 1792)	

The water ewer illustrated in Plate 209 is typical, but a finer shape was probably made with a graceful turned top, as such an unglazed ewer-top was found on the factory site. Large jugs were also made as an alternative to the handleless ewer (which must have presented difficulties in handling with wet, soapy hands). Such a jug and basin are shown in Plates 210 and 211, with a mahogany wash-stand of the type made to accommodate these porcelain ewers and basins. When the bowl was in use the empty ewer or jug could be placed on the bottom shelf.

The wash-basins always have a wide, slightly turned-over flange to fit stands whose tops were made to hold bowls of different sizes.

It is rather a surprise to find that miniature water-ewers and basins were made (Colour Plate IV), but these charming toys are now of extreme rarity.

CHAPTER VIII

POST-1799 CAUGHLEY-COALPORT PORCELAINS

As related in Chapter I, the partners in the nearby Coalport porcelain factory took over the Caughley factory in October 1799, with all fixtures, working materials (including the engraved copper-plates) and the unglazed, partly finished Caughley porcelain. The Coalport partners, then Edward Blakeway, John Rose and Richard Rose, continued the Caughley factory, with their original works at Coalport, until about 1814 when the Coalport factory was enlarged and the Caughley works demolished.

The porcelains made at Caughley from October 1799 to 1814 by the Coalport management were sold as 'Coalport', or as 'Coalbrook Dale', but it has been thought advisable to include in this book a resumé of the later 'Coalport' porcelains made at Caughley, especially as some pieces were decorated with the former Caughley engraved designs, and some forms are very close copies of pre-1799 shapes as first introduced by Thomas Turner.

The new 'Coalport' porcelain made at Caughley is vastly different from the pre-1799 Caughley body, which was a soft-paste, soap-stone body containing a relatively high percentage (approximately 11 per cent) of magnesia. The new body is a type of hard-paste porcelain with only a trace of magnesia. It is cold and heavy, and pieces are thicker in the potting than related pre-1799 porcelains, while the covering glaze, which was more generously applied, is glittery and much thicker than Turner's. The glaze that collects inside the footrims, which, incidentally, are generally shallower than those on pre-1799 Caughley porcelains, was not wiped away, so that the line of glaze-free porcelain inside the angle of these rims is not present on post-1799 pieces, also the inside rims of teapot (or other) covers are now glazed, not wiped clean of glaze as were the Caughley rims.

The well-known cabbage-leaf jug shape with the mask spout (Plate 215) was employed by the new management, and the 'BRIMSTREE LOYAL LEGION' example in the Schreiber Collection at the Victoria and Albert Museum is of the new hard-paste body. Leaf dishes and 'Chelsea ewers' were made for a few years from 1799, the 'Chelsea ewers' being a plainer version of the earlier Caughley shape. The handle is simplified and no longer has the animal-head finial at the lower end, the foot is flat, without the shallow feet found on pre-1799 examples (Plate 216).

The new teawares are of different shapes from the earlier Caughley examples, with the teapots and covered sugar bowls now oval, not circular. Spoon trays and tea caddies were not supplied with post-1799 teasets and straight-sided coffee cans replaced the earlier shaped-sided coffee cups.

Re-used former Caughley printed designs include the View of the Ironbridge, just upstream from Coalport, the birds in a tree designs, and various fruit and floral engravings. Strangely, the once popular Fisherman or 'Pleasure Boat' design does not seem to have been re-used by the Coalport partners after October 1799. It is noteworthy that the post-1799 porcelains do not bear the 'S' or 'C' marks associated with the same designs on pre-1799 Caughley porcelain.

The underglaze-blue pigment when applied to the post-1799 hard-paste porcelain, although it can be quite vivid, is of noticeably paler tone than the normal inky-blue Caughley colour.

The teawares illustrated in Plate 217, with oval teapots and sugar bowl, represent a class of porcelain which some authorities regard as pre-1799 Caughley, and very many fragments of these basic shapes were certainly found on the factory site, but I believe them to be of the post-1799 Coalport period. My main reasons are:

The oval teawares are of hard-paste porcelain.
The potting characteristics—glazed, shallow, footrims match Coalport, not Caughley, porcelains:
The make-up of these services also matches Coalport sets, in that while neither spoon trays nor tea caddies are included, coffee cans, instead of shaped coffee cups, are normally present.
Very similar shapes were employed by the rival Anstice, Horton and Rose factory at Coalport and there is no evidence to suggest that this rival factory was established before 1800.

but it cannot be denied that further evidence may come to light which will indicate that tea services of the basic forms shown in Plate 217 were, in fact, made in the 1790s, during the closing years of Thomas Turner's ownership of the Caughley factory.

A fine range of early Coalport porcelain of the 1799–1814 period which was made at the Caughley site will be illustrated in my forthcoming *Coalport and Coalbrookdale Porcelain*. These are, in the main, unmarked and have in the past been attributed to the Chamberlain Worcester factory.

The Coalport management in the second half of the nineteenth century also 115 re-used some of the pre-1799 engraved copper-plates. Whereas the early Coal-port wares may bear the Caughley engravings on the heavy, thick, hard-paste porcelain, the later pieces are on a very white, soft-paste porcelain. Examples often bear an open crescent or 'C' mark in underglaze-blue, and pieces have been mistaken for original Caughley porcelain by collectors who have compared the two different bodies or noticed the network of fine crazing so often found on the glaze of the late pieces. A selection of these later pieces is shown in Plates 218 to 221.

As previously stated, the Caughley factory was demolished in about 1814, the usable materials being transferred to Coalport. Some materials or clay from the site were, however, sold to Messrs Chamberlains at Worcester at a slightly later date, for the following two entries appear in the Chamberlain records:

September 16th 1816.
    Purchased from Messrs Rose & Blaze, Caughley.
    4 Tons, 5 cwts Fire Clay at 15/6d.   £3. 5. $10\frac{1}{2}$
    2000 Fire Bricks at 56/-   5. 12. 0.
    700 best   do. at 70/-   2. 9. 0.

September 30th 1816.
    Thomas Rose & Co. Caughley. Shropshire.
    For 20 Ton, 6 cwt Fire clay at 15/6   £15. 14. 8.

The subject of clay is a fitting one to close the Caughley section, for not only are the two clay accounts quoted above the last contemporary references to the Caughley factory site, but today, over one hundred and fifty years after the closure of the factory, the site is alive again, with mechanical excavators moving the very clay on which the Caughley factory was built (Plate 4). This Caughley clay is being used for brick making and therefore helps to build homes for the descendants of eighteenth-century families who may well have enjoyed their 'dish of tea' from a blue-printed Caughley 'tea sett'.

The self-same modern clay excavations have brought to light a mass of dis-carded factory wasters, which have helped considerably to identify positively the true Caughley porcelains and by a process of elimination have helped to show which versions of Caughley-type designs were made at Worcester (see the following Chapter).

116

CHAPTER IX

CAUGHLEY OR WORCESTER?

Many collectors have great difficulty in distinguishing between Worcester and Caughley porcelains, for the body, shapes and patterns are often remarkably similar. My recent research has suggested that the problem is even more difficult than is generally supposed, and that much porcelain that has traditionally been ascribed to Caughley is, in fact, of Worcester manufacture. The new divisions put forward in this chapter will surprise many collectors, and it may well be some years before these fresh attributions are fully accepted, but I feel that the evidence is quite clear and conclusive once one has rid the mind of old prejudices and is willing to approach the problem objectively.

The main traditional fallacy is the widely-held belief that all Worcester porcelain is of fine quality and that all Caughley is comparatively coarse, but the truth is that some Worcester of the 1770–90 period is of quite ordinary commercial quality, while Caughley porcelain can be very finely potted and delicately decorated.

Over many years I amassed a collection of porcelains that have been traditionally attributed to the Caughley factory, of shapes and patterns illustrated in most reference books as of Salopian manufacture. From this large assembly I separated out those specimens which bore either the impressed 'SALOPIAN' marks, a clear 'C' mark, or the various versions of the 'S' mark—and also those pieces which exactly matched any of the numerous factory wasters found on the Caughley site; these true Salopian porcelains are discussed in Chapters II to VII.

I was, however, left with about one third of my collection which did not bear a clear Caughley mark nor match any excavated material. These pieces fell into two major categories:

(a) The blue printed specimens bearing one of the Chinese-style disguised numeral marks—examples of which are reproduced below:

(b) Blue printed porcelains bearing the filled-in crescent mark, that is the printed crescent mark with close lines running crosswise to form shading (see Pages 9 and 11).

These two basic classes of porcelain with some related objects will be discussed separately in the following pages but first I shall list certain characteristics of *Caughley* porcelain as shown by marked specimens:

(1) The porcelain is of the soapstone variety, containing a relatively high percentage of magnesia. A recent analysis[1] gave the following result:

Silica	(SiO_2)	75.25 per cent
Magnesia	(Mgo)	11.06 per cent
Alumina	$Al_2O_3)$	5.54 per cent
Potash	(K_2O)	2.14 per cent
Phosphate	(P_2O_5)	1.78 per cent
Lime	(CaO)	1.75 per cent
Soda	(Na_2O)	1.68 per cent
Ferric Oxide	(Fe_2O_3)	0.49 per cent

(2) By transmitted light (using a standard 240v. 40 watt bulb), the body normally has an orange tint. The degree of translucency depends largely on the thickness of the piece being tested, and also on the firing temperature—an underfired specimen appearing more opaque than a correctly fired piece.

(3) The glaze is normally thinly applied, is close fitting and does not craze or speckle. At normal thinness it is colourless but where the glaze may have gathered in pools it shows a cloudy blue-green colour, green rather than blue. It is often incorrectly stated that the Caughley glaze is blued; this is incorrect although some pieces formerly *attributed* to this factory have such a glaze.

(4) The bottom edge of footrims are normally wiped clean of glaze, as is the inside of the footrim and in wiping away the glaze from inside the rim, the tool (or thumb-nail) has left a line (sometimes a broken rather than a continuous line) free of glaze on the base just inside the rim. This unglazed line is generally considered to be a sign of Worcester workmanship but, in fact, most early pre-1765 Worcester porcelain does NOT show this so-called characteristic. On the other hand, nine-tenths of the 'wasters' found on the Caughley site show this characteristic feature to a marked degree. A yellowish colour very often appears in the angle of the footrim where the glaze has been wiped away.

(6) Pieces are cleanly potted, and bases and footrims neatly turned, but in trimming circular articles, one or more concentric circles have often been left under the bottom of pieces where they have received the attention of

[1] The sample tested by the Ceramic Testing Laboratory at the North Staffordshire College of Technology, Stoke-on-Trent was an 'S' marked fragment of a 'Fisherman' pattern teabowl found on the Caughley factory site.

the turners. These incised circular turning marks sometimes occur on other porcelains and, contrary to general belief, these marks are also found on Worcester porcelains of the 1770s as is proved by unglazed 'wasters' from the Worcester site (Plate 227).

(7) Footrims and bases were fired true and very seldom required the attention of the grind-stone to make the article 'sit'.

(8) The inside rims of teapots and covers were wiped clean of glaze, so that a cover could fit on its teapot during firing ensuring a clean fit and lack of distortion.

Apart from documentary Caughley specimens bearing the impressed 'SALO-PIAN marks, the blue printed 'C' and 'S' marks and the pieces which link directly with 'wasters' found on the factory site (particularly the unglazed, partly finished, examples) there is a further source of information on Caughley productions. This source is the impressions taken from the original engraved Caughley copper-plates, several of which bear Thomas Turner's initials as well as the standard 'S' and 'C' marks. Impressions from the original Caughley-engraved copper-plates are preserved in the British, and the Victoria and Albert Museums in London, and in a most interesting 'rag book' preserved by the Coalport China Company which acquired the original copper-plates in October, 1799, when John Rose of Coalport, with his then partners, purchased the Caughley factory with 'all the materials, implements, fixtures, moulds, copper-plates and machinery belonging to the said manufactory. . . .' These copper-plates and the impressions taken from them will be referred to in subsequent pages.

To return to the porcelains which were left in my collection after segregating the pieces with clear, undisputed Caughley marks, or which matched factory wasters, I found that many of these articles bore the series of nine disguised numeral marks which comprise the numbers 1–9, with fancy Chinese style scrolls and embellishments (see the drawings reproduced on Page 117 and the printed patterns bearing these marks illustrated on Plates 228, 233, 235–47, 251, 267 and 285). In the main these designs occur on teawares and dessert services, but may also be applied to other objects. Most of them are Chinese-style landscapes of Willow-pattern type—the commonest being:

(1) The Vase (or Bat) pattern, comprising a large centre vase of flowers with a bat-like bird flying above, and one to the left. A table with a basket of fruit stands on the right of the centre with an openwork fence running across the design, and the whole is enclosed by a wide ornate Chinese-style border. Typical specimens are shown in Plates 236 to 240.

(2) The Temple design of general Willow-pattern type (without a bridge) showing two tall, temple-like, Chinese-style buildings on an island, with two pairs of figures standing in the foreground, the whole being enclosed with a wide, Chinese-style, ornate border. See Plates 241 and 305 for typical specimens. Perhaps this is the 'Temple', or 'New Temple', pattern mentioned in accounts of 1789 and 1790. This design should not be confused with the Caughley 'Temple' pattern (see Plate 16 and Page 17.)   119

(3) The Bandstand pattern, again of general Willow-pattern style with a tall Chinese temple on the right, to the left of which is a bandstand-like structure in which stands a man at the top of a flight of steps. A secondary design comprises two islands jointed by a bridge, with one figure crossing it. (See Plate 242 for typical specimens.) This pattern also links with the contemporary descriptions 'Temple', 'New Temple' or 'Pagoda' (see Page 128).

(4) The 'Argument' pattern, which is also of general Willow-pattern style with a centre apple (?) tree, and an open-ended Chinese building on its left, while on its right an open-fronted, low building contains two figures posed as if in fierce argument and about to fight. A secondary design shows a bridge joining two islands with a figure crossing from right to left. Various ornate, wide, Chinese-style borders enclose this design. See Plates 243–5 for typical specimens. Incidentally, a similar blue-printed design is found on Lowestoft porcelain but not on Caughley.

Then there are the following designs, which are much rarer than the four previously mentioned:

(5) European ruin and landscape designs, several different prints of which show European figures posed in front of elaborate ruins of classical feeling with statues. Attractive and elaborate borders are found with these prints, and in the case of dessert wares, the centre panel is framed by delicate tracing. Typical specimens are shown in Plates 246–7, 251–2. A related series of prints show landscape subjects, often with a horseman in the foreground, and these are sometimes found on moulded teawares (Plates 248 to 250).

(6) The Milk Maid pattern, showing two milk maids, each with a wooden pail of milk on her head, and a central male figure arranged in landscape with cows and farm buildings. A secondary print shows three cows. Similar overglaze prints are found on undoubted Worcester porcelain, and some examples bear the initials R.H. (for Robert Hancock) with the place-name 'Worcester' or the abbreviation 'Worc'. A cup and saucer in the Schreiber Collection at the Victoria and Albert Museum is signed in full 'Hancock fecit'. A blue printed specimen is shown in Plate 253.

(7) The Fruit design, depicting a group of fruit, a central peach, a gooseberry, two cherries, a bunch of round berries or grapes and three berries on long stalks surrounded by a border of six-sided Chinese-style diapers. (See Plate 285.)

Whereas the patterns listed above as numbers 1 to 7 do *not* occur on marked Caughley porcelain, and no matching unglazed fragments were found on the factory site,[1] the following three designs are variations of underglaze blue prints

[1] Since writing this section one <u>glazed</u> fragment of a milk jug bearing the blue printed Milk Maid subject has been discovered on the Caughley site but this piece appears to be of a Worcester shape and it may have been Worcester porcelain purchased by Turner of Caughley for re-sale to his own customers, or even sent up river by Chamberlain as a sample (see Page 128

which are found on marked Caughley porcelains but are printed from different copper-plates and display variations in subject and technique.

(8) The Fisherman pattern, a version of the best known Caughley printed design, called in contemporary accounts the 'Pleasure Boat' pattern, showing a Chinese man standing on the stern of a sailing boat holding a fish. A secondary print shows a seated figure fishing from an island (see Plates 229 and 230, and Page 131).

(9) Mother with child (or 'Image') pattern. Again a variation of a subject found on marked Caughley porcelain but with basic differences between the two, especially on the reverse side (see Plate 255). The design features a seated mother with a standing child on the right and a vase of fruit on the left of the central figure. The secondary print normally features a tall vase, and a pedestal with a protruding handle of a ladle and kettle, or teapot.

(10) Parrot and fruit pattern. An attractive and popular print found on Worcester and on marked Caughley porcelain mugs, jugs, etc but not on teawares. On examples bearing the disguised numeral marks some of the shading has been achieved by cross-hatching, that is, crossed lines; this is seen in the shaded rocks in the central foreground (see Plate 260 and compare with Plate 40), and in several other sections of the design. The same basic subject, when found on initial-marked Caughley porcelain, or on fragments from the factory site, shows no cross-hatching, as, although the parallel lines of shading may be curved, or follow the shape of the object depicted, they are never crossed, a feature that is clearly seen in the pull from the original Caughley engraved copper-plate shown in Plate 40. Several other minor differences exist between the Caughley and the disguised numeral marked specimens, such as lighter fruit, with areas of high lighting on Caughley examples, but the main difference is in the engraving technique, the use of cross-hatching on the pieces here attributed to Worcester.

In addition to these ten subjects, some fruit and floral designs are found occasionally with the disguised numeral marks (Plate 285), but, in general, these floral designs are normally marked with the filled-in, or shaded, crescent mark.

It must be pointed out that most of these ten designs are also found on seemingly identical porcelains which bear a filled in, or shaded crescent, mark rather than one of the disguised numeral marks. Matching cups and saucers in the Victoria and Albert Museum, for example, have one mark on the saucer and the

---

where extracts from Chamberlains accounts for September, 1789, show that a cup and saucer 'Milk Maids' was sent to Caughley 'as patterns'). Several fragments of *glazed* porcelain were found at Caughley which appear to be of Worcester origin and it must be remembered that only *unglazed* (or obviously spoilt glazed) wasters can be taken as wholly reliable evidence of the wares made at any factory site. The Caughley site, for instance, yielded many broken fragments of Chinese porcelain, see Page 14 and Plate 9.

other on the cup (or teabowl) but it is now impossible to say if the cup or the saucer have been 'married' during the last 150 years, or if they were always together, and were originally issued with the two different types of mark. The shaded crescent mark examples are discussed separately on Pages 125 to 135.

The basic characteristics of the most common patterns found with the disguised numeral marks are listed below:

(*a*) a bright deep blue pigment, different from the standard Caughley inky blue.

(*b*) In the common patterns listed under 1–3 the rocks, hills and other features in the foreground, such as shading on water, are represented by a light wash of underglaze-blue applied by hand, often filling in a printed outline. Similar features on marked Caughley porcelains, on factory wasters and on the impressions from the original Caughley copper-plates are represented by closely engraved parallel lines or cross-hatching, not by hand-applied washes of light blue.

(*c*) The glaze, often distinctly blued, has often been disfigured by numerous brownish specks and bubbles where the glaze has been too thickly applied, or has run into pools.

My reasons for rejecting the traditional attribution of these pieces to Caughley rests on the following points:

(1) No unglazed fragments of any of the patterns bearing the disguised numeral marks were found on the Caughley factory site, although many thousands of blue printed wasters were found.

(2) No marked Caughley porcelain shows the hand-applied light blue shading on the numeral marked specimens, and no factory wasters show this characteristic.

(3) The shapes on which the printed patterns were applied are different from the standard Caughley forms and do not match the Caughley factory wasters. These points will be enlarged upon later in the chapter.

(4) None of the printed designs associated with the disguised numeral marks is to be found on the existing impressions taken from the original Caughley copper-plates, although very many copper-plates must have been engraved for the various patterns, and for each different article and the various sizes of object.

(5) Marked Caughley porcelains do not normally show the bubbled, speckled glaze found on many of the pieces bearing the disguised numeral marks (Plate 269) nor is the Caughley glaze blued to such an extent as the glaze on pieces bearing the numeral marks.

(6) Although the 'Vase' or 'Bat' pattern (see Plates 236–40) is the most common of the designs found with disguised numeral marks, no reference to it appears in the Chamberlain-Turner correspondence, or in the lists of Caughley goods purchased by Chamberlain (see Chapter V). References

in these records to 'Temple', 'Image', and 'Pleasure Boat' designs could possibly relate to patterns found with the disguised numerals, but it is more probable that they refer to known Caughley versions of these same patterns.

A further characteristic of many pieces of this general class, is the button, or stud-like knob applied to teapots, coffee pots, covered creamers and covered sugar bowls (see Plates 238, 239, 241 and 244). This is not found on any marked Caughley porcelain, nor is it found on wares bearing a known Caughley print, although it is found on *non*-Caughley versions of some designs, such as the Fisherman pattern employed by two or more different factories.

Having given my main reasons for discounting the previous Caughley attribution for these porcelains, it remains to suggest their true source. I believe that they are of Worcester origin, but of a period neglected by most collectors of 1st period (or Dr Wall) Worcester. This is the ten years from 1773 until 1783, when the Flights took over the Worcester factory from the earlier partnership, and some pieces may even be early Flight porcelains of the 1780s.

These porcelains of the 1770s and 1780s are different in many respects from the fine quality Worcester porcelains of the 1750s and 1760s, in the same way that gold anchor marked Chelsea porcelain of the 1760s differs from the Red anchor marked Chelsea porcelain of the early 1750s. There is the further point that these blue-printed objects would represent the inexpensive 'bread and butter' products of the Worcester factory, and the finish might well be inferior to the more expensive enamelled porcelains. An interesting comment in a letter from Chamberlain of Worcester to Thomas Turner at Caughley underlines the low cost of the blue-printed porcelains, and also shows that the main Worcester factory made such wares (see Page 126).

Joseph Lygo, a trained observer, being the London agent to the Derby Porcelain Company, took a poor view of the Flight-Worcester wares of the 1787–90 period, for he reported to William Duesbury in Derby '. . . Mr Turner . . . manufactures more fine goods than Flights . . .' and referring to Chamber-pots '. . . I have not had an opportunity of going into the city to enquire at the Worcester warehouse if they have them, but if they have they will be much worse than the Staffordshire ware ones'.

The points that lead me to attribute these porcelains bearing the disguised numeral marks to the Worcester factory are:

(1) The body is of the soapstone variety containing a relatively high percentage of magnesia (some 7.5 per cent, see following analysis) and according to present research on ceramic bodies, only two factories, Worcester and Caughley, used a body containing this percentage of magnesia. My reasons for discounting Caughley are given on Page 122. A fragment of a blue printed bowl of the 'Fisherman' pattern bearing the disguised numeral 8 was tested by Herbert Eccles, F.C.S., with the following result (published in the Victoria and Albert Museum booklet *Analysed Specimens of English Porcelain.* (1922)):

123

Silica	74.22
Alumina	8.50
Magnesia	7.62
Oxide of lead	3.73
Lime	2.78
Soda	2.27
Potash	1.28
Phosphoric acid	.20
	———
	100.60

(2) Some prints with disguised numeral marks appear on shapes which match typical Worcester specimens decorated with standard Worcester over-glaze enamel patterns. As already stated on Page 120, the prints do not occur on Caughley forms.

(3) Many of the pieces bearing disguised numeral marks are thinly potted and in this respect correspond with Worcester rather than Caughley, which is relatively thick.

(4) Fragments recently found on the Worcester factory site match pieces bearing the disguised numeral mark[1] and these Worcester fragments differ from the more numerous wasters from the Caughley site, and from designs found on 'S' or 'C' marked Caughley porcelains.

(5) At least one example with a disguised numeral mark in underglaze blue also bears an overglaze Worcester mark—'Worcester Manufactory. Flight'. It has been suggested in the past (probably because of the numeral mark) that this specimen[2] was of Caughley manufacture, that the under-glaze blue decoration was applied there, and that the mug was then sent to Worcester where the red overglaze printing in the reserve panels was added, together with the gilt edges and the Worcester mark. Apart from the fact that there is no evidence that the two factories carried out any inter-trading, and several pointers lead one to suppose that they were rivals, it would seem likely that the Worcester firm would have obliterated the numeral mark (if, in fact, it was a Caughley mark) when they applied their own printed mark.

The most likely explanation is surely the simplest; that the mug, the blue printing and the disguised numeral mark are all of the late Dr Wall period, made a few years or months prior to 1783 when the Flights purchased the factory, together with the existing stock and copper-plates, and that it was completed, made saleable and the second mark added after Flight took over in 1783, a theory which, if accepted, lends further weight to the suggestion that the numeral marks are of Worcester origin. The Flight management certainly made after 1783, blue printed porcelains as is evidenced by the jug illustrated in Plate 287.

The reader may wonder why these disguised numeral marks were attributed

---

[1] An unglazed fragment found on the Worcester site bears a typical blue-printed disguised numeral mark (Plate 228).

[2] A mug formerly in the Dyson Perrins Collection, illustrated in the *Transactions of the English Ceramic Circle*, No. 5 (1937), Plate XIV.

to Caughley in the first place, and the simple answer is that they were not! The nineteenth century writer on ceramic subjects, Llewellyn Jewitt, contributed in the 1860s an interesting series of articles on English porcelain factories to the *Art Journal* magazine. In the issue of February, 1862, Jewitt wrote of the 'History of the Worcester Porcelain Works' and, having listed the early and well-known Worcester factory marks, the crescent, the square mark, the 'W' marks and some of the workmen's personal signs, he continued:

> Other marks adopted were figures disguised in Oriental looking flourishes. Examples from 1 up to 9 are known. . . .

Jewitt then reproduced four of these disguised numeral marks.

However, Jewitt was very soon to change his opinion, for in the next issue of the *Art Journal* (of March 1862), while discussing 'Salopian China', he wrote:

> On two mugs from the same engraved plate which I have seen one bears the 'S' and the other the accompanying curious mark, which is evidently of the same character as the example of assimilated Chinese one which I have given in my article on Worcester.

These *Art Journal* articles were later incorporated in Jewitt's monumental work *The Ceramic Art of Great Britain*. The first edition, of 1878, repeats most of the paragraph quoted above, but after 'assimilated Chinese ones', Jewitt added 'which are occasionally ascribed to Worcester, but which are in reality, I believe, those of Caughley. . . .

Subsequent writers appear to have taken Jewitt's belief as fact, without troubling to delve deeper into the subject, so that twentieth century ceramic reference books give these numeral marks as Caughley.

We cannot now re-examine Jewitt's two mugs, for we have no means of telling which examples he was comparing, but I do not know of any two specimens printed from the same engraved copper-plate which bear the 'S' mark, and any of disguised numeral marks. Several examples could be cited which *appear* to be from the same plates, if the two objects are seen separately, or not *closely* compared (there are, for example, the two versions of the popular Fisherman pattern, the Mother and Child prints, the parrot and fruit design, and the Fishing subject, and I believe it was two different versions of one of these designs found on both Caughley and on Worcester porcelain, which Jewitt compared (without spotting the tell-tale differences) and so caused him to change this original, and correct, opinion that these numeral marks signified a Worcester origin.

Crescent Marked Worcester and Caughley

I have already mentioned that some pieces matching, in form and decoration, examples bearing the disguised numeral marks sometimes bear a filled-in or cross-hatched crescent mark and that some cups and saucers have one piece with one mark and the other with the alternate mark. It seems quite clear that the factory that used the series of disguised numeral marks (and I believe this to be Worcester) also used the filled-in crescent mark.

125

While it is generally acknowledged that both the Worcester and the Caughley factories employed this mark on blue-printed porcelain, the general impression seems to be that most examples bearing the printed, filled-in crescent are of Caughley origin, but my researches show that this was not the case, and that most, if not all, blue-printed porcelains bearing filled-in or shaded crescent marks are Worcester of the 1770–90 period.

Taking first for consideration the popular Fisherman pattern (or 'Pleasure Boat' to use a contemporary term), in company with other writers I had thought that all examples were of Caughley origin (apart from the rather poor Liverpool copies). It would now seem that Worcester also made the design, for one of Chamberlains' letters to Turner at Caughley appears to refer to Worcester versions of this subject:

> . . . [send] no more teas P Boat [standard abbreviation for Pleasure Boat, the original name for the pattern we now call Fisherman] unless they can be sent at the Worcester price 5/6. . . .

Chamberlains also sold Worcester Pleasure Boat patterned porcelains, as is shown by entries in the sales books, when on rare occasions the make of the article sold was added:

> 1 small plate P B [standard abbreviation for Pleasure Boat] Worc^r 1/3d. (Dec. 1789)
> 1 Short sett of Pleasure Boat, Worc^r 8/- (Jan. 1790)
> 2 cups & saucers, Worc^r Pleasure Boat 1/2d. (Aug. 1790)

Further proof that the Worcester factory produced this pattern is provided by fragments, both glazed and unglazed, found on the site of the *Worcester* factory and few readers would not accept that the fragment shown in Plate 231 was not made there. At the time of writing (Spring, 1968) little excavation has been possible on the Worcester site and the shards, a selection of which is shown in Plate 226, found in 1959 during the building of the new Worcester Technical College, represent only a very small proportion of the possible total, many very common shapes and styles of decoration not being represented at all in the discovered wasters.

Several of the fragments found at Worcester are of patterns which also occur on Caughley porcelain and previous writers have suggested that these were of Caughley make. My opinion, however, is that these fragments are of true Worcester make, of the period reviewed in this chapter, that is, *c.* 1770–90.

This opinion is based on the three following basic points:

(1) The Caughley-*type* fragments found at Worcester differ in detail from Caughley fragments and marked Caughley porcelains.

(2) For technical reasons it is very difficult (although not impossible) to transport porcelains bearing unglazed patterns on unglazed porcelain, and yet blue decorated *unglazed* fragments were found at Worcester. It is

practically certain that these underglaze prints were added at Worcester—
to Worcester porcelain.

(3) Several fragments were so spoilt that they would have been dumped at
their place of manufacture.

Several writers have also suggested that Caughley supplied unglazed porcelain
to the so-called Dr Wall Worcester factory and that the Worcester firm sent their
wares to Caughley to be decorated in underglaze-blue. I do not, however, believe
that any *unglazed* porcelain was transported between the two places. The extent
of intertrading between the *Chamberlain* firm at Worcester and Turner at Caughley can be gauged from the original Chamberlain accounts, and not one item of
unglazed porcelain is listed. I also very much doubt if the main, Dr Wall-Flight,
Worcester firm was on friendly terms with Turner at Caughley. It is likely that
they were very keen rivals, each trying to undercut the other on the cheaper
wares and each copying the other's standard patterns and shapes.

When Messrs Flights purchased the former Dr Wall factory in 1783 they
continued their predecessor's practice of decorating their wares with underglaze-
blue prints. John Flight recorded in his diary[1] on July 19th, 1789— '. . . Have
had a good deal of trouble last week about the Blue printing, the Colours peel
off (*sic*) in the burning-in and spoils a vast deal of ware. Every possible attention
is payed to it to find out the cause and remedy it, but hitherto without success. . . .' Later in the diary John Flight notes the death of Lewis, 'he managed
the printing'.

It is difficult to tell which blue-printing John Flight was referring to in 1789
when a 'vast deal of ware' was being spoilt. It is, however, quite possible that the
blue-printed wares were the later pieces bearing the disguised numeral (and the
crescent) marks, for some of the designs were still popular and saleable in the
late 1780s and 1790s as is evidenced by the Chamberlain orders and sales books,
also by the impressed marked 'FLIGHTS' jug shown in Plate 287, with the
blue printed crescent mark and blue printed floral design.

It is clear from the Chamberlain accounts, to be quoted, that on occasions
Chamberlain purchased and sold Worcester porcelain as well as the standard
wares from Caughley. Perhaps these purchases of readily available Worcester
wares were forced on Chamberlain by the delays sometimes experienced in pro-
curing the most saleable items from Turner at Caughley. On several occasions
Chamberlains had cause to complain to Turner:

I unpacked three casks yesterday and was much surprised to find such a
small quantity of Blue goods—can only say we are every day disobliging
our customers & injuring ourselves for want of them—in reality we find
more difficulty in getting the goods than we do in selling them . . .' (letter
written on August 23rd, 1789, see Page 50.)

We are greatly distressed for want of new fluted white. . . .' (letter written
on October 5th, 1789, see Page 53.)

[1] See 'John Flight of Worcester', an article by Geoffrey Wills in *The Connoisseur*, June,
1947.

and in July, 1792, the Chamberlains ran completely out of porcelain to decorate, for a letter from Ann Chamberlain related:

> . . . Our shop is unfurnished & we have long been oblig'd to turn customers away for half they ask for . . .
>
> P.S. Mr Barnes has just been up to say he can no longer find ware for the boys to work on, a circumstance too distressing for to bear writing upon long—pray write what we are to do.

Although in the Chamberlain sales ledgers there is an unfortunate lack of detail concerning the origin of the wares sold, some descriptions do have the abbreviation 'Worc^r' added. These rare entries with the added description include:

September 21st 1789.   Goods sent to Caughley
1 cup & saucer N (new) Temple, Worc^r. } 1/2d. [plus 3/-
1 do.   do. Milk Maids, as patterns } for gilding]

(It is most interesting to see that these two designs were sent to Turner at Caughley, by Chamberlains 'as patterns', so that quite apart from the description 'Worc^r', it is clear that these two designs would be new to Turner and not of his own manufacture).

September 30th, 1789.   Shop Cash book
6 Teas, Temple, Worc^r.   1/9d.

November 24th, 1789.   Shop Cash book
3 Teas, Worc^r., Temple   10½d.

December 2nd, 1789.   Shop Cash book
1 small plate, P.B. [Pleasure Boat] Worc^r.   1/3d.

December 9th, 1789.   Shop order & sales books
1 complete sett, Worc^r. Pagoda, gilt.   £2. 16. 0.

December 17th, 1789.   Shop order & sales books
2 Teapots, Worc^r. @ 2/3d.   4/6d.

January 30th, 1790.   Shop cash book
Short sett of Pleasure Boat Worc^r.   8/-
3 cups & saucers, common   do.   2/6d.

February 5th, 1790.   Shop order & sales books
1 sett of Teas, Worc^r. gilt, and basons   12/6d.

February 21st, 1790.   Shop order & sales books
Gilt Goods

2 setts of teas, Worc^r Temple   15/-
2 pint basons   do.   do.   4/6d.
2 half pint do.   do.   do.   2/8d.
1 Teapot, 2nd [size] do.   do.   3/6d.
2 ewers   do.   do.   2/6d.

February 24th, 1790.   *Shop order & sales books*

8 saucers 2nd [size] Worc^r Temple		3/8d.
2 cups 2nd [size] do. do.		11d.
1 Pint bason do. do.		1/-

July 15th, 1790.   *Shop order & sales books*

1 complete sett, Worc^r. new shanked, gold
edge & line, except (tea) cannister &
(spoon) tray.   £2. 17. 0.

July 26th, 1790.   *Shop order & sales books*

6 cups & saucers ⎫
6 coffee cups   ⎪
1 Teapot & cover   ⎬ Worc^r. Pomegranate
1 spoon tray & plate ⎪
2 basons   ⎪
1 Pint coffee pot ⎭

August 13th, 1790.   *Shop cash book*

To Worc^r Temple	15/10d.
to do. P. Boat	3/-

August 31st, 1790.   *Shop cash book*

2 cups & saucers, Worc^r. Pleasure Boat   1/2d.

September 6th, 1790.   *Shop cash book*

To a complete sett, Worc^r Temple   £1. 3. 6d.

November 6th, 1790.   *Shop cash book*

2 Ewers Worc^r Temple   1/6d.

August 31st, 1791.   *Shop cash book*

12 cups & saucers, 12 coffees &
bason, Worc^r Temple   15/6d.

December 13th, 1791.   *Shop order & sales books*

4 setts (of cups & saucers)	
Worc^r Temple	@ 3/6d.
4 pint basons, Worc^r Temple	@ 1/2d.
4 half pint do.	@ 8d.

Apart from the odd entries where the description 'Worc^r' happened to be
added, there are many more where it is reasonable to assume that the porcelain
was of Worcester, not Caughley, manufacture. For example, on November 13th,
1788, Chamberlains sold to 'Mr Willm. Taylor of Warington'—

2 setts (tea cups & saucers) Birds, blue	4/8d.
2 setts of Landscape, blue edge	5/4d.
2 setts of Ruins	5/4d.
2 setts of New Temple	5/4d.
2 setts of Fruit blue edge	6/-
2 setts of Birds Brown & gold edge	9/-
2 setts of Milk Maid, gold edge	12/-

All these patterns are known with the disguised numeral marks or with the   129

Worcester crescent mark. The 'New Temple' design is one linked with the desig-
nation 'Worc^r' in the Chamberlain accounts and this, with the Milk Maid design,
was sent to Caughley 'as patterns' by Chamberlain in September, 1788. The
'Ruins' and 'Milk Maid' patterns do not feature in the very long lists of goods
sent to Chamberlain from Turner at Caughley, while the other names included
in this November, 1788, sale are of patterns found on both Caughley and on
Worcester porcelains. As late as 1793 the Chamberlain stock-taking lists included
Worcester porcelain, then written as 'old Worcester', and it is interesting to read
that much of this was in the undecorated state, so that Flight-period (c. 1783–92)
or even late Dr Wall period (up to 1783) porcelains probably exist bearing overglaze decoration added at the Chamberlain establishment.

The question now arises, how did Chamberlain acquire these Worcester
porcelains, including named designs such as 'Ruins', which are not shown in the
Caughley lists? Some of this Worcester ware was probably acquired direct from
Messrs Flights, for several entries such as 'China from F . . . t's' are found in
the Chamberlain cash books. A more detailed list of Worcester-type porcelains
occurs under the heading 'Goods Bought' on July 30th, 1788, with the name
'William Broadfoot, High Street, Worcester', which included:

24 Teas, Pleasure Boat, Gilt		13/-
1 half pint bason	do.	1/-
1 pint bason	do.	1/8d.
2 sets Birds, Gilt		9/-
1 half pint bason	do.	9d.
1 Pint bason	do.	1/2d.
1 cream jug	do.	9d.

and on August 6th 1788:

1 complete set of Pagoda, New ribbed, gilt edge		16/-
24 Teas New Temple		9/-
1 Pint Bason	do.	9d.
1 half pint bason	do.	6½d.
1 milk	do.	4½d.

with more articles of the same Temple design purchased on September 27th 1788:

12 tea cups, New Temple		4/6d.
12 saucers	do.	4/6d.
2 Pint basons	do.	1/6d.
1 sugar box	do.	10½d.
1 Teapot	do.	1/3½d.

On December 20th, 1788, Chamberlain purchased further teawares decorated
with 'New Temple, Gilt', and on April 27th, 1789, '1 complete set of Temple,
Gilt'.

Although no direct mention is made of the fact that these purchases were of
Worcester porcelain, it was probably quite clear to the clerks, and the fact did
not seem worth recording. Both Flights and Chamberlains had retail shops in
High Street, and William Broadfoot may have managed the Flight establishment, for a person of the same name was apprenticed to Flights' predecessors at

the Worcester factory on December 17th, 1765, when he would have been in his teens.

Quite apart from the fact that the designs listed are known on Worcester porcelains, there is the point that Chamberlain would hardly have purchased his own, or the Caughley porcelain in which he dealt, from any other establishment. There is also the important fact that some of the goods acquired from William Broadfoot of High Street were already gilt—'Pleasure Boat, gilt'; 'Pagoda, new ribbed, gilt edge'; '1 complete set of Temple, gilt', whereas all blue-printed porcelains of this type from Caughley were supplied without the gilding, which, in fact, Chamberlain himself subsequently added. It was only when he had occasion to buy from a rival establishment that he had to take completed items. It will be remembered that a large proportion of the blue-printed porcelains, here attributed to Worcester, which bear the disguised numeral (or the filled-in crescent) marks do, in fact, bear gilt borders, etc. This Flight gilding is often of fine quality, and applied not merely to the gilt edges and inner borders added by Chamberlain, but often to panels in the ornate borders and in some cases to the main part of the blue printed design.

To return to the question of differentiating between the Caughley and Worcester porcelains, which look alike, I have already referred to the fact that the Worcester fragments differ from the same designs on Caughley porcelain. Although as yet the Worcester site has not been fully excavated, it is a fact that some of the patterns found there match those on porcelains bearing the filled-in crescent mark and the disguised numeral marks. Certain key features help to distinguish between the Caughley and the Worcester versions of the popular Fisherman or 'Pleasure Boat' pattern. The easiest identifying feature is the fishing line held by the seated figure above the standing Fisherman. In Caughley prints the line is tight going in an angled line from the tip of the rod *straight* into the top line of the shading representing the water (clearly seen in impressions from the original Caughley copper-plates, in wasters found at Caughley, and on specimens bearing the impressed 'SALOPIAN' mark). On specimens bearing disguised numeral marks and filled-in crescent marks the line is slack, going from the rod in a wavy manner, crossing several of the shading lines representing the water, compare Plate 229 with Plate 230.

The border found with the Fisherman or 'Pleasure Boat' patterns comprises a line of diaper cells with a line of linked upside down 'fleur de lis' or dagger-like motifs. The Caughley examples and wasters all show these motifs completely filled-in, with solid pigment, whereas the Worcester examples (that is, those pieces with the disguised numeral marks, the filled-in crescent, as well as the Worcester factory wasters) all have these motifs shaded with closely engraved parallel lines (Plate 232).

The central standing Fisherman on Caughley copper-plates, factory wasters and marked specimens is always tall and lean but holds a short, plump fish, whereas the same main figure when depicted on pieces bearing the disguised numeral marks or the filled-in crescent is shorter, but holds a longer and more slender fish than his Caughley counterpart. The stern of the boat on which the main figure stands is longer on the Caughley examples than that engraved on Worcester specimens.

The reader will be able to pick out for himself several other distinguishing features by comparing a marked Caughley Fisherman saucer or plate with one bearing the filled-in crescent or one of the disguised numeral marks, but it must be pointed out that *slight* variations can often be found between prints from the same source, as each copper-plate was engraved by hand and different ones were required for each individual shape or size of article. There is also the point that over the years the copper-plates became worn and had to be replaced or re-engraved. However, the differences listed above for the two types of Fisherman pattern are fundamental differences, applying to all articles of each type.

Patterns, other than the Fisherman, that are common to both the Worcester and Caughley factories include:

> The Fence pattern (Plates 262, 263, 288 and 290)
> The flower sprays (Plate 265)
> The fisher girl (La Pêche) and women with sunshade (La Promenade
>   Chînoise) (Plates 258 and 259)
> Birds on a tree (Plate 304)
> Seated Chinese mother and child

These designs and the differing points of identification are discussed in the following pages. The differences are not confined to the different versions of the added print, as the porcelain articles are also distinguishable, and these differences in shape or manufacturing technique are discussed between Pages 135 and 147.

Fence Pattern

The two versions of the fence pattern are very similar; the most obvious distinguishing point to look for occurs in the secondary print normally found with this subject, which depicts a small island containing two (or three) trees and a thatched hut. On Caughley examples the right-hand tree, that is, the one nearest the hut, is shown with leaves represented with dots. The Worcester versions often show a bare tree, but to complicate the position some Worcester versions also have a tree in full 'dotted' leaf. We must then search for other features. The pair of flying birds sometimes provide guidance, as on Worcester prints the birds are depicted stretched out in nearly straight flight, whereas the Caughley birds are often (but not always) shown in an impossible tail-up attitude (see Plate 262A).

Another secondary print (not included on saucers) shows a mass of rock shaped like a cornucopia with trees growing from the top. The shading on these

---

[1] A further distinguishing feature has recently been pointed out to me; this is the fact that the Caughley standing fisherman holds his fish by a loop of line, or string, one end of which normally protrudes to form a hook-like projection from his outstretched hand. This feature does not occur on examples bearing the numeral marks, or on pieces bearing the Worcester crescent mark, where the fish appears to be held almost directly by its lips (see Plates 229 and 230).

rocks is far heavier on Worcester versions, and that of the rock at the right of the main mass, at the foot of the 'cornucopia', extends down to the ground on Worcester prints, whereas on Caughley versions it appears as a slight central shadow with an unshaded portion surrounding the shaded section. (Plate 262 illustrates this difference). It must be mentioned that so many different plates were engraved at both the Worcester and the Caughley factories for this Fence design that, if a specimen is unmarked, it is one of the most difficult to identify correctly. With marked specimens the task is relatively simple for Worcester versions normally bear the shaded crescent mark or, rarely, the initial 'W', while Caughley porcelains bearing this printed subject are normally marked with the initial 'C' or, very infrequently, the printed 'S' mark. Both the Caughley and the Worcester factory sites have yielded fragments of this design. In finished specimens the Caughley pieces are much rarer than those from Worcester.

Flower Prints

The most common of the Caughley and Worcester flower prints are shown in Plates 265, 272, 282, 287 and 295, probably the most popular being that shown in Plate 272, with three central flowers from which runs to the right a full-blown rose below two rose buds, while to the left a downward-pointing convolvulus type of flower and leaves can be seen.

The two versions are extremely alike apart from the marks, which are a shaded crescent on Worcester specimens, or the 'C' or 'S' initial marks on Caughley examples. The best guide is probably the different shape, although a study of the printed butterfly will be found rewarding.

'La Pêche'—Fishing Subject and 'La Promenade Chînoise'

The print depicting the seated Chinese-woman fishing, sometimes known as 'La Pêche', is normally found with one showing a tall, standing Chinese-woman with sunshade, 'La Promenade Chînoise' (Plates 258 and 259). Taking first the angling print, the main difference is that on the crescent-marked Worcester specimens the fishing-line tapers off from the rod in a continuous curve, whereas on marked Caughley specimens the join between the tip of the rod and the line is quite distinct.

With the companion print several variations are evident; the chin of the child runs into the woman's skirt on Caughley examples whereas it is separate on crescent-marked Worcester specimens (Plate 259). Two trees to the left of the standing figure are far larger on Caughley prints than the trees on Worcester engravings. Many other slight differences will be seen in Plates 258 and 259, where the Caughley and the Worcester versions are shown side by side.

The tankard from the Derby Museum, illustrated in Franklin A. Barrett's *Caughley and Coalport Porcelain* (1951), bears the filled-in crescent mark and, having the Worcester features listed above, clearly does not match the Caughley engraved copper-plates, impressions from which Mr Barrett illustrated. A Worcester mug bearing these two companion prints, dated 1780 (Colour Plate X), shows that Worcester blue-printed porcelains were still being produced at this period. A Caughley example of 1790 in the British Museum is shown in Plate 31.

Bird Design

One of the most attractive of the Caughley blue-printed designs is surely that showing birds (normally three) in the branches of a tree, set in a landscape background (see Colour Plate III, and Plates 39, 14 1and 304). Both the Worcester and the Caughley factories issued several different versions of this popular pattern, in which so many slight variations occur that it is difficult to lay down hard and fast rules, though the Caughley versions do not normally have the birds flying in the sky, while the Worcester, crescent-marked specimens have two. In general the hills or mountains in the background to the left of the tree are heavily shaded on Worcester specimens and only slightly so on Caughley examples (Plate 39).

The centre hill or mountain on Caughley examples often shows a dark patch as if it were a hollow-topped volcano, whereas the same hill on Worcester specimens is quite normal. On several examples from both factories small rocks are shown in the centre foreground, the central rock often showing cross-hatching when on Worcester specimens, whereas the shading on Caughley examples is composed only of parallel lines. Worcester specimens are normally marked with the filled-in crescent and several wasters were found on the factory site, while Caughley examples, when marked, will bear the printed initial 'C' or 'S' marks.

Both factories produced wares of this pattern which have either a single line border, or no border of any type. The device was justly popular over a long period, and is mentioned many times in the Chamberlain accounts, the engraved copper-plates being re-used by John Rose on his hard-paste porcelain after he took over the Caughley factory and working materials in 1799 (see Chapter VIII). A hard-paste footed bowl with these prints is dated 1802.

Mother and Child or Seated-figure Design

The Chinese mother and child design is shown in Plate 35, and has already been discussed on Page 121, when Worcester pieces bearing the disguised numeral marks were referred to. Similar Worcester prints also bear filled-in crescent marks. The main print, whether Caughley or Worcester, is very similar, but the secondary one found on the reverse side of cups, bowls and other objects is vastly different. While the Worcester secondary prints have, from left to right, a tall vase of flowers, a tall pedestal, a large jar with spoon handle protruding and a tea kettle, the Caughley version shows a wide vase or jardinière of flowers, a bottle-shaped, vase-like object, and a pot of flowers on a tripod-based stand. These basic differences are clearly shown in Plate 255.

Fruit, within Panel

One of the most attractive Worcester and Caughley designs depicts a pumpkin-type of fruit, with flowers and foliage set within oval or circular panels. Scattered small sprays are printed between the panels and the whole is enclosed within an attractive looped-scroll border incorporating a running garland of flowers

(Plates 43, 268 and 299). The contemporary name for this design was 'fruit and wreath'.

Caughley versions bear either the 'S' or 'C' initial marks, and the central fruit shows very much less shading than on the Worcester versions, having also the lower right-hand portion completely clear of shading, so that two flowers which overlap the edge of the fruit at this point have a clear-cut outline. With Worcester prints, which bear the crescent mark, these two flowers run into shaped portions of the fruit (Plates 268 and 299).

Standard Shapes, Caughley-Worcester

I have already explained on Page 122 that pieces bearing known Caughley marks differ in details of form from similar pieces bearing the disguised numeral marks. It is clear that minor differences enable Caughley specimens to be distinguished from Worcester pieces, although to the casual observer the two forms appear identical.

On the following pages these minor, but all important, differentiating details will be set out and illustrated in Plates 263 to 314.

Bowls

It is difficult to differentiate between Caughley and Worcester bowls, both occurring in different sizes, ranging from half pint waste-bowls supplied in teasets, to very large punch bowls capable of containing several gallons of liquid.

In general, however, the Worcester specimens are thinner in the sides than Caughley bowls of the same size. In addition, the top edge of Worcester bowls often appear to have been slightly chamfered or sharpened by a turning tool, whereas the top edge of Caughley bowls is finished with a shallow dome without angled facets.

The bowls are normally 'thrown' by hand on the potter's wheel, not mass-produced from moulds, the shapes, height and angle of footrims are not constant, offering little guide to place of manufacture. The glaze-free line inside the footrim may occur on both Caughley and on Worcester specimens.

Butter Pots, Tubs or Tureens

The circular blue-printed 'butter tub' shown in Plate 263 is a Worcester version of a shape also made at Caughley and Lowestoft (examples should stand on a circular dish, as those shown in Plate 262). Note the thin, rather flat, applied leaves which contrast with the thicker ones on the rare Caughley examples (Plate 93). Blue printed Worcester 'butter tubs' normally bear the filled-in, shaded crescent mark, while the Caughley examples have a 'C' or 'S' initial mark.

The oval butter tureen cover and stand form shown in Plate 265 is again found in Caughley and Lowestoft porcelains but both these versions are rarer than the Worcester tureens which are themselves by no means common. Note the thin, rather pointed, applied leaves on the Worcester specimens shown in Plates 263 to 266, and compare with Plate 93.

135

Coffee-pots

Coffee pots were originally included in some Worcester and Caughley tea and coffee services, and it can be very difficult to differentiate between the two makes.

The cover of Caughley coffee pots normally has a higher dome, with a smaller overhang to the rim, than those found on the Worcester equivalents, the large overlap of the latter making it look a size too large for the coffee pot. The Caughley handle often shows moulded ribbing (similar to that found on the jugs shown in Plate 136), compare Plate 104 with Plates 267–8.

The coffee pot shape shown in Plate 106, with ring knobs, is apparently of a shape confined to the Caughley factory, also that shown in Plate 105. The coffee pot shown in Colour Plate VII, is a very rare Caughley shape of the 1780s, note the high domed cover and small rim. Coffee pots with button-knobs are of Worcester origin.

Cream-Boats

The charming, moulded cream-boats shown in Plate 270 could well be taken as of the same shape when seen separately but they are clearly different when compared side by side. That on the left is the Worcester version, decorated with one of the attractive landscape prints, and bears a disguised numeral mark. It also shows a surfeit of bubbled and speckled glaze under the base (Plate 269). In contrast, the 'S' marked Caughley cream-boat has a clean glazed underside.

Other basic differences in the shape of these cream boats are: (*a*) The Worcester specimen is wider in the body ($2\frac{2}{8}$ at the top against $2\frac{1}{10}$ in.). (*b*) Several differences are apparent in the moulded handle, the most pronounced pointers being the thumb rest at the top of the handle, and the centre ornamental junction of the handle, clearly seen in Plate 270.

As with all other objects, these two basic forms are of course to be found with other patterns, both in underglaze-blue and in overglaze enamel colours.

The popular 'Chelsea-ewer' (Page 91) was made at both Caughley and Worcester. The Worcester examples are thinner in the potting than the Caughley ewers and the top return to the handle has a distinct backward curl, as found on the chocolate cup handles (see Plate 273) and this feature is not apparent on the Worcester version.

Cress Dishes

A crescent marked, Worcester cress dish and stand is shown in Plate 271. These rare objects sometimes bear one of the disguised numeral marks, and are sometimes attributed to the Caughley factory.

All examples I have seen have been of Worcester (or very occasionally of Lowestoft) porcelain, and I have yet to find a true Caughley example. If these pierced cress dishes were made at Caughley one would expect them to be rather thick in the potting, with an impressed 'SALOPIAN' name mark or with the initial 'C' or 'S'. Some Caughley examples may be unmarked, but they will not bear the Worcester crescent or disguised numeral mark.

Cups and Saucers

The elegant, large-sized single or double handled chocolate cups shown in Plate 272 are rather rare, especially when they bear underglaze-blue designs.

The main difference between the Worcester and the Caughley examples occurs in the handle. In the typical Worcester specimen, seen in Plate 272, the return at the very top of the handle points upwards and the snake-like moulded-head at the lower end is turned outwards, away from the side of the cup. The Caughley handle is more detailed, and is normally more sharply moulded, with the return at the top of the handle curled away from the rim, and the outside part moulded with fluting, the whole appearing to be formed of two parts fixed together by an overlapping joint (see Plate 273). The moulded snake-head finial at the lower end of the handle is rather smaller than the same feature on Worcester cups and points straight downwards without being slightly turned outwards. These differentiating features apply to both the single and the double handled cups.

The normal tea or coffee cups shown in Plates 64, 191 and 195, would appear only to have been made at Caughley, but the cups with double curved handles as depicted in Plates 75, 192, 196 and 275, were made at both Worcester and Caughley as can be seen in the comparative illustration (Plate 274). The inward curve to the Caughley handle is much more pronounced than that of the Worcester version, and also the shape of these cups varies, and the Worcester specimens are thinner in the potting. More Worcester cups with this type of handle are included in Plates 275, 308 and 309, and Caughley specimens are shown in Plates 82, 192 and 196. This standard shape of Worcester cup was continued into the post-1783 Flight period, as can be seen from a 'Flight' marked example in the Victoria and Albert Museum (ref. no. 3284-1901).

Dessert Services

Dessert services in Caughley and Worcester porcelain varied greatly in make-up. A fine 'full' service would have contained the following pieces, but very many 'short' sets were supplied, as well as sets to suit the buyer's individual needs.

Centrepiece
2 ice pails, liners and covers
2 sugar & cream tureens, covers and stands
2 ladles to do.
4 shell shaped dishes
4 melon shaped dishes
4 square dishes
4 heart shaped dishes
24 plates

The different components are treated separately under the individual names in this section.

Dinner Services

Both Worcester and Caughley dinner (originally termed 'Table') services are very   137 rare, probably because the blue-painted Chinese Nankin ones were so cheap that the English producers could not compete. It is certainly a fact today that the Oriental dinner wares are far more common than our native Worcester or Caughley dinner services.

The English services would have comprised the following articles:

> Tureens, covers and stands
> small do.
> salad bowl
> platters, in various sizes
> meat plates
> soup plates
> small plates

A Caughley part service of the 1785–90 period is shown in Plate 116, but I have yet to find a blue and white Worcester dinner service made between 1770 and 1790 and the factory may not have produced such articles if they could not meet the low price of the imported Chinese Nankin-type porcelains.

Jugs

Cabbage-leaf, Mask-head Jugs

The moulded cabbage-leaf jugs with mask-head spout (originally known as 'Dutch jugs') are perhaps the best-known articles made at Worcester and at Caughley. To most collectors all are alike, but several differentiating points are apparent on close comparison.

The Caughley examples (Colour Plate II) are readily identified, for by fortunate chance a complete unglazed specimen (Plate 276) was found on the factory site, and also numerous fragments of similar jugs in various stages of manufacture. Several completed specimens can be identified by the Caughley 'S' or 'C' initial marks, which those with underglaze-blue decoration normally bear, while those sold in the white to the Chamberlains and other decorators without underglaze-blue are unmarked. Dated specimens show that the basic Caughley form of cabbage-leaf jug remained constant from at least the early 1780s, and hard-paste specimens indicate that the same moulds were used after the Coalport partners took over the Caughley factory in October, 1799, (Plate 215).

The Worcester versions are identified by plainly marked specimens with known Worcester styles of decoration, for example, square-marked scale-blue ground jugs. The same characteristics are found on marked 'Flight' or 'Flight & Barr' Worcester examples made after 1783.

The Caughley cabbage-leaf jugs appear taller and slimmer than the Worcester examples, the bulbous lower part of the body being lemon-shaped, whereas the Worcester specimens show a more rotund or orange-shaped lower part. The mask-head spouts show several slight differences; for instance, the eyes on Caughley pieces are open and protruding but the Worcester eyes appear recessed and closed, or slit-eyed. The eye-brows on Worcester mask-heads are flat in

comparison with the relief-moulded Caughley eye-brows. The lips of the Caughley mask-head are quite prominent and puckered, while the brow of Caughley
heads is heavily furrowed. Close-up photographs of these different mask-head
spouts are shown in Plate 278.

The handles are also different, those from Caughley displaying three main
types of moulded handle. One has a ribbed section while a rarer version has
moulded ornamentation on the outside, top-half, see Plate 40. Very large jugs
with a strong, thick handle of almost circular section, provide yet another
variation, but these specimens are rare. The top and bottom junctions of the
handle have slight returns from the body. The Worcester handles have several
variations, in section some Worcester handles are thick and nearly round, others
are of very thin section, ribbon-like, without the ribbing found on Caughley
handles. The top junction of these ribbon-like Worcester handles goes directly
into the body, without the outward return of Caughley, but the outward kick at
the bottom is more generous on Worcester specimens. The Worcester handle
is fuller than the Caughley version, the main hand grip section being nearly
circular rather than the oval of the Caughley hand grip. These points can be
clearly seen in Plates 277 and 280.

Jugs

Mask-head, Plain

One of the most graceful of Caughley objects is the simple, mask-head jug
(Plates 134–6), and although similar jugs were made at Worcester, in most
instances the Caughley form is the more satisfying, with a graceful flare to the
top. Several different handle forms were employed, and the different mask-head
spouts enable one to distinguish between the Caughley and the Worcester specimens (Plate 281).

Like the masks on the cabbage-leaf jugs, the Caughley faces have a heavily
furrowed brow, protruding open eyes (as opposed to the Worcester closed, slit-
eyes) with relief-moulded eye-brows and thick, puckered lips, points clearly seen
in Plates 134–6 and 282.

Leaf-dishes

The leaf-shaped dish form shown in Plate 284, which is a Worcester example,
does not appear to have been made at Caughley. The rare Caughley leaf dish,
illustrated in Plate 137, is very finely moulded, with veining, and although a very
similar form was made at Worcester (see Plate 283), in the Worcester examples
the main vein is to the right of centre, and has a relief-moulded projection where
the stalk meets the handle.

The standard Caughley, leaf-shaped dish, or pickle-tray, which often bears the
Shropshire version of the Fisherman design and the 'S' mark, is shown in Plate
138. The late Worcester version differs slightly in basic form in that the short
stalk-handle is set-in, and does not protrude nearly as much as does the Caughley
handle. The Caughley examples are much thicker in the potting than the Worcester specimens, and the segregated edge is more pronounced on Caughley leaf-

dishes. The clearest indication of origin occurs on the reverse side, with the differences in shape of the foot, the moulding of the veining and of the stalk-handle, all of which are clearly illustrated in Plate 285.

A small, deep, leaf-shaped dish was also made by both factories (Plate 140) and, in general, the Worcester examples are squarer in plan than the longer, elongated Caughley specimens, and the Caughley leaves are thicker in the potting than the very trim, neatly finished Worcester versions.

A further shape of small, deep leaf dish is shown in Plate 286, the Caughley examples being slightly larger than the Worcester and thicker in the potting. The Caughley handle is larger than the Worcester at the top edge of the stalk, but the main difference lies in the shaped top edge: the Worcester edge is deeply shaped whereas the Caughley rim is relatively smooth (Plate 286). Caughley examples of this model are very much rarer than the Worcester.

Milk Jugs

Milk jugs differ from cream boats (see Page 136) in that the milks stand upright whereas the creamers are low, and of general boat-shape.

The sparrow-beak milk jugs, with a simple loop handle, found with Worcester and Caughley teasets are very difficult to distinguish one from the other when they have been divorced from the set, which would include more easily identifiable objects such as teapot-stands. In general, however, the Worcester sparrow-beak creamers have the main curve to the body settling well below the middle, in a pot-bellied manner, whereas the Caughley creamers have a more uniform profile. Plate 288 illustrates this basic difference, while the other Worcester creamers are included in Plates 234, 238, 241, 249, 275, 305 and 309. Other differences are seen in the shape of the footrim, triangular for Worcester, straight-sided for Caughley. The top edge of Worcester creamers is often slightly faceted, resulting in a rather sharp line. Some small jugs were equipped with covers and when these are still present the button-shaped knob indicates a Worcester origin, but both Caughley and Worcester factories used the floral knob. Worcester milk jugs normally bear a blue crescent mark or one of the disguised numeral marks while the Caughley ones, if marked, will bear a blue initial 'C' or 'S'.

Some, mainly fluted, milk jugs have a moulded handle with an inward kick, the extent of which, as with other handles of this type, indicates the origin for the Caughley version is indented further than that of Worcester. Plates 275 and 309 show Worcester milk jugs, but other low jugs also have this type of handle (Plates 310 and 311).

A bucket-shape Worcester milk jug seems at first sight identical to the standard Caughley version but the handle is vastly different, compare Plate 308 with Plates 143 and 145.

The milk jug form shown in Plate 287 is rare in Worcester porcelain (the shape was also employed at Caughley and Lowestoft) although the blue print was very popular. This example in the Victoria and Albert Museum is very interesting in that apart from the normal blue printed, shaded, crescent mark this jug also bears the impressed mark 'Flight' as used at Worcester from 1783.

It is therefore apparent that this type of Worcester blue printing was continued into the 1780s, and perhaps even into the 1790s.

Mugs

In general the Worcester mugs are turned to a thinner gauge than comparable Caughley examples, and the Worcester specimens are also normally narrower and taller than the Shropshire ones; Plates 258 and 259 show this distinction clearly.

One Caughley handle is characteristic, in that an overlapping strap-like section appears at the top of the handle (Plates 31 and 32). Others have a convex section with indented lines at each side near the edge, and on small mugs the Caughley handle consists of a simple strap, slightly indented in the middle, see below.

Two basic types of Caughley mug handle.

Worcester handles of this type have a deeper concave indentation, and a further pointer to their origin lies in the finish of the top edge of mugs, for the Caughley examples have a simple curved top edge, whereas many (but not all) of the Worcester tankards have been trimmed, or chamfered, giving a sharp line or edge rather than the curved top found on marked 'Salopian' specimens.

The Worcester and Caughley mugs can also often be distinguished by the differences in the patterns they bear (see Pages 131–5). The fine prints of shooting subjects (Plate 254) which are attributed in several books to the Caughley factory, have all the characteristics of Worcester porcelain and the subjects are not included in the lengthy lists of blue-printed Caughley porcelains sent to Chamberlain. The dated 1780 blue-printed Worcester mug shown in Colour Plate X, illustrates the point that typical styles of the 1770s were continued into the 1780s.

Mustard-pots

Both the Caughley and the Worcester firms produced these rare articles, often bearing similar underglaze-blue prints, but the Caughley examples normally bear the 'C' or 'S' underglaze-blue initial marks, whereas the Worcester specimens often have the filled-in crescent mark. While the Worcester mustard pots stand 4 in, high, the Caughley examples measure only $3\frac{3}{4}$ in. high, or $2\frac{7}{8}$ in. to the top rim of the body. As can be seen in Plate 290, the handle on Caughley specimens is slightly longer so that, with the lower body, the bottom end of the handle is nearer the base than that of the Worcester example.

A rare Worcester mustard pot, decorated with the Worcester version of the Fisherman pattern, having a button-knob (instead of the normal flower-knob) is shown in Plate 289.

Plates

Plates present many problems of identification, and it is often the different patterns, or variations of shared designs, that help to differentiate between Caughley and Worcester specimens.

In general, those of Worcester are thinner in the potting than the Caughley pieces, and consequently lighter. The footrim of Caughley plates is nearly always of square section, whereas the Worcester foot is angular or of wedge shape (see Page 12).

Worcester blue and white plates are normally marked with the crescent or with the disguised numerals. The Caughley examples sometimes bear the impressed 'SALOPIAN' name mark, the printed initial 'S' or 'C', but many plates are unmarked.

The two saucer-shaped plates found with teasets are normally of different sizes and are often of plain form, like an enlarged saucer, and it should also be noted that each shape of plate was made in different sizes, dessert plates being normally made in four sizes, the customer choosing which he required. The shapes shown in Plates 52, 56 and 159 are believed to be peculiar to the Caughley factory.

Both factories also made plates with a shaped-edge, having twenty-four depressions in the rim (Plates 26, 37 and 238), the footrim of Caughley specimens being normally deeper than that on Worcester specimens, and the depth of the central depression in the centre of the plate deeper on Worcester examples, which normally bear a crescent or disguised numeral mark rather than the Caughley 'C' or 'S' signs.

Plates with moulded basket-work rims were made at both Worcester and at Caughley, and a marked 'SALOPIAN' example is shown in Plate 160.

Salad Bowls

One of the most ornate moulded forms made by the Caughley and Worcester factories comprises the interior moulded salad bowls such as are illustrated in Plates 167 and 291. It should be noted that the design of each of three shell-like panels differs slightly but these differences in the moulding are constant to all examples.

The Caughley salad bowls of this design are rarer than those of Worcester, which normally bear the filled-in crescent mark or a disguised numeral device, but the Worcester examples themselves are by no means common. The Caughley salad bowls are rather thicker (4 mm.), and therefore heavier, and the bowl is slightly deeper (3 in.) than in the Worcester specimens, which normally show a height of about $2\frac{3}{4}$ in. Several slight differences are apparent in the blue-printed floral, fruit and vegetable motifs which are found on these bowls, and the hand-painted blue border normally has more solid blue pigment on Caughley specimens.

The Lowestoft factory also made rare copies of these moulded salad bowls (see Plate 362 of the *Illustrated Encyclopaedia of British Pottery & Porcelain*). The design was also, though very rarely, copied by the Chinese potters, in hard-paste porcelain.

Other Caughley salad bowls are illustrated in Plates 168–70, but these seem to have been restricted to the Shropshire factory.

Sauce-boats

Many finely moulded sauce-boats were made at Worcester and at Caughley in several different sizes ranging in length from about 8 to 5 in. Smaller boat-shaped articles are creamers, rather than sauce-boats, and are treated under 'Cream Boats' on Page 136.

Caughley sauce-boats are of three basic shapes. Firstly, there is the intricate, moulded design shown in Plate 172, where the Fisherman pattern sometimes found tends to hide much of the moulding, especially the framework to the panel on each side of the body. Fortunately, an unglazed fragment from the Caughley site, included in Plate 172, shows clearly a portion of this relief moulding. The very rare Worcester version of this sauceboat shape is very similar to the Caughley one, the main difference appears in the handle where the inward kick is very near the lower junction of the body on Worcester specimens, compare Plates 172 and 292.

A second shape of Caughley sauce-boat has relief moulding round the lower part of the body only, of which numerous unglazed fragments were found on the Shropshire site (Plate 173). A rare variation of this basic shape has a top border of moulded basket-work and a half mould for such a sauce-boat was also found at Caughley (Plate 174).

This second basic shape of Caughley sauce-boats does not seem to have been employed at Worcester, but a third form was copied there and at Lowestoft and Derby. It is low and wide, with six convex ribs each side of the body, and normally decorated with Oriental designs, the shape, in fact, occurring in Chinese export market porcelains. It is shown in Plate 176 with related fragments, and a Derby example is illustrated in S. W. Fisher's *English Blue & White Porcelain of the 18th Century* (1947), Plate 15. Apart from the differences in paste, it will be observed that the spout has a higher curve than the Caughley example, and also that the bottom of the handle ends in a scroll. A Lowestoft specimen is shown in Plate 86C of Dr B. Watney's book *English Blue & White Porcelain of the 18th Century* (1963) with a distinctive loop handle joining the body at the lower junction only just above the footrim.

Shell-dishes

Although both the Worcester and the Caughley factory made shell-dishes, the shapes are quite different. The deep dish shown in Plate 294 is Worcester, but

143

of a very rare form, whereas the standard Caughley shell-shaped dish, as seen in Plate 177, does not appear to have been made at Worcester.

Spittoons or Saffer-pots

The globular bowls with a wide spreading lip, as shown in Plates 165, 166 and 295, are often referred to as Spittoons although they may have been bulb-pots (see Page 103). They were made both at Worcester and Caughley.

The Worcester examples are rather graceful, because they normally have turned decorative bands below the neck which contrasts with the plain form of the rare 'S' or 'C' marked Caughley examples. The Worcester examples also normally bear the printed crescent mark, but may have one of the disguised numeral marks.

Spoon Trays

The Worcester spoon tray form is shown in Plate 296, together with Caughley examples. The outline shapes are quite clear and afford a ready means of identification, but other pointers are that the walls of the Worcester specimens are thinner than the Caughley trays, and their shaped sides are more upright than the outward sloping Caughley trays. Both factories left the flat bases unglazed.

Sugar-bowls

It is often difficult to distinguish between the earliest Caughley sugar-bowls, issued with teasets which included the globular teapots, and their Worcester counterparts, so that the different patterns, or different versions of shared designs, afford the best clue to origin. Many Worcester specimens bearing the blue-printed crescent mark are classed as Caughley in error.

Some of the finer, enamelled Worcester teasets have fluted sugar-bowls of the type shown in Plates 310 and 311, while the standard Caughley forms are shown in Plates 14, 58, 59, 75, 182, 183, 195 and 196, and these Caughley shapes were not copied at Worcester. Several Worcester sugar-bowl forms were equipped with characteristic stud-knobs, as shown in Plates 244 and 297, and these were not employed at the Caughley factory.

Tart (or Patty) Pans

A rare, but typically shaped, Worcester blue and white tart or patty pan is illustrated in Plate 298. Note the flat, turnover flange, quite unlike the thick reinforced edge that appears on the unique Caughley shape in Plates 184 and 185.

Teapots

The standard forms of Worcester and Caughley globular teapots (Plates 21, 44, 58, 59, 299–301) are very near copies of each other, and it is often extremely difficult to separate the two kinds. The footrims of those from Caughley are normally deeper than those from Worcester, being 6 mm against 5 mm. In addition, the globular part of the body is more completely round on Worcester pots, as the short foot and top rim are smaller than those which cut into the circular outline of the elevation of Caughley pots (see Plates 21, 44 and 197) and, as the top rim of the Caughley pots is set lower than on Worcester specimens, the Caughley opening is larger, being 68 mm (inside measurement on standard 1¼ pint pots) against 60 to 62 mm for a Worcester pot of the same capacity. The handle on Caughley teapots is rather thicker than the handle on a similar Worcester pot, a measurement taken at the top point of the loop will give a reading of 13.5 × 10.5 mm for a Caughley handle but only about 12 × 10 for a typical Worcester example.

The Caughley globular teapots have knobs to the cover in two varieties, a flower knob and a characteristic, wide, squat, turned conical knob, as shown in Plates 21, 44 and 197. The Worcester knobs may also be floral or of flat button-type or have an elegant, tall, slender, turned, conical finial (Plates 234, 299 and 300).

The globular bodied teapots shown in Plates 64, 74, 81, 195 and 198, with the characteristic moulded spouts and ornately moulded handles are Caughley, for the form does not appear in Worcester porcelain. The basic shape, with this spout and handle, also occurs in Chinese Nankin-type export porcelain (Plate 11), and probably served as a prototype for Turner, but these oriental examples are of hard-paste porcelain. It is noteworthy that the same moulded handle was re-used on post-1799 Coalport porcelain mugs.

Barrel-shaped teapots were made in several varieties by both the Worcester and the Caughley factories (the new forms largely superseding the plain, globular pots), the E-shaped handle found with these barrel-shaped pots being a helpful guide to origin. The standard Worcester handle is 13 mm wide at the highest point, whereas the Caughley handle is larger, about 16 mm wide. The curve of the handle also varies greatly, that of Caughley having a more generous outline with a pronounced inward kick, whereas the Worcester outline is gentler and nearer to the body of the pot, and with a gentler inward kick, compare Plate 201 with 307. This difference is also found on the handles of the matching cups (Plate 274).

The Worcester spouts to the barrel-shaped teapots are normally long and elegant, with moulded fluting running along the whole length (see Plates 302 to 307) and the end of the spout is also cut to form a lip-like opening. Although the Caughley factory did occasionally employ this elegant, clean, sweeping spout, the standard one on their barrel-shaped teapots has relief moulding for only half the length, and also the end of the spout is cut-off in a straight, angled line (see Plates 62, 72, 196 and 201 and compare with the Worcester version shown in Plate 308).

The knobs on Worcester barrel-shaped teapots may take the form of an open flower, or be of button shape (Plates 239, 303 to 311), whereas the Caughley finials are of more conventional, fat, knob-shape, slightly moulded on pots which are themselves fluted or ribbed (Plates 62, 72, 196 and 201). The ribbed Worcester teapots have twenty-four convex ribs but the Caughley examples have thirty.

Several slight variations of shape occur in both Worcester and Caughley barrel-shaped teapots but the differences in handle and spout should enable the two makes to be distinguished without difficulty.

Teapot Stands

The Worcester teapot stands are of the same basic shape as those of the normal Caughley shape (Plate 312). As with other Worcester porcelains, they are thinner in the potting than the companion Caughley examples, which are correspondingly slightly heavier, normally 6 oz as opposed to 5 oz. The Caughley stands are an eighth of an inch higher than the Worcester pieces, that is, about nine-tenths of an inch high, although slight variations may occur between individual specimens.

Other basic shapes of Caughley teapot stands are illustrated in Plate 203, but these forms do not seem to have been made at Worcester.

Tea Canisters

The vase-shaped tea canisters, or 'tea-vases', were originally part of 'full' teasets but their use declined in the 1780s, and by 1800 their manufacture had been entirely discontinued.

Fortunately, the shapes favoured by the Worcester manufacturers differ from those made at Caughley. A selection of the different Worcester shapes is shown in Plates 240, 241, 261, 303, 309 and 313, and the Caughley ones in Plates 189 and 190, and these should enable a true identification to be made without difficulty; once again it can be stated that porcelains with the button knobs are Worcester.

Tea Services

Worcester and Caughley tea services normally included the following items:

> Teapot and cover
> Teapot stand
> Spoon tray
> Tea canister and cover
> Sugar bowl and cover
> Slop bowl
> 2 bread and butter plates (of differing size)
> 12 tea bowls
> 12 handled coffee cups
> 12 saucers

Some services also included a coffee pot and cover but these are rather rare. The individual make-up of services could, of course, be modified to suit the original customer's requirements, some had only eight cups and saucers, for instance.

The different items are listed separately in this section under their individual descriptions, but part services showing linked shapes are shown in Plates 234, 275, 303 and 308–311.

Tureens

The dessert service, covered tureens shown in Plate 314, were made at both the Caughley and the Worcester factories and the two versions are remarkably similar. The Caughley examples are rather thicker in the potting, as are the applied leaves on the cover, the latter, therefore, standing higher on the cover than the Worcester leaves.

In concluding this controversial chapter I must deal with the question of the translucency, or colour, of the body against a light, for this is a matter that has caused great confusion due to the fact that collectors have the old rule firmly in their mind that the Worcester body shows green against a light, but that Caughley porcelain has a distinct orange tint.

This belief, however, is largely false.

The early pre-1775 Worcester porcelains do indeed show a green translucency, but we are concerned, when comparing contemporary Caughley and Worcester porcelains, with post-1775 wares and in many cases with wares of the 1780s and these are vastly different. In general terms, the Caughley and the Worcester porcelains are very similar in basic make-up, as is proved by chemical analysis (see Pages 118, 124) and also by recent experiments with analysis by radiation, which result in a circular graph-like identifying design, showing Worcester and Caughley designs to be very similar. I believe that the reason for this is that both factories used largely the same raw materials, gathered from much the same locality, and we have evidence in the form of a letter that Chamberlain sent clay from *Worcester* to Caughley.

We are left with the fact that not *all* Caughley porcelain (see also Page 150) shows an orange translucency, although it very often does, but the Worcester of the post-1775 period *can* show this characteristic, so that the orange translucency simply points in the main to a later period *c.* 1770–90 of either Caughley *or Worcester* porcelain.

The dark, rather bright, blue found on so many pieces bearing the disguised numeral marks, has formerly been thought to be a characteristic late Caughley colour, but this belief is not borne out by marked Caughley porcelains, and it is characteristic of Worcester, not Caughley, wares of the 1770–90 period.

In brief, then, I believe that the best guide to the identification of these two very similar porcelains lies in the different shapes, especially the moulded forms which are constant over a lengthy period and also in the printed patterns, or rather the difference between the two versions of shared designs, points which have been enlarged upon in the preceding pages.

One outcome of this re-attribution is that true Caughley porcelains are revealed to be much rarer than we had thought, for nearly a third of the so-called Caughley wares are now seen to be Worcester. Of 158 units[1] in the blue and white Caughley case at the Victoria and Albert Museum I am now unable to accept forty-eight, and several standard designs are now found to be very rare on Caughley porcelain but relatively common on Worcester.

---

[1] Counting cups and saucers as one unit, and the three tea services as three units.

A result of the recent researches published in this Chapter is that it will now be necessary to change the descriptions of several illustrations contained in standard reference books. The reader may find the following notes helpful in correcting the old captions in the light of recent discoveries.

A History and Description of English Porcelain by William Burton, 1902. Fig. 66. 'Fisherman' pattern spoon-tray is Worcester, not Caughley.

The First Century of English Porcelain by W. Moore Binns, 1906. Colour Plate facing Page 182. Ten objects are arranged in two rows. As no details of marks are given it is difficult to make a definite judgment on some pieces which bear blue-printed designs used both at Caughley and at Worcester, but the plate in the top row is definitely Worcester, as is the 'Fisherman' teabowl and saucer in the lower row.

Transfer Printing on Enamels, Porcelain and Pottery by W. Turner, 1907. Plate XXXVIII. Fig. D.3. Not Caughley.
Plate XXXVII. Fig. D.2. This 'Chelsea-ewer' bearing the Pleasure boat or Fisherman pattern is Caughley, not Bristol. The attribution to Bristol was no doubt due to the fact that it bears the painter's cross, without the normal 'S' initial mark, and a cross is a Bristol mark.

Catalogue of the Schreiber Collection. Vol. I. Victoria & Albert Museum publication. Revised edition 1928. Plate 74. Item 682, the blue-printed 'Brimstree Loyal Legion' jug is of hard-paste porcelain and is therefore likely to be of Coalport manufacture rather than pre-1799 Caughley porcelain.
Plate 74. Item 680, the blue and gold floral pattern jug is of the Worcester model, not the similar Caughley shape (see Page 138 and Plates 276 and 277).

English Blue and White Porcelain of the 18th Century by Stanley W. Fisher, 1947.
Plate 3C. Probably Worcester rather than Caughley.
Plate 36 A to F. All these examples appear to be of Worcester manufacture, the source of the creamer 'g' being open to doubt.
Plate 38. The reproduction of this small-size cabbage-leaf jug is not particularly clear, but it appears to be a Worcester version of a shared form and pattern, but only a study of the original piece will confirm this attribution.
Plate 40. This butter dish and stand appears to be of Worcester manufacture. The pattern on the stand does not match the covered dish although it is of the correct form.
Plate 41 b. This mug appears to be Worcester, not Caughley, although both factories produced this carnation pattern.

Caughley and Coalport Porcelain by Franklin A. Barrett, 1951
Plate 1.   Very probably Worcester, not Caughley.
Plate 2.   Covered sugar bowl is Worcester but the 'Chelsea-ewer' shown with it is Caughley.

Plate 4.	Worcester version of shared design.
Plate 12.	Very probably Worcester.
Plate 17.	Both teabowls and saucers are Worcester.
Plate 18.	The left and right-hand teabowls and saucers are probably Worcester versions of shared designs.
Plate 19.	Worcester, not Caughley.
Plate 21.	Possibly post-1799 John Rose Coalport porcelain, not true Caughley.
Plate 22.	Worcester, not Caughley.
Plates 27, 28	This mug is Worcester, not Caughley.
Plates 29, 30.	Worcester versions of shared subjects (see Plates 258 and 259 in this book).
Plate 33.	Worcester, not Caughley.
Plate 34.	Worcester, not Caughley.
Plate 42.	This mask-head jug is of Coalport-type, hard-paste porcelain and is consequently unlikely to be of true Caughley make.
Plate 53.	Although it is impossible to be certain, the present writer considers that this part teaset, in the Victoria and Albert Museum, is of Worcester make (see Page 45) although some pieces bear a 'C'-like open crescent mark.
Plate 66.	This moulded cabbage-leaf jug (illustrated in this book as Plate 280), appears to be of the Worcester version of this shared form (See Pages 138–9 and Plates 276 and 277).
Plate 69.	Worcester version of cabbage-leaf jug.
Plate 70.	Worcester, not Caughley, although this teapot and stand has been illustrated as Caughley in several books and magazine articles.
Plates 71–72.	I consider that this bowl is Worcester, not Caughley.

English Blue and White Porcelain of the 18th Century by Dr B. Watney, 1963.

Plate 90 B (2) Blue-printed bowl, Worcester not Caughley.
Plate 90 C (1) Blue-printed mug, Worcester not Caughley.

English Porcelain 1745–1850 Edited by R. J. Charleston (Caughley-Coalport Chapter by Franklin A. Barrett) 1965.

Plate 39A.	This teapot is of Worcester shape, not Caughley (see Page 145 and Plates 275, 309 and 311) although some pieces of this set bear a 'C'-like crescent mark.

English Ceramics by S. W. Fisher, 1966.

Plate 149.	Three cups and saucers. The 'Image' pattern cup and saucer on the left is Worcester, not Caughley, and the Fisherman pattern cup and saucer on the right shows the Worcester version of this shared subject.

An Illustrated Encyclopaedia of British Pottery and Porcelain by G. A. Godden, 1966.

Plate 95. A group of eleven subjects. From top left to bottom right, the plate is Worcester as are the four tea bowls to its right. The two waste bowls in the bottom row are also Worcester, not Caughley.

Plate 97. The plate, bottom left, is Worcester as is the Fisherman pattern creamer and the covered tea-caddy to the right.

Postscript

Regarding the colour of Caughley and Worcester porcelain by transmitted light, Dr Watney has pointed out to me that the similarity, or otherwise, of the colour does not *only* depend on the basic raw materials but also if cobalt was introduced to the mix, as a whitening agent. The method of firing also has a bearing, for different results would be obtained from a reducing kiln, to that obtained in a kiln fired in an oxidizing atmosphere. The fact still remains that the colour of Caughley and some late eighteenth-century Worcester porcelain can be very similar.

CONTEMPORARY REFERENCES TO CAUGHLEY PORCELAINS
CAUGHLEY PORCELAINS SOLD BY AUCTION

Several sale catalogues from 1780 included 'Lots' of Salopian porcelain, and in the following list these are arranged in chronological order.

The first 'Lots' of Salopian porcelain that I have been able to trace in the original Christie catalogues (still so fortunately preserved at Messrs Christie, Manson & Wood's London premises) are included in a sale of Bristol porcelain held on February 28th, 1780.

One complete Salopian table (dinner) set, 126 pieces, the new Salopian sprigs.	£27.	16.	6.
One dessert set, ditto, 66 pieces.	10.	10.	0.
A Salopian table (dinner) service with chantille sprigs, containing 115 pieces	19.	19.	0.
6 new spriged Salopian cups & saucers	1.	3.	0.
6 ditto.	1.	5.	0.

Other lots included in this sale seem likely to be of Caughley, rather than Bristol manufacture, although the description Salopian is not used:

18 blue & white chocolate cups & saucers, Chantille pattern		16.	0.
A fine blue teaset, 50 pieces	£6.	17.	6.
18 breakfast cups, chantille sprigs	1.	9.	0.

Mr Christie   *23rd March, 1781*

               Part of the Valuable and extensive stock in trade
               of Mr Hussey of Coventry Street.   *China man.*

A dessert (service) of Salopian blue & white 13 compôtiers (side dishes) and 2 dozen plates.	£4.	18.	0.
A Salopian Table (Dinner) service, consisting of 18 long dishes, 5 dozen flat plates, 18 soup plates, 1 tureen, 2 small tureens, 2 salad dishes, 4 sauce boats. Reserve price	£24.	0.	0.
12 Salopian cups & saucers	1.	1.	0.
12 Salopian breakfast cups & saucers, 12 plates.		no price.	

151

Mr Christie *Sale 6th November, 1782*

*Stock in Trade of Mr Thomas Morgan,
china man, late of Dover Street, London.*

Lot 106.
A Capital table (Dinner) service of the Salopian Manufactory
containing 20 dishes in five sizes, 2 tureens, covers & stands,
72 table plates, 24 soups, 4 salad dishes & 4 sauce boats.   £18. 0. 0.
(see also sale of February 26th, 1783).

Mr Christie *26th February, 1783*
Further stock in trade of Thomas Morgan, China man
(see also sale of 6th November, 1782)

A Salopian blue & gold dessert service, containing
15 comports (side dishes) various shapes, 2 cream bowls
(tureens), covers, stands & spoons, and 24 plates.   £2. 0. 0.
A tea & coffee equipage of the Salopian manufactory,
blue & gold, 40 pieces.   £6. 6. 0.

Mr Christie *27th November, 1783.*

A Salopian blue & gold dessert service containing 15
comports (side dishes), 2 cream bowls (small tureens),
covers, stands & spoons & 24 plates.   £18. 18. 0.
A Salopian blue & gold déjeune   £1. 2. 0.

Mr Christie *16th April, 1792.*

. . . The Property of a Man of Fashion

A very elegant white and gold Salopian dessert service
comprising of 13 compôtiers (side dishes), 2 cream
bowls (tureens) stands & spoons and 18 plates.   £11. 0. 0.

Mr Christie *2nd March, 1796.*

*The Extensive Stock of Trade of Mr Thomas
Williams, china man, deceased.*

Forty-two blue & white Salopian butter boats, 3 milk
ewers, 10 milk pots (& 10 Wedgwood sauceboats).   £1. 4. 0.
7 three pint quilted Salopian jugs, 4 quart do. and
5 pint do.   £1. 4. 0.
A Salopian dessert service, 44 pieces.   £2. 14. 0.
Six very elegant caudle basons & plates of the
Salopian manufacture   £2. 8. 0.
A Salopian tea & coffee equipage, blue celeste border
enriched with burnished gold.   £4. 4. 0.
A white and gold Salopian coffee and tea equipage,
42 pieces.   £3. 11. 0.
Seven elegant Salopian breakfast basons & saucers,
richly gilt.   £2. 12. 6.
Twenty-two Salopian custard cups and covers, 12 various
cups, 13 saucers, 3 sugar dishes, 5 milk pots, a butter
pot and cover and 2 plates.   £2. 10. 0.
16 Salopian dishes, 2 sauce tureens, covers & stands,
40 dessert plates, 13 saucers & 2 ice pails.   £2. 5. 0.
12 Salopian dishes, a tureen and cover, and 9 dozen
plates.   £4. 15. 0.
A Salopian tureen & cover, 4 dishes, 8 dozen plates,
2 sauce tureens and stands and 3 sauce boats.   £3. 17. 0.

Mr Phillips (now Messrs Phillips, Son & Neale)   *9th May, 1796.*

'*All the genuine Elegant Household Furniture of a Gentleman*'

A Capital and extensive Table (Dinner) service of
Nankin porcelain . . . an oval Salopian dish and
fish tray, nearly to correspond in pattern.   £27. 16. 6.
Fifteen Salopian custard cups and saucers.   9. 0.

Mr Phillips   *11th December, 1801.*

. . . *the prime part of the Stock in Trade of
Mr Joseph Tansley, a bankrupt* (see also sale of
12th January, 1802).

A Dinner service, Salopian carnation sprig, containing
15 dishes in sizes, a round tureen & cover, 48 meat
plates, 24 soup do. 4 sauce boats, 12 patties, 12 small
plates, 2 square dishes & covers, 1 dish cover and a
triple muffin plate.   £3. 13. 6.
A Dessert set containing a centrepiece, 12 compôtiers,
2 sugar tureens & stands, 12 plates, en suite, with
the preceeding lot.   £1. 1. 0.

The Salopian porcelains were, of course, still being auctioned after Turner
had sold the works to the Coalport partners in October 1799, as the items had
been originally acquired before this date. It is interesting to see in one 1802
catalogue of the 'elegant Household Furniture . . . of the late R^t. Honble.
Lady Jane Ferry' both Thomas Turner Caughley porcelains, and John Rose's
Coalport or 'Coalbrook Dale' porcelains:

A blue & white Salopian dessert service, consisting of 12 compôtiers (side dishes),
a centrepiece, 2 sugar & cream tureens, covers and stands, a wine stand [query,
an ice pail] and 23 plates.
   A Coalbrook Dale sandwich set, 4 compôtiers (fan-shaped side dishes) centrepiece & cover, and 7 plates.

Mr Phillips   *12th January, 1802.*

'. . . *the extensive stock in Trade of Mr Joseph Tansley, a bankrupt* . . .
comprising a general assortment of Porcelain, Glass and earthenwares' (see
also sale of 11th December, 1801).

Six sets of Salopian tea cups and saucers, 48 basons, a teapot and stand, 14 milks,
6 preserving pots, 24 artichoke cups, 12 pickle stands, 3 asparagus trays, 2 dishes,
12 breakfast cups & saucers, 11 chocolate ditto, 48 coffees, 6 custards, 2 sugar
boxes, 6 plates, 4 inks.   £2. 2. 0.

Six sets of Salopian tea cups and saucers, 21 handled cups & saucers, a teapot &
stand, 4 sugar boxes, a tea jar, 3 plates, a caudle cup & stand, 12 milk pots, 6
basons & saucers, 12 chocolates, 67 coffee and 36 artichoke cups, 30 bowls, a mug,
9 asparagus trays, a butter boat and 2 ladles.   £2. 10. 0.

APPENDIX II

LYGO-DUESBURY & EGAN CORRESPONDENCE

A further source of contemporary information on Caughley porcelain is the letters and accounts which passed between Joseph Lygo, the London agent for the Derby firm, and Duesbury at Derby, and between Lygo and Richard Egan, the Bath retailer. Lygo apparently purchased, from the London warehouse of the Caughley factory (and from sales) articles of Caughley or Salopian make and forwarded them to Egan. The Salopian china warehouse in London was then trading under the title Turner & Shaw.

Relevant extracts from these papers (preserved at the Derby Library) read:

Lygo to Duesbury   October 9th, 1788.

. . . The two toy sets white & gold wrote for on the 16th September are very much wanted, please to say when they will be here (in London), if they are detained for want of the coffee pots think I could get them done here from the Salopian warehouse. . . .

October 22nd, 1788.

. . . Mr Donovan (the Dublin decorator and retailer) stay'd but a few days and purchased very little goods he just called here (the Derby shop) one day but did not buy anything and Burgin at the Salopian House informs me he only bought a few common things there. . . .

Lygo to Duesbury   8th September, 1786.

In this box is one pound of fine blue and one ounce of gold agreeable to your request . . . there is no other samples of blue to be got at present, inclosed is a list of the prices of different Cobalts from T. & H. (Tuish & Hickers) they show me many different trials of Mr Turners both from the smalts & Cobalts, I understand they have served him for some time, the Cobalt at 50/- produces a strong colour under the glaze . . .

154   The reference to 'many different trials of Mr Turners' available at a London

colour suppliers' premises is very interesting and may well account for the trial-mugs still in existence (one dated 22nd May, 1787, is illustrated in the *Antique Collector* magazine of May, 1944, and shows eight identical Chinese landscapes in different tones of blue, lettered 'Cobalt B', 'Cobalt L', etc.). Another trial-mug is illustrated in Dr Watney's *English Blue and White Porcelain of the 18th Century* (1963). These were probably made for the colour suppliers, or for the use of the retail suppliers who could take orders for special pieces in stipulated tones of blue. If the mugs were intended, as has previously been suggested, as factory trials it is difficult to see how they came to be preserved and sold outside the factory. Most factory trials were on odd scraps of porcelain, not on completed objects.

Lygo to Duesbury   8th September, 1786.

. . . Mr Templeton from Dublin called . . . could not do any business with him his price was so very low, they all of them go to the Worcester & Salopian Warehouses and buy goods unfinished, and then have them gilt, which most makes it impossible to do any business with them, to do any good, there is still more and more of the goods made, laid with the blue only, which I think the Manufacturers will one day see their error in so doing!

Lygo to Duesbury   2nd January, 1787.

. . . Mr Turner the Salop manufacturer is out of Town. I have seen Mr Flight the Worcester manufacturer and informed him what you propose doing [with regard to the proposed reduction in import duty on Foreign wares] but he does not seem inclined to do anything in the business and does not think there is a possibility of you succeeding, if I read Mr Flight right I think he had rather the present treaty took place than not on account of their making a great deal of common goods, which is not made in France. I should not wonder if Mr Turner [of Caughley] was of the same opinion tho. he manufactures more fine goods than Flight but on the other hand he manufactures a great deal of common goods.

Lygo to Duesbury   30th June, 1787.

. . . I am inform'd Mr Turner, the china manufacturer is gone over to France.

Lygo to Duesbury   26th August, 1790.

I have been to the Salopian Warehouse to enquire about the wash hand bason & jugs blue & white, they have got 4 common ones only and the price is 10/6d. each. Chamber pots they have none, they have not made any for some time and the reason is foreign Nankeen ones are so much cheaper than theirs, and so much better. You will please to say if you would have them in foreign china, I have not had an opportunity of going into the city 155 to enquire at the Worcester warehouse if they have them, but if they have they will be much worse than the Staffordshire [earthen] ware ones . . .

Lygo to Egan (the Bath retailer).   *25th January, 1794.*

. . . I have laid out £16 odd at the Salopian Sale for you. I will send you the account of what they are and if there should be any thing that you think will not suit you they may remain here they are on 6 months credit, or 5 per cent for (ready) money.

Account sent to Richard Egan of Bath, by Lygo for goods purchased by Lygo on Egan's behalf from Thomas Turner.

'Feby 24th, 1794.

6 Pint basons, Dresden flower border	@ 1/6d.	9/-
4 ½ pint do.	do.	1/-	4/-
24 dessert plates 2nd (size)	do.	1/3	30/-
6 Pint basons Chantille sprig		1/6	9/-

Lygo to Egan   25th March, 1794.

. . . You will see by the inclosed account I have made another purchase for you at the Salopian Sale, of such goods that I think will suit you, china dishes are very scarce and dear of the small sizes . . .

Lygo to Egan   1st June, 1794.

Please to inform me if there is anything wanting from the Salopian Warehouse as they are going to have another sale on Thursday next . . .

Lygo to Egan   2nd August, 1794.

On Monday last I paid Turner & Shaw [under whose name the Salopian London warehouse traded] £16.2.0 for your account for the goods bought at the first sale . . . I have this day sent in two boxes some goods which I bought at Turners and [at] Christies sales . . .

Lygo to Egan   17th November, 1794.

. . . what cups & saucers they have at the Salopian warehouse with the Dresden flower & border are so very bad, that I cannot send them.

Lygo to Egan   10th January, 1795.

. . . have done all in my power to get the 12 Salopian breakfast cups & saucers but without success, they have cups at the warehouse but no saucers . . .

I have this day sent some gilt goods of Spodes and the 2 Salopian blue sets bought at Sale . . .

156   The following entries relate to Thomas Turner's porcelains purchased by Lygo

in London on behalf of Richard Egan, the Bath retailer, and have been gleaned
from the original Lygo correspondence preserved at the Derby Library:

June 10th, 1795.
  1 set Teas 1st [size] Basket [border?] Chantille sprig   8/-
  1 Pint Bason New fluted Shrewsbury   2/-

July 15th, 1795.
  1 Sugar box, bell fluted, fine blue edge.   2/-

August 26th, 1795.
  1 Saucer 2nd [size] new fluted shrewsbury   8d.
  1 B & B [bread & butter plate] 2nd [size] do.   2/-

March 22nd, 1796.
  4 cups & saucers 2nd [size] new fluted white @ 6½d.   4/4
  1 Pint bason   do.   1/3
  1 teapot 4th [size]   do.   3/6
  2 B & B [bread & butter] plates do.   @ 1/9d.   3/6

September 7th, 1796.
  2 cups 2nd [size] handled, new fluted blue border @ 1/6d. 3/-
  1 cream ewer   2/6
  6 coffee cups   new fluted sprig border   9/-

December 17th, 1796.
  1 B & B [bread & butter] plate 2nd [size] Bute [shape]
    sprig border   2/-
  3 cups & saucers 2nd [size] Brosely Nankeen @ 7½d. 3/9
  5 caudle cups Bell fluted dagger border   @ 2/6d. 12/6
  2 stands for do.   do.   @ 2/6d. 5/-

SOME POPULAR MYTHS

Most standard reference books contain many misleading and incorrect statements relating to the Caughley products. This is probably due to the fact that up to the present time nobody has carried out original research on this neglected factory and writers have been content to repeat statements first made in nineteenth century books.

Many of these erroneous statements can be traced back to Llewellyn Jewitt's *The Ceramic Art of Great Britain*, first published in 1878 and largely based on material incorporated in an article in the *Art Journal* magazine of March 1862, and it may be helpful to collectors and subsequent writers to list some of these statements which I consider were incorrect:

Jewitt wrote—

> In 1780 Mr Turner introduced the making of the famous 'Willow Pattern'—the first made in England—at Caughley, and about the same time the 'Broseley Blue Dragon' pattern. . . .

I have explained on Page 15 that no known Caughley marked porcelain bears a representation of the Willow pattern as it is known today, although of course several different Chinese-styled landscape designs do occur *without* the main features of this well-known Willow pattern. The Broseley Dragon design occurs on much post-1799 Coalport porcelain but I have yet to find it on a marked example of pre-1799 Caughley porcelain.

The same authority also attributed the disguised numeral marks to the Worcester factory but this point is dealt with in Chapter IX and in particular on Pages 122 and 125. Jewitt then followed with a long, complicated discussion on printed Caughley porcelain. I shall have to break-up these extracts in order to deal with the various points but these are important as they show the confused state of knowledge when Jewitt wrote these statements, which have been repeated and rephrased by writer after writer so that most collectors have accepted these statements as fact.

> I (Jewitt) have already shown that transfer-printing was used as early as 1757 on Worcester porcelain, and I have little doubt that quite as early, if not a few years before that period, it was practised at Caughley. Indeed, in

the early years of the manufactory, the two works, Caughley and Worcester, seem to have been closely connected, and to have worked 'in and in', . . .

Although a pottery was probably working at Caughley in the 1750s we have no evidence at all that it produced anything but utilitarian pottery, certainly not transfer printed porcelain, as Turner did not come from Worcester to establish the porcelain factory until the 1770s, see Page 2.

Jewitt continues:

> . . . and I believe, with ample reason, that a great proportion of the printed goods bearing the Worcester mark were printed at Caughley. Indeed, it is known that the ware was sent up from Worcester by barge to be printed at Caughley, and returned, when finished, by the same mode of conveyance. I have closely examined the style of engraving and the patterns of a large number of examples, and I am clearly of opinion that they are the work of the same hands.

Jewitt did not state his 'ample reason' for believing that Worcester porcelain was printed at Caughley and I am unable to trace any evidence to support this contention,[1] in fact all indications point to the fact that the Caughley and the Worcester managements were keen rivals. Jewitt stated, without elaboration, 'it is known that the ware was sent up from Worcester by barge to be printed at Caughley and returned, when finished, by the same mode of conveyance'. What is known is that Chamberlain of Worcester, the independent decorator and retailer, received vast quantities of Caughley porcelain to decorate and stock his Worcester shop from 1789 (see Chapter V) but I cannot trace any evidence that intertrading was practised between Caughley and the main Worcester porcelain factory, and it would appear that Jewitt presumed that the evidence relating to Chamberlain applied to the Worcester Porcelain Works. Excavations on the site of the Worcester factory show that blue-printing was carried on at the factory for 'wasters' show all stages of manufacture. Printed specimens so distorted in the firing that they can only have been discarded at the place of manufacture (see Plate 231) and numerous printed pieces bearing traces of unfired glaze which could only have been added at Worcester, not at Caughley or any other factory. If further facts are needed to show that the Worcester porcelains were not printed at Caughley, we can cite the point that no fragments of any Worcester shape were found amongst the thousands of unglazed fragments found at the Caughley site, all were of Caughley shapes and it is inconceivable that none of the Worcester wares were spoilt if they had been printed and refired at Caughley.

Jewitt followed by commenting that he had 'closely examined the style of engraving and the patterns of a large number of examples, and I am clearly of opinion that they are the work of the same hands'. I can only state that my own

---

[1] As early as 1865, R. W. Binns, the ceramic authority and then owner of the Royal Worcester Factory, sought to correct this belief, for in his *A Century of Potting in the City of Worcester* he noted 'we can find no evidence, nor do we believe that Worcester porcelain was ever sent to Caughley to be decorated either by printing or painting. . . .' but unfortunately the belief remained in some quarters and has since been spread as fact.

observations are completely different from Jewitt's and I cannot but think that Jewitt did not *closely* examine the two classes of porcelain. I would refer the reader to Plates 255, 258, 259 and 262, where the two versions of shared patterns are shown, in other patterns the Worcester engraver used cross-hatching where the Caughley engraver used only parallel lines. Many Worcester designs were engraved with clear areas which were intended to be shaded in by hand applied washes; these washes do not occur on Caughley designs where engraved parallel lines were used when shading was required (see Plates 258, 259 and 262). Again we have the several major differences between the Worcester version of the Fisherman or 'Pleasure Boat' design (see Plates 229 and 230, and Pages 131–132) which underline my point that the printed designs on Worcester porcelain are different from those found on the contemporary Caughley articles.

Llewellyn Jewitt also stated:

> Collectors . . . must not be too hasty in ascribing, from appearance alone, examples to either one or the other make (he was referring here to Worcester and Caughley), but must be guided, in a great measure, by the body on which the engraving occurs.

I do not know if by 'body' Jewitt meant the appearance and colour by transmitted light of the porcelain, or if he was referring to the shape of the article. If Jewitt was referring to the appearance, then this method presents great difficulty, for it would seem that the make-up of the two porcelain bodies was substantially the same and the materials may well have come from the same source, for we have evidence in the form of letters, that clay for the Caughley factory was shipped up river from Worcester, neither factory used local materials, each had to purchase the ingredients to make their porcelains. Factory 'wasters' found at the Worcester site show that the orangish translucency, so often cited as a Caughley characteristic, is to be seen in some *Worcester* specimens, seemingly of the 1770–90 period. If Jewitt was referring to the shape of the article when he used the term 'body', then I am pleased to agree, for as I have shown (see, for example, Plates 269 and 270 or 273) each factory used slightly different forms, of handle, or of moulded articles. For example, the two different versions of the popular moulded cabbage-leaf jug are illustrated in Plates 276 and 277. These differences in shape help to show which patterns were Worcester and which are Caughley.

I would not wish the reader to believe that all Jewitt's material is untrustworthy, on the contrary most is correct, in particular that information relating to nineteenth century potters. It is probably this fact that has led subsequent writers to repeat his statements without rechecking of the available facts.

Other popular myths include the belief that the Caughley body contained less soapstone than Worcester, so that the Caughley management could undersell the Worcester products. An analysis of a marked Fisherman pattern 'waster' from the factory site disproves this myth, see Page 118.

There is also the popular misconception that Thomas Turner at Caughley employed copies of other factories' marks, the Worcester crescent is often cited, also the Worcester 'W' mark and the hunting horn mark of the Chantilly factory. No wasters bearing such marks were found on the Caughley site (only pieces with the impressed 'SALOPIAN' name mark and the blue-printed 'S' or 'C' initial marks) and I have not seen any Caughley porcelain bearing a fake mark. All examples which I have seen have been Worcester, not Caughley, although these pieces have been called Caughley in error for very many years.

Now that we have been able to differentiate between comparable Worcester and Caughley porcelains, we can see the Caughley wares in their true light, not as inferior copies of Worcester, and having discarded a large number of Worcester specimens we find that Caughley porcelains are much rarer than we had previously thought.

I trust the researches published in this book will stimulate interest in these Salopian wares and perhaps lead to further research on these interesting and varied porcelains.

BIBLIOGRAPHY

Although the author finds himself unable to accept all the attributions suggested by most other writers on the subject, he feels that no serious work of reference can be complete without a bibliography. The interested reader is therefore invited to consult the following and to form his own judgment on the several points of divergence.

The Ceramic Art of Great Britain. L. Jewitt. (1878, revised edition 1883).
English Blue and White Porcelain of the Eighteenth century. S. W. Fisher. (1947).
Caughley and Coalport Porcelain. F. A. Barrett. (1951).
The House of Coalport 1750–1950. Sir Compton Mackenzie. (1951).
English Blue and White Porcelain of the Eighteenth century. Dr B. Watney. (1963).
English Porcelain 1745–1850 (edited by R. J. Charleston) Chapter 7 by F. A. Barrett. (1965).

A book to appear shortly in Messrs Herbert Jenkins new series of *Illustrated Guides* will feature Worcester porcelains, including some examples hitherto attributed to the Caughley factory. Like the present work, it will be based on finds made during recent excavations, in this case at the Worcester factory site.

INDEX

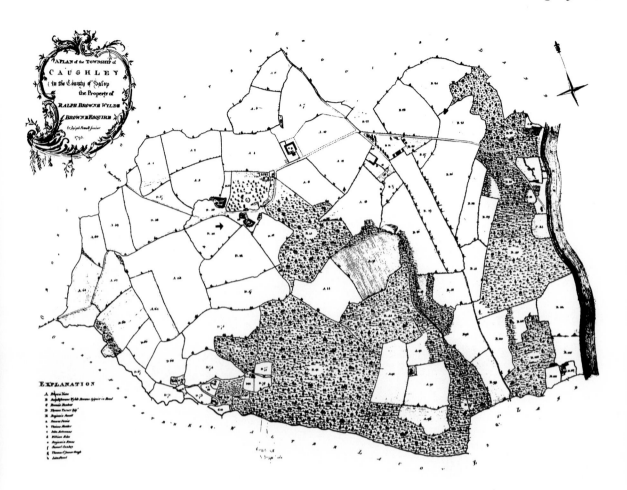

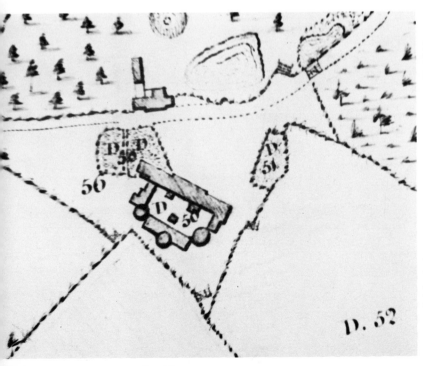

1. Map of Caughley (dated 1793) showing at 'D' the china factory owned by Thomas Turner. The coal mine was in the field just to the north. The River Severn is seen on the extreme right.

2. Enlarged detail of the 1793 map (Plate 1) showing the open plan of the factory, with three circular kilns.

3. Engraving of the front elevation of the factory, reproduced from L. Jewitt's *Ceramic Art of Great Britain* (1878).

4. View of the factory site in 1967 with clay mining in progress. The camera is pointing north and part of the 'road' shown in Plate 2 can be seen on the far side of the pit. Most of the factory 'wasters' illustrated in this book were found among the kiln ash in the foreground, and by the hedge running along the boundary with the 'road'. Note the country setting.

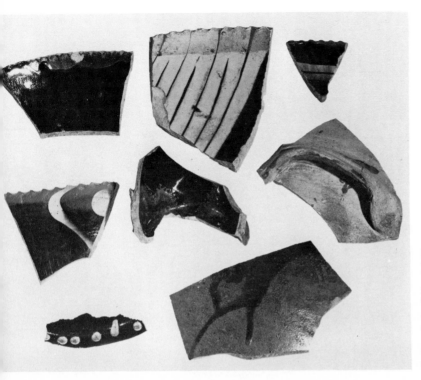

5. Pottery found on the Caughley site, including traditional 'slip' decorated dishes made at many 18th-century potteries. These wares may have been produced at the pottery before Turner came from Worcester and commenced the production of porcelain (see Page 2).

6. Fragments of blue and white Caughley porcelain, from the factory site, including the popular 'Fisherman' pattern (*top and bottom, left*). British Museum (Crown Copyright).

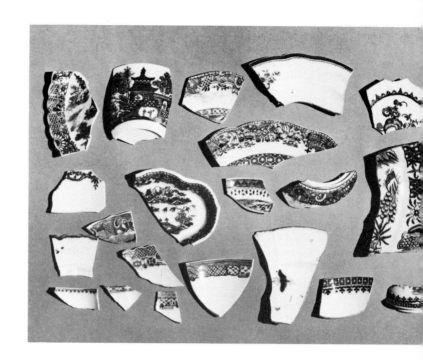

7. Selection of Caughley factory 'wasters' showing typical patterns and borders of the 1775-90 period.

8. Caughley factory 'wa[s]showing the underglaze-portions of blue and goldsigns of the 1785-99 pesuch as those illustrate[d]Plates 60, 61, 80, 81, 96, 97and 145. The circular obj[ect]a rare button (see Page 88[,]Plate 94).

9. Fragments of hard-paste Chinese blue and white 'Nankin' porcelains of a type which was imported into England in vast quantities. Most of these Chinese fragments were parts of plates and dishes from dinner services, a line seldom made by English porcelain manufacturers, and it would seem that Turner at Caughley supplied *Chinese* sets as these could be sold for less than the cost of producing his own dinner services (see Page 13).

10. Two Chinese hard-paste blue and white plates. An almost exact copy of the right-hand design was made by Turner at Caughley (see Plate 14 and Page 16). *Godden of Worthing Ltd.*

11. Chinese hard-paste Nankin-type blue and white teaset, *c.* 1780, the gilding on the handles, edges, etc. added in England. The Caughley factory copied these standard shapes, in particular the teapot handle and spout. Compare with the Caughley teaset shown in Plate 195, the creamer with Plate 142 and also the Chinese teapot with Plates 198 and 199. *Godden of Worthing Ltd.*

12. Chinese hard-paste pierced cress-dish and stand, *c.* 1775-80, hand-painted with a standard printed design much used at the Worcester, Caughley and Lowestoft factories in England. Compare with Plate 271. *Godden of Worthing Ltd.*

13. Chinese hard-paste deep centre dish from a dessert service, enriched with gilt inner border added in England. This shape was much used by Turner at the Caughley factory (see Colour Plate V and Plates 99 & 100) but apparently not at any other English factory. $12\frac{1}{2}$ in. long. *Godden of Worthing Ltd.*

14. Caughley blue-printed tea-wares of a rare and attractive pattern which is also found on Chinese hard-paste Nankin porcelains (see Plate 15, below, and Page 16). Plate 8½ in. dia. Blue-printed 'S' marks. *c.* 1780. *Author's Collection.*

15. Chinese hard-paste 'fine old Nankin table service of the fine Willow landscape and dagger border' (see Page 13). Although dinner services of this pattern were NOT made at Caughley, the basic design was used on tea services (see Plate 14, above). Dish 16 in. long. *c.* 1770–80. *Godden of Worthing Ltd.*

I. A selection of Caughley porcelains bearing the 'Pleasure Boat' or 'Fisherman' patterns (see Chapter III) shown with an unglazed 'waster' part saucer and a fragment mug found on the factory site. The Worcester factory made a different version of this popular design (see Page 131). Large dish $12\frac{1}{4}$ in. long. Impressed mark 'SALOPIAN'. c. 1780-90. *Author's Collection.*

16. Caughley fluted teawares of very rare form, bearing the blue-printed 'Temple' pattern (see Page 17). This *printed* pattern occurs only on Caughley porcelains although a hand-painted version is very occasionally found on Worcester wares (see Plate 261). Creamer $5\frac{1}{4}$ in. Blue-printed 'S' mark and gilder's number '5'. *c.* 1780–5. *Godden of Worthing Ltd.*

17. Caughley tea-caddy decorated with the rare 'Striped Temple' pattern (see Page 18), a design not employed at Worcester. 5 in. high. *c.* 1780–5. *Author's Collection.*

Caughley Blue-Printed
Porcelains

8. *Right*. Caughley moulded
bread and butter plate from a
tea service as shown in Plate
95, bearing the blue-printed
'Pagoda' pattern (see Page 18)
copied from a Chinese original.
The design is also found on
later Coalport wares but not on
Worcester porcelains. 8½ in.
dia. Blue 'Sx' mark. *c.* 1780.
Author's Collection.

9. *Below left*. Caughley tea
cannister bearing the underglaze blue-printed 'Fence' pattern (see Page 19). 5 in. high.
c. 1780–5. *Godden of Worthing
Ltd*.

10. *Below right*. Caughley teawares bearing the rare 'Fenced
Garden' design (see Page 19).
The pattern is not found on
Worcester porcelains. Large
saucer 6 in. dia. Blue 'Sx'
marks. *c.* 1780–5. *Author's Collection*.

II. A selection of Caughley 'cabbage-leaf' mask-head jugs showing popular underglaze blue patterns and the different sizes. This moulded jug form was also made at Worcester but with important differences in the moulding (see Pages 98, 138 & 139). Large Parrot pattern jug 8¾ in. high. Underglaze blue 'Sx' mark. *c.* 1775-90. *Author's Collection.*

21. Caughley teapot decorated with the blue-printed 'Fence and House' design (see Page 20), a pattern not found on Worcester porcelains. 5¾ in. high. Blue-printed 'S' mark. *c.* 1780. *Godden of Worthing Ltd.*

22. A 'sandwich service' dish decorated with the blue-printed 'Full Nankin' design. A popular pattern, found on a variety of wares and, along with the 'Conversation' subject, apparently the only blue-printed designs applied to Caughley dinner services (see Plates 117 & 118 and Pages 20, 21 & 94). This design is not found on Worcester wares. 13½ in. long. Impressed 'Salopian' name mark and blue-printed 'S' mark. *c.* 1780. *J. Cronk Collection.*

23. A Caughley small-sized plate from a dinner service, bearing the blue-printed Conversation pattern (see Page 21). This design is not found on Worcester porcelains. 6½ in. dia. Blue-printed 'S' mark. *c.* 1780–5. *Author's Collection.*

24. A Caughley moulded waste-bowl decorated with the very rare blue-printed 'Uninhabited Pagoda' design (see Page 21). Gilt border inside and gilt footrim. Diameter at top 6 in. Gilder's number '55' inside footrim. *c.* 1780–5. *Author's Collection.*

25. Caughley teawares showing the ornate, so-called 'Fitzhugh'-type border (see Page 22) found with several patterns, and occasionally, as in this case, without other decoration apart from gilt inner border. Creamer $3\frac{3}{4}$ in. high. Printed 'S' mark. *c.* 1785. *Godden of Worthing Ltd.*

26. Caughley plate decorated with powder-blue ground (see Page 22) and hand-painted panels. The powder-blue examples are rare but the process was employed at several other factories including Worcester. $8\frac{1}{8}$ in. dia. Impressed 'Salopian' name mark and mock Chinese signs (see Page 10). *c.* 1775–85. *Victoria & Albert Museum (Crown Copyright).*

27. Caughley tureen-stand, hand-painted in a bright under-glaze blue with child-like Chinese-styled landscape (see Page 23), shown with Caughley factory 'wasters'. This pattern has in the past been attributed to the Derby factory. Stand 9½ in. long. Painter's dash mark inside footrim. *c.* 1785–90. *Godden of Worthing Ltd.*

28. Caughley bread and butter plate from a tea service, hand-painted in underglaze blue with the child-like 'Tower' pattern (see Page 23). Note the trees seemingly floating in the sky. 7½ in. dia. Unmarked. *c.* 1780–90. *Author's Collection.*

29. Caughley tea bowl, hand-painted with a rare underglaze blue bridge design (see Page 23) and also factory 'waster' of thickly-potted saucer-like object painted with simple but rare design (see Page 24). Unmarked. *c.* 1780–90. *Author's Collection.*

30. Caughley miniature dish from a child's toy dinner service, shown with factory 'wasters', including an unglazed small plate, bottom left. Dish 4 in. long. Painted 'S' mark. *c.* 1785–90. *Author's Collection.*

31. Caughley blue-printed mug showing the 'La Pêche' design, also employed at the Worcester factory (see Colour Plate IX, Plate 258 and Pages 24 & 133). Note handle form. Inscribed 'Sus^h French. 1790'. $4\frac{3}{10}$ in. high. Blue-printed 'S' mark. *British Museum (Crown Copyright)*.

32. Caughley blue-printed mug showing the 'La Promenade Chînoise' pattern, which is normally found on the same article as 'La Pêche' (shown above) that is, one print on each side of an object. Again, this design is found also on Worcester porcelains (see Plate 259 and Pages 24 & 133). $5\frac{1}{2}$ in. high. *c.* 1790. *Godden of Worthing Ltd.*

33. Caughley moulded, cabbage-leaf jug, one of numerous objects found with the 'Pleasure Boat' or 'Fisherman' design printed in underglaze-blue (see Chapter III, Colour Plate II and Plates 85–88, 91, 95, etc.). A variation of this design is also found on Worcester porcelains (see Pages 27 & 133). 8½ in. high. Blue 'Sx' mark. *c.* 1785. *Author's Collection.*

34. Caughley saucer, bearing the blue-printed 'Bell-toy' pattern (see Page 25), an attractive design not found on Worcester porcelains. $4\frac{7}{8}$ in. dia. Blue 'Sx' mark. *c.* 1780–90. *Author's Collection.*

35. Caughley tea bowl and factory 'waster', showing the blue-printed 'Mother & Child' pattern. This design is sometimes mistaken for the Bell-toy pattern (see above) but in this design the child holds a fan-like object in the crook of his elbow, not the bell-toy (see Page 26). This design is found also on Worcester porcelains (see Plate 255 and Pages 26 & 134). *c.* 1780–90. *Author's Collection.*

36. Caughley bowl, the interior with an underglaze blue print of the Ironbridge over the River Severn at Coalbrookdale. This print is also found on jugs of both Caughley and later Coalport porcelains, but not on Worcester wares (see Page 38). Diameter 7 in. Blue 'S' mark. *c.* 1780–5. *Author's Collection.*

7. Caughley dessert plate bearing the rare underglaze blue print, originally called 'Travellers' (see Page 38). The printed border is similar to that found on the popular 'Fisherman' pattern. 6$\frac{3}{8}$ in. dia. Impressed 'Salopian' mark. *c.* 1780–5. *Victoria & Albert Museum (Crown Copyright).*

38. Detail, showing the centre of a Caughley tureen-stand, similar in outline to that seen in Plate 27. Hand-painted farm scene in light, bright blue (see Colour Plate V for the same colour and style, and see also Page 39). Panel 5 × 3½ in. Impressed 'Salopian' mark. *c.* 1785. *Author's Collection.*

39. Saucer, showing the Caughley version 'A' of the 'Birds in a tree' design, and also a Worcester version 'B' (see Pages 39 & 134). 4¾ in. dia. Blue-printed, shaded crescent mark on Worcester saucer 'B'. *c.* 1775–85. *Author's Collection.*

Parrot and Fruit Design

40. *Above.* Reproduction of a 'pull' from an original Caughley engraved copper-plate of the attractive Parrot and fruit design. This print was also employed at Worcester, but note the parallel-line shading of rocks (in foreground) on this Caughley engraving. *Left.* Caughley moulded cabbage-leaf jug, bearing the Salopian version of the Parrot print. Compare this with Plate 260, and note the restraint of the shading on the fruit. $7\frac{3}{4}$ in. high. *c.* 1780–5. *Messrs Sotheby & Co.*

189

Blue-Printed Designs

41. Detail, of centre of Caughley basket (as Plate 90), showing the popular so-called 'Pine Cone' design, much favoured at the Worcester factory. Caughley versions bear 'S' or 'C' marks (see Page 40), not the Worcester shaded crescent or disguised numeral marks (see Plate 90). Impressed 'Salopian' mark and blue-printed 'C'. *c.* 1780–5. *K. Middlemas Collection.*

42. Reproduction of 'pull' from an original Caughley engraved copper-plate, showing two popular fruit designs. The small sprays were separated and spread over the object. Note 'S' and 'C' marks found with these designs (see also Plate 44, opposite, Plate 197 and Page 42). *Messrs Coalport China Ltd.*

43. Reproduction of 'pull' from an original Caughley engraved copper-plate, showing one of the 'Fruit and wreath' designs (see also Page 42). These attractive designs were also employed on crescent-marked Worcester porcelains, but note here the Caughley 'S' and clear 'C' marks. *Messrs Coalport China Ltd.*

44. Caughley teapot and cover bearing an underglaze blue print of fruit, taken from the same engraved copper-plate as the 'pull' reproduced opposite (Plate 42A). 5¼ in. high. Blue-printed 'S' mark. *c.* 1775–80. *Author's Collection.*

45. A Caughley mug, showing the 'Full-blown rose' blue-printed design, one of the rarer floral designs (see also Plate 135). $5\frac{1}{4}$ in. high. Blue-printed 'S' mark. *c.* 1780. *J. Cronk Collection.*

46. Caughley mug (note handle form) bearing a rare blue-printed floral design. $4\frac{1}{5}$ in. high. *c.* 1785-90. *Godden of Worthing Ltd.*

47. *Top left.* A fine and early Caughley mask-head jug, hand-painted with floral sprays. Dated 1778. $7\frac{1}{8}$ in. high. Blue 'C' mark. *Victoria & Albert Museum (Crown Copyright).*

48. *Top right.* A rare and very early Caughley blue-painted mug. Inscribed, in front, with initial monogram below crossed branches and doves (as seen on the jug above) with date '1776' below. $5\frac{1}{4}$ in. high. Blue-painted open crescent or 'C' mark (see Page 9). *F. Baxendale Collection.*

49. *Left.* A rare form of Caughley teapot, hand-painted with flowers in a bright tone of underglaze blue. The same pattern is seen on the cup and saucer in Plate 51. $5\frac{1}{2}$ in. high. Blue 'S' mark. *c.* 1785–90. *Godden of Worthing Ltd.*

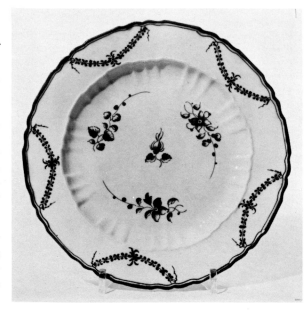

50. *Top.* A rare Caughley fluted tea-
bowl and saucer, and an egg-strainer,
hand-painted with a bright tone of
underglaze blue. Blue-painted 'S'
marks. *c.* 1785-90. *Godden of Worthing Ltd.*

51. *Centre.* A Caughley tea cup and
saucer, hand-painted with flowers,
and a rare coffee-cup with French-
style moulded basket edge, shown
with factory 'wasters'. Blue-painted
'S' marks. *c.* 1785-95. *Author's Collection.*

52. *Bottom.* A rare shape of Caughley
moulded plate, hand-painted with
flowers and festoons. $7\frac{1}{2}$ in. dia. Impressed 'Salopian' mark. *c.* 1785-95.
Godden of Worthing Ltd.

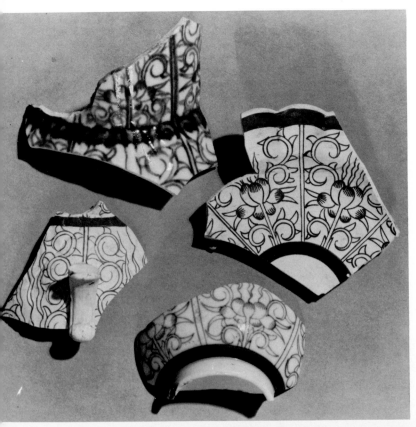

53. Caughley factory 'wasters' (both glazed and unglazed) of the popular 'Lily', 'Royal Lily' or 'Queen Charlotte' pattern (see Page 44). This design was heightened with gilding and was employed at other factories including Worcester.

54. Caughley tea-bowl and saucer showing the completed 'Lily' pattern (see above), with gilding over the blue borders. Blue-painted 'S' mark. *c.* 1785-90. *Victoria & Albert Museum (Crown Copyright)*.

55. Caughley small-sized mug, hand-painted with the carnation design (printed variations occur both on Caughley and on Worcester porcelains). 3½ in. high. Blue-painted open crescent or 'C' mark (see Page 9). Dated 1778. *Godden of Worthing Ltd.*

56. Rare Caughley moulded plate with basket-work edge, in the French style. Hand-painted in underglaze blue. 8½ in. dia. Impressed 'Salopian' mark. *c.* 1790. *Author's Collection.*

57. Caughley small tureen, from a dessert service, with rare addition of moulded basket-work edge, in the French style. Painted with underglaze blue. Chantilly sprigs (see Plates 120, 129 & 146 and Page 45). 5½ in. long. *c.* 1785-95. *J. Cronk Collection.*

58. Representative pieces from a Caughley tea service enamelled with slight floral sprays. Such enamelled examples are quite rare. Teapot 6 in. high. Unmarked. *c.* 1780. *Godden of Worthing Ltd.*

Representative pieces from Caughley tea service deco-
ed with overglaze black or
t' enamelled floral design
h gilt borders and knobs.
ntemporary Chinese porce-
s sometimes bore similar
oration, and the saucer
wn with these Caughley
ces is Chinese. Perhaps the
ughley pieces were decorated
match an Oriental service.
pot 6 in. high. Unmarked.
1780-5. *Godden of Worthing*

Blue and Gold Designs

60. Caughley cup and saucer decorated in underglaze blue and overglaze gilding, a style of pattern known as 'Dresden flower' (see Page 64). Underglaze blue 'S' mark. *c.* 1785–95 *Author's Collection.*

61. Caughley spoon tray with underglaze blue border and overglaze gilding. Perhaps the design called 'blue & gold Fly' in the Chamberlain correspondence (see Page 52). Note the gilt border around the fly and compare with the Chamberlain decorated objects shown in Plates 69–74. 6½ in. long. Underglaze blue 'S' mark. *c.* 1785–90. *Godden of Worthing Ltd.*

Enamelled Floral Designs

62. Caughley teapot with good quality floral painting and gilding, probably decorated outside the factory. $5\frac{1}{4}$ in. high. Unmarked. *c.* 1785–95. *J. Waring, Brighton.*

63. Caughley mug (note handle form) enamelled in the same style as the teapot shown above. It is inscribed on the front 'Edward Turner. 1795'. $5\frac{1}{2}$ in. high. Unmarked. *Messrs Christies.*

64. Representative pieces from a Caughley tea service of moulded, half-fluted form, decorated with enamelled sprigs, gilt borders, etc. perhaps a design called 'French sprigs' or 'Lady's Sprigs' mentioned in the Chamberlain accounts as being applied to Caughley porcelains (see Page 74). Teapot $5\frac{3}{4}$ in. high. Gilder's 'T' mark inside footrims. *c.* 1785-95. *Godden of Worthing Ltd.*

65. Caughley shaped dish from a dessert service enamelled with the colourful 'Bishop Sumner', 'Bengal Tiger' or 'Dragon' pattern (see Page 75). 8¾ in. Impressed 'Salopian' mark. *c.* 1785–90. *Godden of Worthing Ltd.*

66. Caughley covered tureen, stand and ladle, enamelled with red Oriental-styled design, perhaps the 'Scarllet & gold Japan' dessert pattern invoiced by Chamberlains in 1789 (see Page 74). Impressed 'Salopian' mark on stand. *c.* 1785–90. *Messrs Sotheby & Co.*

67. A Caughley moulded cabbage-leaf jug, very probably decorated in Chamberlains' decorating workshop at Worcester. The centre panel enamelled with 'View of Worcester' (taken from Nash's 'Worcestershire' of 1782). Note the gilt floral sprays at the sides and compare with Plates 69 and 70. $7\frac{1}{2}$ in. high. Unmarked. *c.* 1785–90. *Dyson Perrins Museum. Worcester Royal Porcelain Works.*

68. A superb Caughley cabbage-leaf jug, finely enamelled in Chamberlains' decorating establishment at Worcester, the exotic birds in the style of George Davis (see Page 76). 7¾ in. high. Unmarked. *c.* 1785–90. *Messrs Delomosne & Son Ltd.*

69. A fine Caughley cabbage-leaf jug, probably enamelled in Chamberlains' decorating establishment at Worcester (see Chapter V). Compare the top border with that on Plate 70, and the panel-surround with Plates 70–74. 7½ in. high. Unmarked. *c.* 1785–90. *Victoria & Albert Museum (Crown Copyright).*

70. A Caughley cabbage-leaf jug, enamelled in the same general style as those shown in Plates 67–69 attributed to Chamberlains' decorators. Title 'Sherborne Castle, Oxfordshire' enamelled on base. 7¾ in. high. Unmarked. *c.* 1785–90. *Victoria & Albert Museum (Crown Copyright)*.

71. A superb Caughley cabbage-leaf jug, very finely gilt (also with overglaze blue enamel) with crowned Royal Garter and motto (see Page 76). The same panel-surround is seen in Plates 69–74. Decoration attributed to Chamberlain (see Page 77). 9¼ in. high. Unmarked. *c.* 1785–90. *Messrs Sotheby & Co.*

Chamberlain Decorated Wares

72. *Top*. A teapot, from a superb Caughley tea service, with underglaze blue border and finely gilt in the manner of the cabbage-leaf jugs illustrated in Plates 69–71, which are attributed to Chamberlains' decorating establishment. $5\frac{3}{4}$ in. high. Underglaze-blue 'S' mark. *c.* 1785–90. *Messrs Christies.*

73. *Middle*. Large Caughley cup decorated in gold and blue enamel in the same manner as the Royal pieces shown in Plates 71 and 74. Prices for Chamberlains' decoration of Caughley porcelains with 'Princes Feather' are given on Page 77. 3 in. high. Unmarked. *c.* 1790. *Victoria & Albert Museum (Crown Copyright).*

74. *Bottom*. Caughley teapot and stand (from a tea service), decorated in the same style as the jug shown in Plate 71. This decoration is attributed to the Chamberlain decorating establishment at Worcester, where much Caughley porcelain was enamelled (see Chapter V, and Page 76). Teapot $5\frac{3}{4}$ in. high. Unmarked. *c.* 1785–90. *Messrs Sotheby & Co.*

75. Representative pieces from a fine Caughley fluted teaset enamelled with the attractive 'Amitie' design. This word is enamelled on a ribbon, above the two doves. Chamberlains' prices for enamelling this design are quoted on Page 77, but the design (after about 1795) was also applied to Chamberlains' own porcelain tea services, with their oval teapots and oval covered sugar boxes. Tea caddy 4¼ in. high. Unmarked. *c.* 1792. *Godden of Worthing Ltd.*

76. A Caughley handled dish (one of the standard dessert service shapes, see Plates 113 & 115), finely enamelled, perhaps by Chamberlain of Worcester, or by one of the London decorators (see Page 78). Impressed 'Salopian' mark. *c.* 1780–90. *Victoria & Albert Museum (Crown Copyright).*

77. A very rare Caughley oval dish or stand with relief moulding, finely enamelled with yellow border and flowers. Probably decorated in London or by Chamberlain of Worcester. 13 × 10 in. Impressed 'Salopian' mark. *c.* 1780–90. *Victoria & Albert Museum (Crown Copyright).*

78. Caughley covered sugar bowl decorated with gilt design, perhaps the 'white & gold wreath' added by Chamberlain to Caughley teawares (see Page 79). 4½ in. high. Unmarked. *c.* 1785–90. *Author's Collection.*

79. Caughley bowl, from a tea service, of moulded half-fluted form. Decorated with a gold design, perhaps 'White & gold festoons' added to Caughley porcelains by Chamberlains (see Page 79). 3 in. high. Unmarked. *c.* 1785–95. *Godden of Worthing Ltd.*

80. Caughley tea-bowl and saucer showing an attractive combination of underglaze blue borders with overglaze gilding. Underglaze blue 'S' mark and also gilder's numbers 16 and 20 (on the inside of the footrim). *c.* 1785–95. *Author's Collection.*

81. Caughley teapot, with relief moulded spout and handle (usually found with a fluted body, see Plates 64, 195 & 198). Underglaze blue border with tasteful and restrained gilt design. 5 in. high. Underglaze blue 'S' mark, also gilder's number 4. *Godden of Worthing Ltd.*

82. A finely gilt Caughley (not Worcester, see Plate 274) cup and saucer, with gold pattern in a style associated with Giles, the London decorator, who purchased both Worcester and Caughley blanks to decorate. Most examples in this style are Worcester. Cup $2\frac{3}{5}$ in. high. *c.* 1780. *Godden of Worthing Ltd.*

209

83. A fine, and very rare, basalt moulded teapot (see Page 84) bearing the impressed mark 'SALOPIAN'. Several fragments of basalt-bodied wares were found on the factory site. 5 in. high. *c.* 1780–5. *D. Holgate Collection.*

84. A blue-printed EARTHENWARE teapot, of a type which sometimes bears crescent or 'S' marks, and which is often attributed to the Caughley factory. However, as far as is known, no creamware or pottery (other than black basalt) was made at Caughley during the Turner period, *c.* 1775–99 (see Page 84). Inscribed under the base is 'March th (sic) 31 1786'. Shaded (Worcester) crescent under the base and inside the cover. *Messrs Martin Hutton, Battle.*

III. A superb Caughley mask-head jug bearing the attractive 'birds in tree' underglaze blue-printed pattern (see Page 39). A special inscribed presentation jug, dated 1780. This shape and design were also employed at Worcester (see Page 139). 7 in. high. *Mr and Mrs J. Manning Collection.*

85. Caughley ARTICHOKE-CU bearing the popular 'Fishe man' pattern (see Page 28). in. high. Blue 'Sx' marks. 1780-90. *Victoria & Albert M seum (Crown Copyright)*.

86. Two Caughley ASPARAGU SERVERS (see Page 28), bearin the 'Fisherman' pattern, ap plied in two different position shown with a 'waster' from th site. 3 in. long. Unmarked. 1785-95. *Author's Collection.*

87. Caughley oval BAKING DISH (see Page 28), originally made in several different sizes. 12$\frac{1}{4}$ in. long, 2$\frac{1}{10}$ in. deep. Blue 'So' mark. *c.* 1780–90. *Author's Collection.*

88. A rare, deep shaped-edged Caughley dish, probably a BAKING DISH (see Page 29). 8$\frac{1}{2}$ in. long, 1$\frac{3}{4}$ in. deep. Impressed 'Salopian' mark. *c.* 1780–90. *Mrs R. J. Green Collection.*

IV. A selection of miniature or 'Toy' wares, hand painted in underglaze blue (see Page 24), shown with matching 'wasters' from the factory site. Oval dish $4\frac{1}{5}$ in. long. Blue 'S' marks. *c.* 1780–90. *Mrs M. Stewart-Browne, Miss N. Wilson and Author's Collection.*

89. A very rare Caughley chestnut BASKET (see Page 86), of a moulded form used also at Lowestoft and Worcester. A fragment of a matching pierced stand is shown in Plate 214. The hand-painted underglaze blue flowers on the cover are repeated inside the basket. 8 in. long, over handles. $5\frac{3}{4}$ in. high. Blue-painted 'S' mark. *c.* 1785. *Mrs N. Findlay Collection.*

90. A fine Caughley blue-printed BASKET of a shape made at Worcester and other factories, shown with unglazed 'wasters' and an over-fired fragment. Such baskets were made in several sizes (see Page 86). $8\frac{3}{4}$ in. long. Blue-printed 'C' mark and relief moulded 'IT' (see Page 10). *c.* 1780–5. *Godden of Worthing Ltd.*

91. Two Caughley circular BASKETS of a form made in several sizes, both at Caughley and at Worcester (see Page 86). Note the clear Caughley version of the 'Fisherman' pattern (see Pages 27 & 133). $5\frac{1}{4}$ and $4\frac{1}{4}$ in. in dia. Blue-printed 'S' mark on the smaller basket, shown here upside down. (The number is the Museum reference number.) *c.* 1780–5. *Victoria & Albert Museum (Crown Copyright).*

92. An extremely rare Caughley BOTTLE-STAND, decorated in underglaze blue in the Chantilly style (see Page 87). 11 in. long. Blue 'S' mark and incised initial 'H' (see Page 11). *c.* 1780–5. *Dr B. Watney Collection.*

93. An oval Caughley BUTTER TUREEN and cover (missing the oval stand) decorated with the blue-printed 'Fence' design. Similar tureens with this same design were also made at the Worcester and Lowestoft factories (see Pages 88 & 135). 5½ in. long. Blue-printed 'C' mark. *c.* 1785-90. *Godden of Worthing Ltd.*

94. Four, half-finished Caughley BUTTONS, and an unglazed stud found on the factory site. These would have been finished with gilding, added in some cases by Chamberlain of Worcester (see Page 88). Shown with a penny to indicate small size. *c.* 1790. *Author's Collection.*

95. A very rare moulded 'CHAMBER CANDLESTICK' bearing the Caughley version of the 'Fisherman' pattern (see Pages 29 & 88), shown here with an unglazed fragment of the moulded edge. $5\frac{5}{8}$ in. dia. Unmarked. *c.* 1780–5. *Godden of Worthing Ltd.*

96. A rare Caughley CAUDLE CUP, cover and stand, decorated with underglaze blue and overglaze gilding (see Page 88). $5\frac{3}{4}$ in. high. Unmarked. *c.* 1790–5. *Victoria & Albert Museum (Crown Copyright).*

97. A rare Caughley CAUDLE CUP, cover and stand, decorated in blue and gold (see Page 88). $4\frac{1}{4}$ in. high. Blue 'S' mark. *c.* 1790–5. *Messrs Christies.*

98. *Left.* A large CENTRE-DISH, from a dessert service, bearing the Caughley version of the 'Fisherman' pattern (see Pages 29 & 89). $12\frac{1}{4} \times 8\frac{3}{4}$ in. Impressed 'SALOPIAN' mark. *c.* 1775–85. *Godden of Worthing Ltd.*

Right. A deep, shaped-[d] CENTRE-DISH, from a des[sert] [s]ervice, a standard Caugh[ley fo]rm not made at Worcester [(see a]lso Colour Plate V, Plates [4 and 5 and Pages 29 & 89, and] [comp]are with Plate 13). $12\frac{1}{2}$ in. [long, 3]$\frac{3}{4}$ in. deep. Impressed ['SAL]OPIAN' mark. *c.* 1780–[5.] *Cronk Collection.*

100. *Left.* A slightly different view of the standard Caughley CENTRE-DISH (see Plate 99), in this case decorated with a blue and gold pattern of 'Dresden Flowers and border' type (see Page 89). $12\frac{1}{2}$ in. long. Blue 'S' mark. *c.* 1790–5. *Godden of Worthing Ltd.*

219

101. A Caughley CHOCOLATE CUP and saucer, bearing the blue-printed 'Temple' pattern (see Page 90). Compare with Worcester shape shown in Plate 272. Diameter of saucer 6 in. Blue 'Sx' marks. *c.* 1785-90. *Author's Collection.*

102. Caughley gilt CHOCOLATE CUP and saucer (see Page 90), the saucer turned to show moulded form. An unglazed factory 'waster' of a handle is also shown, and should be compared with the Worcester form of handle illustrated in Plate 273A. Cup 3 in. high. Unmarked. *c.* 1790-5. *Godden of Worthing Ltd.*

103. A graceful Caughley gilt COFFEE POT. Note the slightly enlarged return at the end of the handle (see Page 90) and shape of knob. $8\frac{3}{4}$ in. high. Unmarked. *c.* 1785–95. *Godden of Worthing Ltd.*

104. A fine, blue-printed Caughley COFFEE POT, with floral knob in the Worcester style. Note the enlarged return at the end of the handle (see Page 90). $9\frac{1}{4}$ in. high. Blue-printed 'C' mark. *c.* 1775–85. *Godden of Worthing Ltd.*

105. A fine and rare Caughley COFFEE POT bearing the blue-printed 'Pagoda' pattern (see Plate 18 and Page 90). Note the moulded, Chinese-style handle and spout, not found on Worcester examples. $9\frac{3}{4}$ in. high. Blue 'Sx' mark. *c.* 1780–5. *Author's Collection.*

106. A rare form of Caughley COFFEE POT, hand-painted in underglaze blue. $6\frac{3}{4}$ in. high. Blue 'S' mark. *c.* 1780–90. *Victoria & Albert Museum (Crown Copyright).*

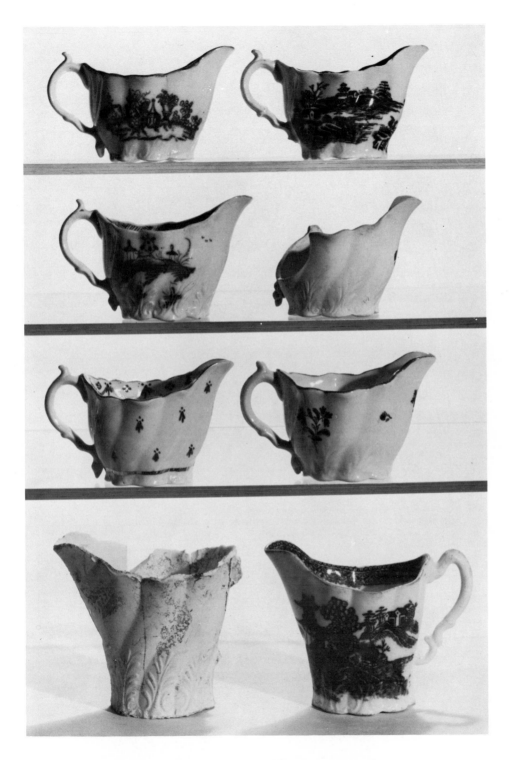

107. A selection of Caughley 'Chelsea-ewer' CREAM BOATS. The top six examples are 'low Chelsea-ewers' (see Page 91), the other is a rare, tall version, shown with an unglazed factory 'waster'. Several factories, including Worcester, made cream boats of this basic shape (see Page 136). Low ewers $2\frac{7}{10}$ in. high; tall $3\frac{2}{5}$ in. high. *c.* 1780–95. *Author's Collection.*

108. Caughley CREAM BOAT of a form originally known as 'Gadroon boats' (see Page 91). 4 in. long. Impressed star mark, see below. *c.* 1785–95. *Godden of Worthing Ltd.*

109. Unglazed Caughley factory 'waster', showing the base of a 'gadroon boat' (as Plate 108, above) turned to show a typical impressed mark often found on these attractive CREAM BOATS.

110. A very rare Caughley CREAM BOAT, originally called a 'dolphin ewer' (see Page 92). 4 in. long. Blue 'S' mark. *c.* 1785–90. *C. Staal Collection.*

111. A selection of Caughley CUSTARD CUPS (see Page 92).
Left: blue-printed 'Cottage' pattern (see Page 21), 'S' mark.
Centre: 'Willow-Nankeen' pattern (see Page 16), 'S' mark.
Right: hand-painted blue floral design, unmarked (see also
Plate 51). $3\frac{1}{10}$ in. high. *c.* 1780–95. *Author's Collection.*

112. Representative shapes from a Caughley DESSERT SERVICE
(see Page 92), finely gilt, perhaps by Chamberlains of Worcester. Ice-pail $10\frac{3}{4}$ in. high. Some pieces with impressed
'SALOPIAN' mark. *c.* 1785–90. *Godden of Worthing Ltd.*

113. Representative shapes from a fine Caughley DESSERT SERVICE (see Page 92). This gilding may have been added at the Caughley factory, as a completed fragment of a tureen stand was found on the Caughley site. Ice-pail $10\frac{1}{2}$ in. high. Some pieces with impressed 'Salopian' mark. *c.* 1785–95. *Godden of Worthing Ltd.*

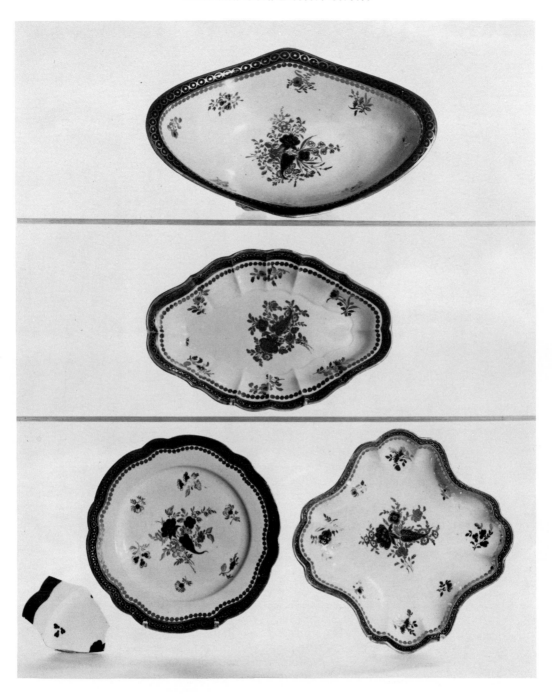

114. Representative pieces from a Caughley DESSERT SERVICE (see Page 92) decorated with underglaze blue and overglaze gold, a type of design known as 'Dresden Flowers and border'. The gilding was probably added by Chamberlains of Worcester, and their accounts list similar wares (see Page 61). The Caughley site yielded many fragments showing only the underglaze blue portions of these designs, see bottom left. Diameter of plate $8\frac{1}{4}$ in. Blue 'S' marks. *c.* 1785–95. *Godden of Worthing Ltd.*

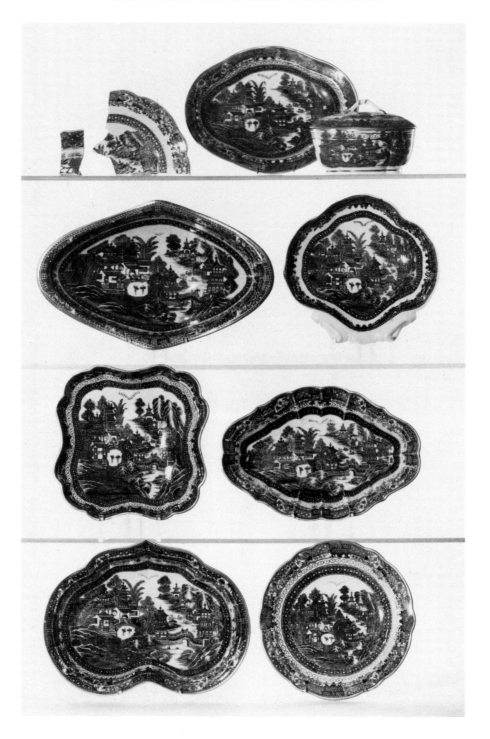

115. Representative pieces from a long Caughley DESSERT SER-
VICE bearing the underglaze blue-printed 'Full Nankin' pattern
(see Pages 58 & 93). They have added gilt inner border and
edging. Many fragments of this popular pattern were found on
the factory site, and the design was not employed at Worcester.
Diameter of plate 8¼ in. Some pieces bear impressed 'Salopian'
marks. *c.* 1785–95. *Godden of Worthing Ltd.*

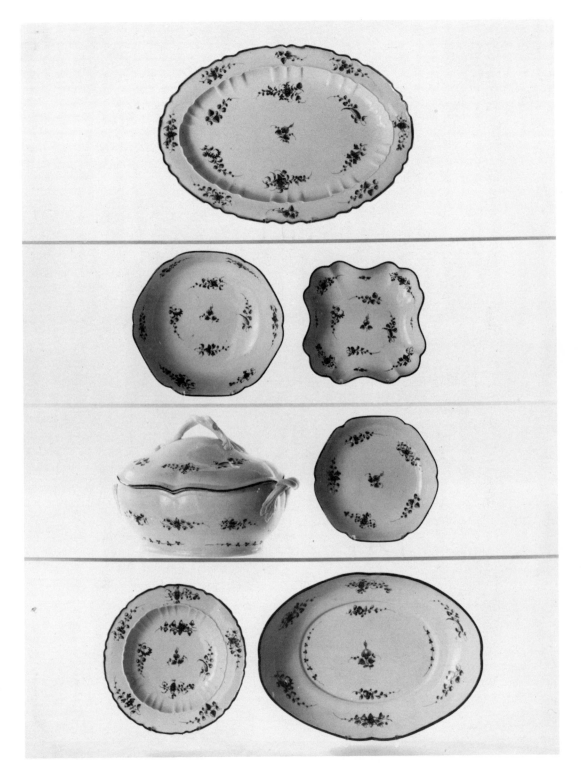

116. Representative pieces from a Caughley DINNER SERVICE (see Page 93), hand-painted in underglaze blue, note moulded large meat dish and plate. Large oval dish 16½ × 12 in. Blue 'S' mark and impressed 'Salopian' mark. *c.* 1785–95. *Godden of Worthing Ltd.*

117. Very large DINNER SERVICE DISH (made in various sizes, see Page 94) bearing the 'Full Nankin' underglaze blue-printed design (see Page 20). 17 × 13 in. *c.* 1785–90. *H. L. Lloyd Collection.*

118. A large, shaped-edged DINNER SERVICE DISH (made in various sizes) bearing the 'Full Nankin' underglaze blue-printed design (see Pages 20 & 94). 16½ × 12 in. *c.* 1785–90. *Author's Collection.*

119. Two Caughley EGG DRAIN-ERS with different handle forms (see Pages 31 & 95). Decorated with the blue-printed 'Fisher-man' design, and shown with unglazed factory 'wasters'. Dia-meter $3\frac{1}{10}$ in. Unmarked. *c.* 1785-99. *Author's Collection.*

Egg Drainers and Egg Cup

120. A rare and graceful Caughley EGG CUP (see Page 95), hand-painted in under-glaze blue, in the French style. $2\frac{1}{2}$ in. high. Blue 'S' mark. *c.* 1790-99. *Godden of Worthing Ltd.*

121. A rare Caughley EYE BATH bearing portions of the 'Fisher-man' design (see Pages 32 & 96), shown with two matching factory 'wasters'. 2 in. high. Unmarked. *c.* 1785–95. *Author's Collection.*

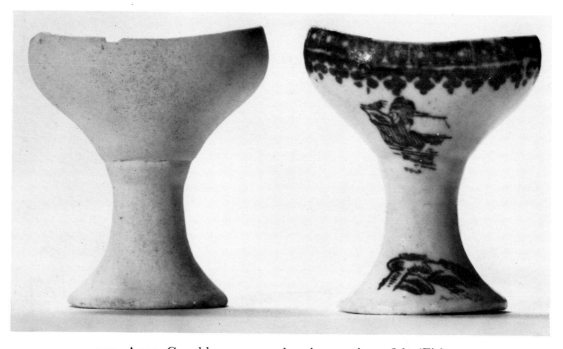

122. A rare Caughley EYE BATH bearing portions of the 'Fisher-man' design (see Pages 32 & 96), shown with an unglazed 'Waster' found on the Caughley site. $1\frac{9}{10}$ in. high. Unmarked. *c.* 1785–90. *Author's Collection.*

123. A rare and finely potted Caughley FINGER BOWL bearing underglaze blue fruit prints (see Page 96). 2½ in. high. Blue-printed 'C' mark. *c.* 1780–5. *Author's Collection.*

. A very rare Caughley ⠀ᴋ (see Page 96), hand-⠀nted in underglaze blue, ⠀ed 1777. 6 in. high. Un-⠀ked. *S. Spero Collection.*

125. A Caughley ICE-PAIL, liner and cover, decorated with 'Dresden flowers and border' in underglaze blue and overglaze gilding (see Page 97). Total height $10\frac{3}{4}$ in. Blue 'S' mark. *c.* 1785-90. *Godden of Worthing Ltd.*

126. A finely gilt Caughle ICE-PAIL, liner (shown correct placed in the pail) and cove from the dessert service show in Plate 113. The side handl are a later variation of tho shown above and this late for was also employed by Joh Rose after 1799 (see Page 97 Total height $10\frac{3}{4}$ in. Unmarke *c.* 1785-95. *Godden of Worthi Ltd.*

127. A very rare Caughley INK-POT with detachable well, shown with two pieces found on the factory site (see Page 97). 3 in. high. *c.* 1780–90. *S. Spero Collection.*

Ink-Wells

128. A rare Caughley INK-POT, decorated with the blue-printed 'Bell toy' pattern (see Pages 25 & 97). Diameter at base 4 in. *c.* 1775–85. *Castle Museum, Norwich.*

129. An extremely rare Caughley small JARDINIÈRE, modelled after a French original (see Page 97) and painted in Chantilly style, in underglaze blue. 4¾ in. high. Blue 'S' mark. *c.* 1780–90. *Author's Collection.*

130. Unglazed Caughley 'waster' showing the Royal Arms impressed, under the base of cabbage-leaf jugs. *D. Holgate Collection.*

131. A fine specimen of the standard Caughley form of moulded cabbage-leaf JUG which was made in several different sizes and enriched with many patterns (see Colour Plate II and Plates 67–71). This basic form of jug was made at several factories, including Worcester (see Plates 277–80 and Pages 98 & 138). $9\frac{1}{8}$ in. high. Blue cross mark (see Page 8). *c.* 1785. *D. Roberts Collection.*

132. *Right.* An extremely rare form of relief-moulded Caughley mask-head JUG, with underglaze blue panels (see Page 98). $5\frac{1}{4}$ in. high. Blue 'S' mark. *c.* 1775–80. *Victoria & Albert Museum (Crown Copyright).*

133. *Below left.* An extremely rare Caughley puzzle JUG, inscribed, dated and decorated in underglaze blue (see Page 98). $7\frac{9}{16}$ in. high. Blue, hand-painted open crescent, or 'C' mark (see Page 9). 1778. *Dr B. Watney Collection.*

134. *Below right.* A Caughley mask-head JUG (see also Plates 281–2 and Pages 98 & 139). Inscribed and dated in underglaze blue and with blue-printed floral sprays, etc. $7\frac{3}{8}$ in. high. 1792. *Dr B. Watney Collection.*

135. Front view of Caughley mask-head JUG decorated with underglaze blue rose print (see Plate 45). 6¾ in. high. Blue-printed 'S' mark. *c.* 1780–90. *J. Cronk Collection.*

136. Side view of Caughley mask-head JUG bearing Caughley version of the popular blue-printed 'Fisherman' pattern (see Pages 27, 32, 131 & 139). Note pronounced return or 'kick' at bottom of handle. 7 in. high. *c.* 1780–90. *D. Roberts Collection.*

137. Extremely rare Caughley relief-moulded LEAF DISH bearing the Caughley version of the popular blue-printed 'Fisherman' pattern (see Pages 32 & 99). Compare shape and moulding with the relatively common Worcester form of leaf dish as shown in Plate 283. $7\frac{3}{4}$ in. high. *c.* 1780-90. *Author's Collection.*

138. Caughley small 'pickle' LEAF DISH decorated with the 'Fisherman' pattern (see Pages 32 & 99), shown with unglazed 'wasters' from the factory site. Compare with Plate 285. $4\frac{1}{4}$ in. high (several different sizes were made). *c.* 1780-95. *Author's Collection.*

139. Caughley LEAF DISH bearing a rare underglaze blue-printed design. 4¾ in. high. *c.* 1785-95. *Godden of Worthing Ltd.*

140. Caughley small LEAF DISH decorated with the 'Fisherman' pattern (see Pages 33, 99 & 140). Shown with original plaster mould and unglazed fragments found on the factory site. 3½ × 2½ in. (several different sizes were made). *c.* 1785-95. *Author's Collection.*

141. Caughley sparrow-beak MILK JUG bearing the attractive bird print (see Pages 39, 99 & 140). See also Plate 39. $3\frac{7}{10}$ in. high. Blue-printed 'C' mark. *c.* 1775–85. *Godden of Worthing Ltd.*

142. Rare Caughley moulded MILK JUG; note the Chinese-style handle (see Page 99). Decorated with the blue-printed 'Pagoda' design (see Plates 18 & 105 and Page 18). $4\frac{1}{5}$ in. high. Blue-printed 'S' mark. *c.* 1780–5. *Godden of Worthing Ltd.*

143. A selection of standard Caughley MILK JUG shapes (see Pages 99 & 100). The very small jug on the centre shelf is from a child's toy teaset. They bear blue 'S' and 'C' marks. The large jug, top left, is 5½ in. high. *c.* 1775–95. *Godden of Worthing Ltd.*

144. A rare fluted Caughley MILK JUG bearing a blue-printed carnation pattern. $3\frac{7}{8}$ in. high. Blue 'S' mark. *c.* 1780–5. *Dr B. Watney Collection*.

145. An attractive Caughley fluted MILK JUG decorated with underglaze blue and overglaze gilding (see Page 100). Jugs of this shape would have been issued with teasets as shown in Plate 196. $2\frac{9}{10}$ in. high. *c.* 1785–95. *Godden of Worthing Ltd*.

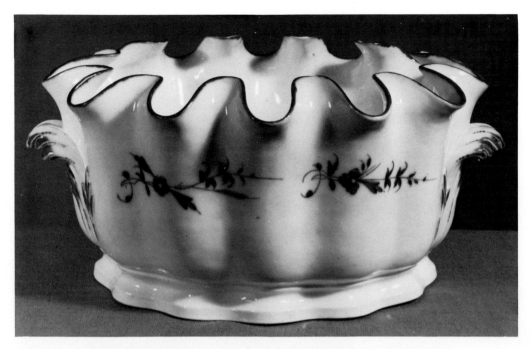

146. An extremely rare Caughley 'Monteith' or 'Verrière' (for cooling wine glasses, see Page 100) decorated in underglaze blue in the French style, as the jardinière shown in Plate 129. 12 in. long. Blue 'S' mark and incised 'H' mark (see Pages 8 & 11). *c.* 1780–90. *Victoria & Albert Museum (Crown Copyright).*

147. A pair of Caughley MUGS of a very rare form (see Page 100). Decorated with the blue-printed 'Fisherman' pattern but with hand-painted initials under the handles. 4 in. high. Blue 'S' marks. *c.* 1780–5. *Messrs Sotheby & Co.*

148. A rare Caughley bell-shaped MUG bearing the 'Fisherman' pattern (see Page 100). 3¾ in. high. Blue-printed 'S' mark. *c.* 1775–80. *Victoria & Albert Museum* (*Crown Copyright*).

149. A Caughley MUG, of standard cylindrical shape, bearing the 'bell toy' blue-printed design (see Pages 25 & 100). Inscribed and dated. 4½ in. high. Blue-printed 'C' mark. 1776. *Victoria & Albert Museum* (*Crown Copyright*).

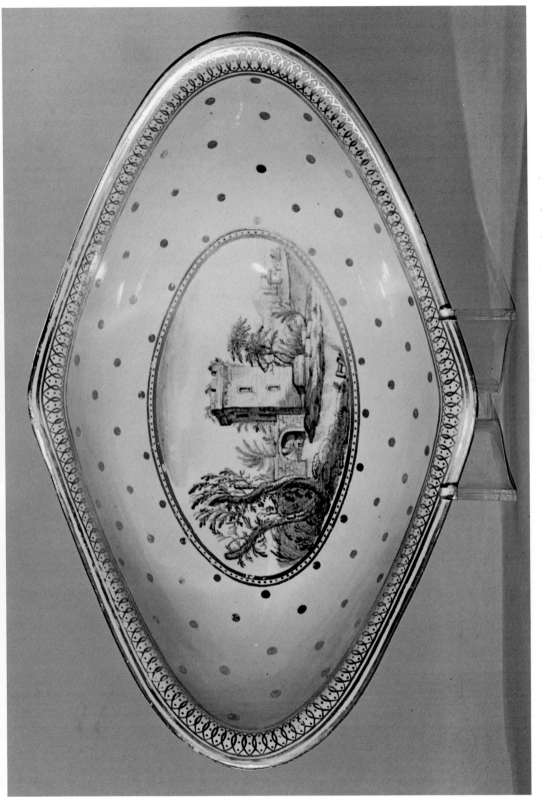

V. A fine centre dish from a dessert service, attractively painted in a bright underglaze blue with gilt enrichments (see Page 39). 12¼ in. long. Impressed mark 'SALOPIAN'. *c.* 1785–90. *Godden of Worthing Ltd.*

150. A small Caughley MUG, bearing a clear impression of one of the fruit prints. $3\frac{2}{5}$ in. high. Printed spray of flowers under base, in 'doodle' style. *c.* 1775–80. *Godden of Worthing Ltd.*

151. Caughley MUG, with characteristic handle, bearing a blue print of the Ironbridge (see Plate 36 and Pages 38 & 101). Inscribed 'The Gift of Mrs. Lee, 25 July. 1794'. $4\frac{11}{16}$ in. high. 1794. *Dr B. Watney Collection.*

152. Three Caughley MUGS (note the characteristic handle), bearing the blue-printed 'Fisherman' design (see Pages 33 & 101). $5\frac{1}{4}$ and $3\frac{1}{4}$ in. high. Blue-printed 'S' marks. *c.* 1785–95. *Godden of Worthing Ltd.*

153. Caughley MUG, with rare moulded Chinese-style handle form (see Page 101). Bearing underglaze blue floral prints. 5¾ in. high. *c.* 1780–90. *Godden of Worthing Ltd.*

154. A rare Caughley MUG, with unusual scroll handle bearing on the front the blue-printed pine-cone design. 5½ in. high. *c.* 1780–90. *Victoria & Albert Museum (Crown Copyright).*

155. A fine Caughley MUG of wide, low form (see Page 101) bearing the blue-printed 'Birds' design. Initialled and dated 1783. Diameter 4¼ in. and 3⅞ in. high. 1783. *Mrs P. G. Ferriday Collection.*

VI. Representative pieces from a Caughley tea service bearing
the blue-printed Pagoda design (see Page 18). The teapot shape
is very similar to the Chinese pot shown in Plate 11. Most pieces
of this set have the gilder's initial 'M' inside the footrim but the
teapot and stand have the name 'Morris' in full (see Page 80).
This set is shown with matching unglazed 'wasters' from the
Caughley factory site. Diameter of plate $8\frac{1}{2}$ in. Underglaze blue
'S', 'Sx' and 'So' marks. c. 1780-90. *Godden of Worthing Ltd.*

156. Caughley MUSTARD POT bearing blue-printed fence design (see also Plate 19 and Pages 19 & 101). $3\frac{3}{4}$ in. high. Blue-printed 'C' mark. *c.* 1780–5. *Godden of Worthing Ltd.*

157. A very rare Caughley dry-MUSTARD POT bearing the rare blue-printed 'Travellers' design (see Pages 38 & 101). $3\frac{1}{2}$ in. high. Blue-printed 'S' mark. *c.* 1780–5. *Messrs Newman & Newman (Antiques) Ltd.*

158. A Caughley shaped-edged PLATE of a standard dessert service shape (see Pages 33 & 102), bearing the Caughley version of the 'Fisherman' design. 6⅗ in. dia. Blue-printed 'S' mark. *c.* 1780–5. *Godden of Worthing Ltd.*

159. A rare and attractive Caughley moulded PLATE shape (see Page 102). 8¼ in. dia. Blue pressed 'Salopian' and blue-printed 'S' marks. *c.* 1785–90. *J. Cronk Collection.*

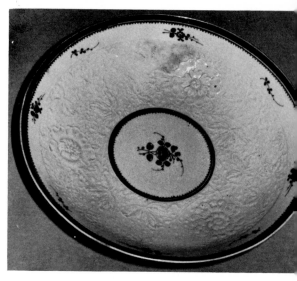

160. A rare Caughley PLATE, with basket moulded French-style edge (see Page 102). 8¼ in. dia. Impressed 'Salopian' and blue-printed 'S' marks. *c.* 1785–90. *J. Cronk Collection.*

161. A very rare Caughley PLATE, with finely moulded Worcester-style floral design (see Page 102). 8¼ in. dia. Blue 'S' mark. *c.* 1775–85. *Dr B. Watney Collection.*

162. Two blue-printed Caughley POUNCE-POTS (see Page 103). The left example bears the 'bell toy' pattern (Page 25) and the right example matches in design the ink pot shown in Plate 127. $3\frac{1}{4}$ and $4\frac{1}{10}$ in. high. *c.* 1780–90. *Author's Collection.*

163. Another shape of rare POUNCE-POT (see Page 103). Shown with similar fragment of a different sized pounce-pot from the Caughley site. $3\frac{1}{2}$ in. high. *c.* 1780–90. *F. Baxendale, Esq. (Chichester Antiques, China Section).*

164. A rare Caughley moulded RADDISH-DISH. Hand-painted with Chinese-styled design (see Pages 23 & 164), shown with unglazed fragment of handle from the factory site. $11\frac{1}{2}$ in. long. Blue-painted 'x' mark. *c.* 1785–90. *Godden of Worthing Ltd.*

165. A rare form of Caughley spittoon or 'SAFFER-POT' (see pages 103 & 144). Decorated with blue fruit and floral prints. $4\frac{1}{4}$ in. high. Blue-printed 'S' mark. *c.* 1780–90. *Victoria & Albert Museum (Crown Copyright).*

166. Caughley spittoon or 'SAFFER-POT' (see Page 103) of standard form. $3\frac{9}{10}$ in. Blue-printed 'S' mark. *c.* 1780–90. *Author's Collection.*

167. A rare Caughley moulded SALAD BOWL similar in general form to a Worcester shape (see Plate 291 and Pages 104 & 142). $10\frac{1}{4}$ in. dia. *c.* 1780–5. *Godden of Worthing Ltd.*

168. A rare Caughley SALAD BOWL (see Pages 34 & 104), decorated with the popular 'Fisherman' pattern. $3\frac{3}{4}$ in. high. Blue-printed 'S' mark. *c.* 1785–90. *J. Riley Collection.*

169. A rare Caughley shallow SALAD BOWL, with shaped edge (see Pages 34 & 169), decorated with the 'Fisherman' pattern. 2¼ in. high. Impressed 'Salopian' mark and also blue-printed 'S' mark. *c.* 1785–90. *Author's Collection.*

170. A rare large-sized, fluted Caughley SALAD BOWL (see Page 104). Painted in underglaze blue in the French style (see Page 45). 10½ in. dia. *c.* 1785–95. *Godden of Worthing Ltd.*

171. Four segment dishes from a Caughley SANDWICH SET (see Page 105) bearing the blue-printed 'Full Nankin' design (see Page 20). Each dish $13\frac{1}{2}$ × $7\frac{1}{2}$ in. Diameter of assembled set $20\frac{1}{2}$ in. One with impressed 'Salopian' mark. *c.* 1780–90. *Author's Collection.*

172. Caughley moulded SAUCE-BOAT (see Page 105) bearing the blue 'Fisherman' pattern and shown with an unglazed 'waster' from the Caughley site. $7\frac{1}{2}$ in. long (all sauce-boats were made in various sizes). Blue-printed 'S' mark. *c.* 1780–5. *Godden of Worthing Ltd.*

173. Caughley moulded SAUCE-BOAT (see Pages 34 & 105) showing reverse side of 'Fisherman' design, shown with two unglazed factory 'wasters'. 7 in. long. *c.* 1785-90. *Godden of Worthing Ltd.*

174. Caughley moulded SAUCE-BOAT, with French-style basket border (see Page 105) shown with part of the original mould found on the factory site. 8 in. long. *c.* 1785-90. *Author's Collection.*

175. A pair of rare Caughley blue-printed SAUCE-BOATS show-ing plan and elevation (see Page 105). $5\frac{9}{10}$ in. high. Blue-printed 'C' mark. *c.* 1780–90. *Godden of Worthing Ltd.*

176. A Caughley moulded SAUCE-BOAT (with factory 'waster') of a basic form also used at Derby, Lowestoft and Worcester (see Page 143). Blue-printed 'Full Nankin' pattern (see Page 20). $8\frac{1}{2}$ in. long. *c.* 1785–90. *Author's Collection.*

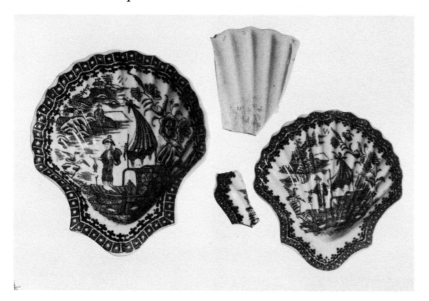

177. Two Caughley moulde
SHELL-SHAPED DISHES of diffe
ent sizes (see Page 106) show
with factory 'wasters'. 4¼ an
5½ in. long. *c.* 1785-95. *Author*
Collection.

178. A rare Caughley small
SPOON-like object (see Page 106)
bearing blue-printed pattern.
4⅛ in. long. *c.* 1780-90. *Dr B.*
Watney Collection.

179. A rare Caughley sugar or
cream SPOON, or ladle originally
sold with tureens in dessert
services (see Page 106). Decorated with the 'Fisherman' design, shown with two factory
'wasters'. 6½ in. long. *c.* 1780-
90. *Author's Collection.*

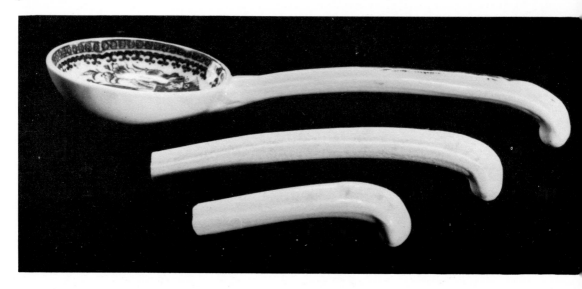

180. A very rare form of Caughley small tray, perhaps a SPOON-TRAY from a teaset (see Page 106), with fine gilt decoration. 6 in. long. Impressed 'Salopian' mark. *c.* 1785–95. *Victoria & Albert Museum (Crown Copyright).*

181. Selection of Caughley SPOON-TRAYS (see Page 106) shown with factory 'wasters', illustrating the two standard shapes. See also Plate 296. Top tray $6\frac{1}{2} \times 3\frac{3}{4}$ in. *c.* 1785–95. *Author's Collection.*

182. A Caughley moulded SUCRIER, or sugar bowl, from a teaset of standard form (see Plate 195 and Page 107). 4¼ in. high. *c.* 1785–90. *Godden of Worthing Ltd.*

183. An attractively gilt Caughley SUCRIER of moulded fluted form (see Page 107) as would accompany teaware shapes shown in Colour Plate VII. 4¼ in. high. *c.* 1785–90. *Godden of Worthing Ltd.*

184. Two Caughley 'patty-pans' or TART-PANS, of different sizes, decorated with the 'Fisherman' pattern (see Pages 35 & 107). $3\frac{1}{2}$ and $4\frac{1}{2}$ in. dia. Blue-printed 'Sx' marks. *c.* 1780–90. *Godden of Worthing Ltd.*

185. *Above.* Interior and underside of two Caughley TART-PANS, decorated with 'fruit and wreath' blue-printed designs (see Pages 42 & 107). 4 in. dia. Blue-printed 'C' mark. *c.* 1780–90. *Author's Collection.*

186. *Below.* A small Caughley TASTER-like object, bearing the 'Fisherman' pattern, shown with unglazed factory 'waster' and penny to indicate size (see Pages 35 & 107). Diameter of bowl 2 in. *c.* 1785–90. *Author's Collection.*

187. A Caughley handleless TEA-BOWL, showing reverse side of 'bell-toy' printed pattern (see Page 25). 1¾ in. high. *c.* 1780–90. *Author's Collection.*

188. A Caughley moulded TEA-BOWL and saucer, with thickened or reinforced edge, as shown in fragment of saucer (see Page 108). Blue-printed 'Temple' pattern (see Page 17). Saucer 5⅔ in. dia. Blue-printed 'S' mark. *c.* 1780–5. *Godden of Worthing Ltd.*

189. A selection of Caughley TEA CANISTERS (see Page 108), showing
typical blue-printed patterns and shapes (compare with Worcester
forms shown in Plates 240, 241, 261 & 313). $4\frac{1}{4}$ to $4\frac{3}{4}$ in. high. Blue
'S' or 'C' marks. *c.* 1775–90. *Godden of Worthing Ltd.*

190. A superb Caughley TEA CANISTER with flower knob (see Page 108) decorated in underglaze blue and overglaze gilding. $4\frac{3}{8}$ in. high. Blue 'S' mark. *c.* 1790. *Victoria & Albert Museum (Crown Copyright)*.

191. A Caughley gilt TEA CUP AND SAUCER with rare moulded handle shape (see Page 108). Cup $2\frac{1}{5}$ in. high. *c.* 1785–95. *Godden of Worthing Ltd.*

192. A fluted Caughley TEA CUP AND SAUCER with Caughley version of indented handle (compare with Plate 274 and see Page 108) decorated with underglaze blue border and added gilding. Cup 2 in. high. Blue 'S' mark and gilder's 'H' initial mark inside footrim. *c.* 1785–95. *J. Cronk Collection.*

193. A Caughley child's toy TEA SERVICE decorated with the blue-printed 'Fisherman' pattern (see Pages 36 & 109) shown with 'wasters' found on the factory site. Teapot $2\frac{9}{10}$ in. high. Blue-printed 'S' marks. *c.* 1780-90. *Author's Collection.*

194. A Caughley toy TEA SERVICE (and ewer) hand-painted in underglaze blue (see also Colour Plate IV and Pages 24 & 109). Several different objects were painted with this attractive design. Teapot 3 in. high. Blue 'S' marks. *c.* 1785-95. *Messrs Christies.*

195. Representative pieces from a Caughley moulded TEA SERVICE, blue-printed 'Pagoda' design (see Page 18) with gilt edges, etc. Diameter of large bread plate 8¼ in. Blue 'S' marks. *c.* 1785. *Godden of Worthing Ltd.*

196. Representative pieces of a Caughley moulded TEA SERVICE with
fluted outline (see Pages 108-9) decorated with underglaze blue
flowers and borders and finished with overglaze gilding (see also
Colour Plate VII). Teapot 6½ in. high. Blue 'S' marks. *c.* 1785-95.
Godden of Worthing Ltd.

197. An early Caughley TEA-POT printed in underglaze blue with cut fruit design (see Plates 42B & 44 and Page 42). 5¼ in. high. Blue-printed 'S' mark. *c.* 1775–80. *Author's Collection.*

198. A Caughley moulded TEAPOT. Note the Chinese-styled spout and handle (see Plates 11 & 74 and Pages 14 & 110). Attractively decorated with gilding. 5¾ in. high. *c.* 1785–90. *Godden of Worthing Ltd.*

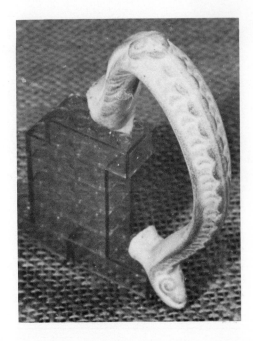

199. Unglazed fragment of a Caughley moulded teapot handle, found on the site. Part of a Chinese handle of the same form was also found and the basic shape occurs on several Caughley shapes (see Plates 9, 11 & 74). *D. Holgate Collection.*

200. An extremely rare shape of Caughley TEAPOT, painted in bright underglaze blue and enriched with gilding (see Page 110). 5¼ in. high. Blue 'S' mark. *c.* 1785-95. *Author's Collection.*

201. A Caughley fluted TEAPOT, of standard form (see Page 110) as would be found with the teawares shown in Plate 196. Compare with the Worcester version shown in Plates 308-11. 5¼ in. high. *c.* 1785-95. *Godden of Worthing Ltd.*

202. An extremely rare oval TEAPOT decorated in underglaze blue with gilding, shown with matching fragments from the site. A transitional piece incorporating an earlier design and spout (see Plates 196 & 201). 10 in. long. *c.* 1795-1800. *Author's Collection.*

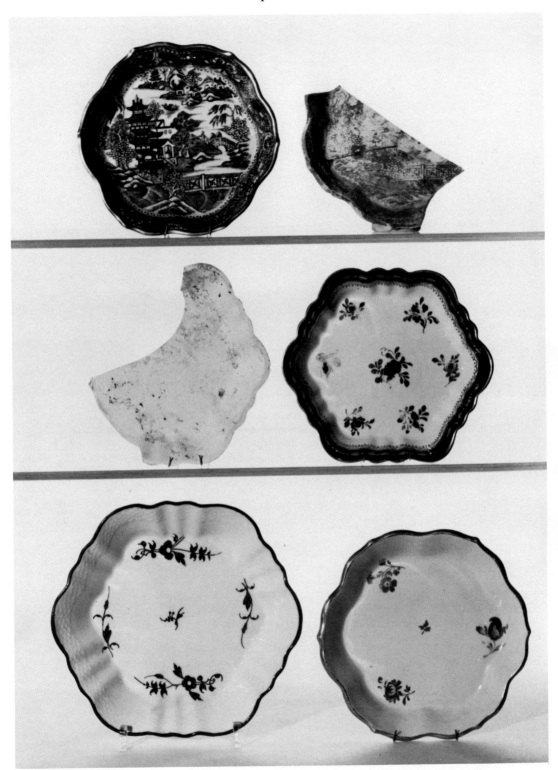

203. A selection of Caughley TEAPOT STANDS, seen with factory 'wasters' showing the two standard shapes (with a rare basket bordered variation, bottom left). Compare with Worcester form (see Plate 312 and Pages 110 & 146). $5\frac{9}{10}$ in. to $6\frac{9}{10}$ in. dia. Blue-painted specimens have 'S' marks. *c.* 1775–95. *Godden of Worthing Ltd.*

204. Caughley large TURE[EN] and cover, from the serv[ice] shown in Plate 116 with mat[ch]ing unglazed 'wasters' from [the] site, also a fragment of [a] superbly-moulded tureen cov[er] (see Page 111). Tureen $13\frac{1}{2}$[in] long. Blue 'S' mark. *c.* 1785-9[0]. *Author's Collection.*

205. An extremely rare mou[ld]ed Caughley TUREEN from [a] dessert service, decorated w[ith] the blue-printed 'Full Nank[in]' pattern (see Page 112). $5\frac{7}{8}$[in] long. *c.* 1780-90. *Victoria [&] Albert Museum (Crown Copyrigh[t)].*

206. An extremely rare Caughley TUREEN from a dessert service (see Page 112) decorated with an intricate blue and gold design. 6¾ in. long. Impressed 'Salopian' mark. *c.* 1785–90. *Victoria & Albert Museum (Crown Copyright)*.

207. The standard shape of Caughley cream or sugar TUREEN (and ladle) as found, in pairs, in dessert services (see Page 112). Decorated with 'Dresden flowers and border' pattern (see Plates 96 & 114 and Pages 61 & 64). 5¾ in. long. Blue 'S' mark. *c.* 1785–95. *Godden of Worthing Ltd.*

208. A rare Caughley beaker-VASE, probably from a set of five, or three (see Page 113), decorated with underglaze blue fruit designs and cell border. The overlap in transferring the border can be seen in the centre of the lower border. 4¾ in. high. Blue-printed 'C' mark. *c.* 1785-90. *Author's Collection.*

209. A Caughley WATER-EWER (see Page 113), decorated with the blue-printed 'Fisherman' design (see Chapter III). A large bowl would have originally been sold with ewers of this shape. 10½ in. high. *c.* 1780–90. *J. Cronk Collection*.

210. A Caughley WATER-JUG AND BASIN, decorated with blue-printed floral and pine-cone designs (see Page 113). Jug 9¾ in. high. Blue-printed 'C' marks. *c.* 1785-95.

211. *Right.* Here the water-jug and basin are shown on an antique mahogany stand. Once the bowl had been filled with hot water from the jug, the jug was placed in the well shown on the bottom shelf. Very few 18th-century porcelain jugs and basins have remained intact. *Godden of Worthing Ltd.*

Caughley Site Fragments

212. *Left*. Double-handled sauce-boat in unglazed state, found on the Caughley site (see Page 105). $7\frac{1}{2}$ in. long.

213. *Below*. An unglazed handle (perhaps for a knife or fork) found on the factory site, with two further glazed 'wasters' (see Page 98). Complete handle $3\frac{3}{4}$ in. long. *D. Holgate Collection.*

214. *Below*. Unglazed 'wasters' of forms not yet identified. *Top*, left to right: turned collar-like fragment, perhaps part of a vase; base of small vase-like object; simple handle to a spoon, with underglaze blue-printed scroll design; scroll end to unknown ornamental object. *Bottom row:* fragment of moulded jug or bowl showing part of handle near top; very finely moulded handle similar to those found on mustard pots (see Plate 156); fragment of a thick, welled object such as a pen, or brush, tray showing unglazed blue-line edge and part of printed flower; moulded and pierced fragment probably to stand of chestnut basket, compare design with Plate 89. Handle 2 in. high. *Author's Collection.*

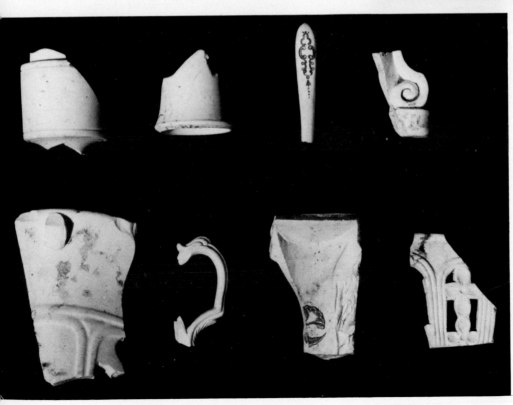

215. Standard shape of Caughley moulded cabbage-leaf jug, but made in the hard-paste body introduced by John Rose of Coalport, or by Thomas Turner, in the last years of the 18th century (see Chapter VIII). 8 in. high. *c.* 1798–1802. *Victoria & Albert Museum (Crown Copyright).*

216. John Rose variation of the Caughley 'Chelsea-ewer' (see Plates 107 and Page 115) in the new hard-paste body, with matching fragment from the Caughley site. 4⅕ in. long. *c.* 1798–1805. *Author's Collection.*

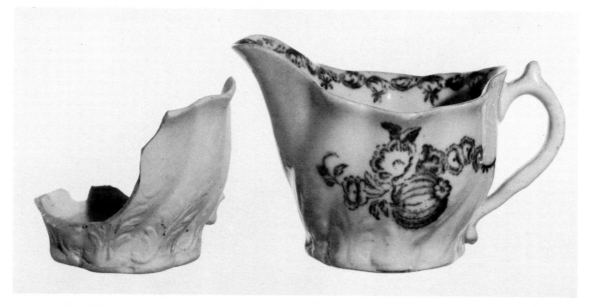

217. Blue-printed and gilt tea service with matching fragments found on the Caughley site, but made under the post-1799 management of the Coalport partners (see Page 115). Note the new teapot, sugar bowl and creamer shapes. The underglaze blue is lighter and brighter than the standard Caughley tint, owing to the new hard-paste porcelain. This printed pattern does not occur on true, pre-1799 Caughley wares. *Godden of Worthing Ltd.*

218. 19th-century Coalport bone-china beaker bearing blue-printed designs taken from the original Caughley engraved copper-plates. Marked with the OPEN crescent mark, NOT the shaded crescent as found on Worcester porcelains (see Pages 9 & 116). *J. Cronk Collection.*

219. The reverse side of the above Coalport beaker showing former Caughley blue-printed design. $3\frac{1}{2}$ in. high. OPEN crescent mark. *c.* 1840–50. *J. Cronk Collection.*

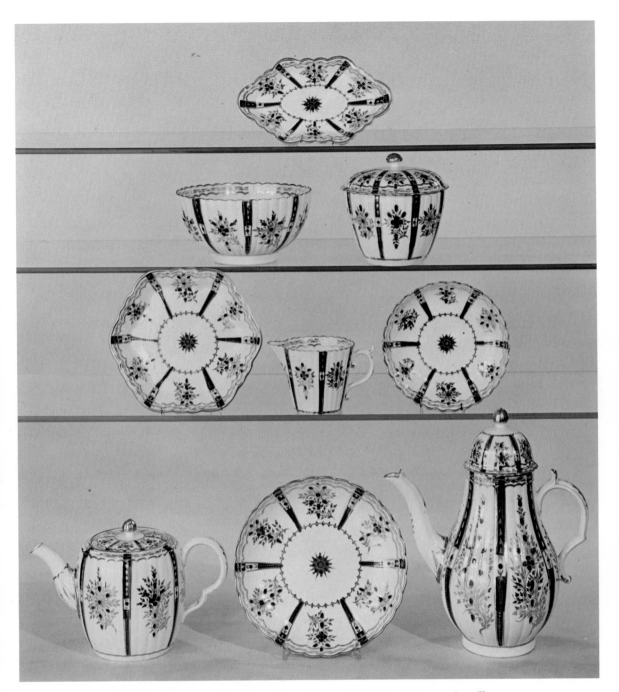

VII. An attractive Caughley blue and gilt part tea and coffee service (see Page 73), including a rare coffee pot which is 10¼ in. high. Underglaze blue 'S' marks. *c.* 1785-90. *Godden of Worthing Ltd.*

220. Coalport bone-china mug bearing the blue-printed, so-called pine-cone design taken from one of the Caughley copper-plates acquired by the Coalport management in 1799 (see Plate 41, page 41 and Chapter VIII). Blue-printed 'C' mark, not the shaded Worcester crescent (see Page 8). *c.* 1840–60. *Author's Collection.*

221. Coalport bone-china small vase bearing prints taken from original Caughley copper-plates, retained up to very recent times (see Plate 43). 5¼ in. high. Blue-printed 'C' mark, not the shaded Worcester crescent (see Page 8). *c.* 1840–60. *Author's Collection.*

222. Sample page from the Chamberlain account books, which list undecorated, partly decorated with underglaze blue, and blue-printed porcelains sent down river from Caughley to Worcester. This page of July 1789 lists standard blue-printed designs (see Chapter V). *Plates 222–5, Worcester Royal Porcelain Co. Ltd.*

223. Continuation page showing blue-printed and white, undecorated Caughley porcelain received by Chamberlain (see Chapter V). The pattern 'P Boat' refers to Pleasure Boat or, as it is known today, the 'Fisherman' pattern (see Chapter III).

VIII. A fine Caughley cabbage-leaf jug with underglaze blue
top and bottom borders (see Page 57). The overglaze enamel
decoration added at Chamberlain's decorating establishment
at Worcester (see Chapter V and Page 76). 8¾ in. high. Underglaze blue 'S' mark. *c.* 1785–90. *Victoria & Albert Museum* (*Crown
Copyright*)

224. Page from Chamberlains' account book of January 1789 listing undecorated Caughley 'second' (or slightly faulty articles, see Pages 62–3) goods received from Thomas Turner. Such white porcelains would have been decorated by Chamberlains' staff (see Chapter V).

225. Further page from the Chamberlain account book, showing Thomas Turner's Caughley porcelain received by Chamberlains in January 1789. The 'Dutch Jugs' listed in various sizes and patterns are the moulded, cabbage-leaf jugs, as shown in Colour Plate II.

226. Selection of blue-printed patterns of a type made both at Caughley and at Worcester. These factory 'wasters' are from the WORCESTER site. Note the line-shaded border to 'Fisherman' pattern, top left (see Page 131) and the shaded crescent mark, 'A', as found on Worcester porcelains, NOT on Caughley examples (see Pages 9 & 125). *Plates 226-37, Worcester Royal Porcelain Co. Ltd.*

227. Two unglazed bases to cups or tea bowls found on the WORCESTER site, illustrating the circular marks left by the 'turners'. These manufacturing signs are often cited as an indication of Caughley origin although they occur on several different makes.

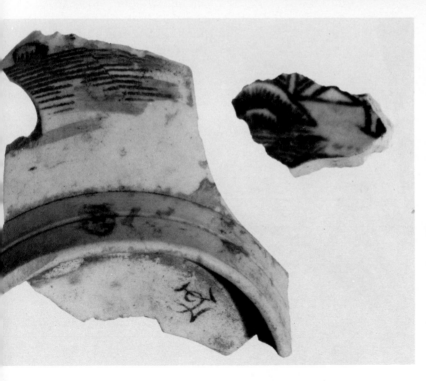

228. An unglazed WORCESTER factory 'waster' showing disguised numeral mark, and also hand-applied washes of light blue (see Page 122). The small fragment also shows this wash of light blue, not found on Caughley porcelain but commonly applied to late Worcester blue-printed designs bearing the numeral marks.

229. Detail of CAUGHLEY version of the 'Fisherman' or 'Pleasure Boat' design. Note especially the straight fishing line 'A', and the short, fat fish held on the line by a tall, thin man 'B' (see Pages 27 & 131).

230. Detail of WORCESTER version of the 'Fisherman' design. Compare this with Plate 229 above, and note the loose wavy line 'A', and the long, slender fish 'B' (see also Plates 233-4 and Page 131).

231. A badly mis-shapen, over-fired fragment of a bowl, showing traces of the 'Fisherman' print, found on the Worcester factory site and obviously made and fired there.

232. Two unglazed fragments of 'Fisherman' pattern saucers showing the differences in the inner border always found with this popular design. The top fragment, from the WORCESTER site, shows line-shading 'A', while the larger fragment, from the CAUGHLEY site, shows both the short, fat fish and the solid inner border 'B'.

233. Large WORCESTER bowl, bearing the popular blue-printed 'Fisherman' pattern, with rare fancy floral festoon border, marked with disguised numeral mark '7'. Shown with un-glazed WORCESTER fragment of matching border, including the line-shaded 'fleur de ly' border 'A'. Note also the wavy fishing line and long slender fish (see Page 131). Diameter of bowl $11\frac{1}{5}$ in. *c.* 1775–80.

234. Representative parts of a WORCESTER tea service, decorated with the Worcester version of the 'Fisherman' or 'Pleasure Boat' pattern (see Page 131). The wavy, loose fishing line can be seen and also the long slender fish. The prints are applied to Worcester shapes, not Caughley porcelain. *c.* 1770–80. *Godden of Worthing Ltd.*

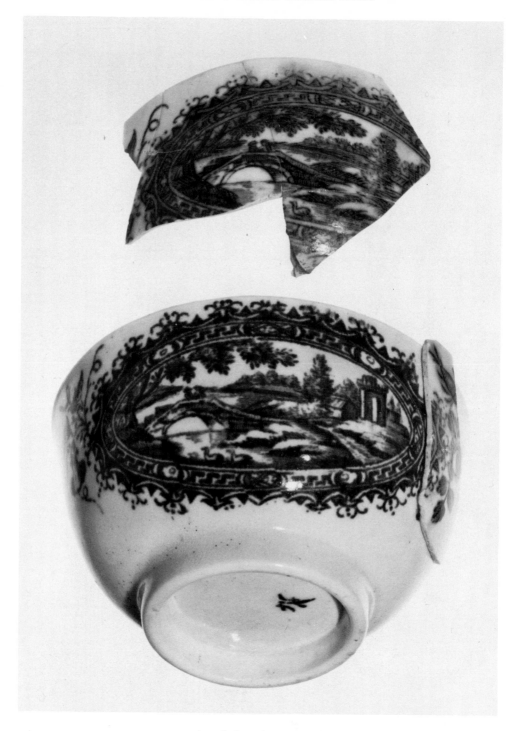

235. WORCESTER tea bowl, bearing one of the panelled European landscape designs (see also Plate 249), shown with matching 'wasters' from the Worcester factory site. Note the typical Worcester disguised numeral mark '7' under the bowl. *c.* 1775–80.

236. WORCESTER bread plate from a tea service, bearing the blue-printed 'vase' or 'bat' design (named after the bat-like bird shown at 'A'). Note also the hand-applied washes of light blue, used to fill in rocks, and to shade the foreground 'B'. On Caughley prints, engraved lines would have been used. See also Worcester 'waster' matching border. Disguised numeral mark '8'. *c.* 1780.

237. Detail of border of above plate, with unglazed 'waster' from the WORCESTER factory site.

238. A selection of WORCESTER porcelains bearing the blue-printed 'vase' or 'bat' pattern (see Plates 236, 237, 239 & 240). Note the stud-like knob on the coffee pot. Central dish $10\frac{1}{4} \times 8\frac{1}{2}$ in. Disguised numeral marks '4' and '8'. *c.* 1775–85. *Godden of Worthing Ltd.*

239. A WORCESTER barrel-shaped teapot (see also Plates 303–5) decorated with the 'vase' or 'bat' pattern. Note the stud knob. 5 in. high. Disguised numeral mark. *c.* 1775–85. *Bulwer Collection. Castle Museum, Norwich.*

240. A WORCESTER tea canister and cover (see Page 146), decorated with the blue-printed 'vase' or 'bat' design (see Plates 236–9 and Pages 119 & 122). 5½ in. high. Disguised mark. *c.* 1775–85. *Victoria & Albert Museum (Crown Copyright).*

241. Worcester blue-printed milk-jug and tea canister, showing both sides of the 'Temple' pattern (see Page 119). Note the stud-like knobs and light-blue painted foreground. $5\frac{1}{2}$ and $4\frac{3}{4}$ in. high. Disguised numeral marks '8' and '7'. *c.* 1770–80. *Godden of Worthing Ltd.*

242. Worcester coffee pot bearing the blue-printed 'bandstand' pattern (see Page 120). Note the stud-like knob and light-blue *painted* shading without engraved lines. $8\frac{1}{4}$ in. high. Disguised numeral mark '2'. *c.* 1770–80. *Godden of Worthing Ltd.*

243. Worcester bowl bearing the blue-printed 'argument' pattern (see figures in window and Page 120). 8 in. dia. Disguised numeral mark '3'. *c.* 1770–80. *Author's Collection.*

244. Worcester sugar bowl and cover, showing the reverse side of the 'Argument' pattern (see above). Note the non-Caughley stud-like knob. $5\frac{1}{4}$ in. high. Disguised numeral mark '7'. *c.* 1770–80. *Godden of Worthing Ltd.*

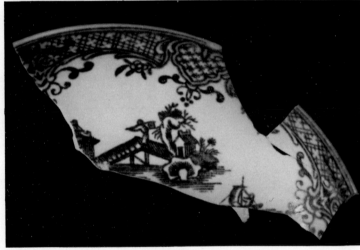

245. Fragment of saucer showing the fancy border found on Worcester 'Argument' pattern teawares, found on the Worcester factory site.

246. Worcester tea bowl and saucer bearing blue-printed European ruins (see also Plates 247, 250-2 and Page 120). Disguised numeral marks '7' and '8'. *c.* 1770-80. *Author's Collection.*

247. Two Worcester bowls showing European ruins and fountain motif inside the bowl. 5 in. dia. Disguised numeral marks '7' and '8'. *c.* 1770-80. *Godden of Worthing Ltd.*

248. *Above left.* A fine Worcester mug decorated with an underglaze blue-print of European landscape (see also Plates 249–50 and Page 120). $4\frac{9}{10}$ in. high. Blue-printed, shaded crescent mark. *c.* 1770–80. *Author's Collection.*

249. *Above right.* Worcester sparrow-beak milk jug, showing blue-printed European landscape pattern. This subject is the same as occurs on the reverse side of the bowl shown, with factory fragments, in Plate 235. $3\frac{3}{5}$ in. high. Disguised numeral mark '7'. *c.* 1775–80. *Author's Collection.*

250. *Below.* Selection of Worcester teawares bearing blue-printed European landscape subjects (see also Plates 248–9 and Page 120). Larger bowl $5\frac{3}{4}$ in. dia. Blue-printed, shaded crescent marks. *c.* 1770–85. *Godden of Worthing Ltd.*

251. A fine Worcester dessert dish bearing a superb underglaze blue-printed landscape within fancy scroll frame. $10\frac{1}{4} \times 7\frac{1}{4}$ in. Disguised numeral mark '7'. c. 1770–80. *Author's Collection.*

252. A fine Worcester dessert dish decorated with *overglaze* print in the same style as the above blue-printed dish bearing the disguised numeral mark. Note especially the same ornate outer border. $9\frac{1}{2}$ in. dia. c. 1770–75. *Dyson Perrins Museum, Worcester Royal Porcelain Works.*

253. Worcester bowls bearing the blue-printed milk-maid subject (see Page 120). The larger bowl shows the reverse of the standard subject as depicted on the small tea bowl. Large bowl $5\frac{1}{2}$ in. dia. Blue-printed, shaded crescent mark. *c.* 1775–85. *Author's Collection.*

254. Two fine Worcester mugs decorated with blue-printed shooting subjects (see Page 141). $4\frac{3}{4}$ and $3\frac{3}{10}$ in. high. Blue-printed shaded crescent marks. *c.* 1770–80. *Godden of Worthing Ltd.*

255. Reverse side of Worcester 'A' and Caughley 'B' tea bowls, the front bearing the 'Mother & Child' design (see Plate 35 and Page 134). Apart from the different design, the thicker section of the Caughley bowl 'B' can be clearly seen. Worcester example bears blue-printed, shaded crescent mark. *c.* 1775–85. *Author's Collection.*

256. *Right.* Worcester bowl showing a rare enlarged version of the 'Mother & Child' design (see Page 134) with extra standing figure. $5\frac{1}{2}$ in. dia. Blue-printed, shaded crescent mark. *c.* 1770–80. *Godden of Worthing Ltd.*

257. *Bottom.* Reverse side of the Worcester bowl shown in Plate 256, bearing rare, blue-printed Chinese-styled figure design, at least two versions of which were made, a variation also occurs on 'S' marked Caughley examples. $5\frac{1}{2}$ in. dia. Blue-printed, shaded crescent mark. *c.* 1770–80. *Godden of Worthing Ltd.*

258. Worcester 'A' and Caughley 'B' mugs bearing slightly different versions of the 'La Pêche' blue-printed design (see Page 133). Note foreground shading and rod-tips. 4⅓ and 4½ in. high. Worcester mug 'A' blue-printed shaded crescent mark, Caughley mug 'B' blue 'Sx' mark. *c.* 1775–85. *Godden of Worthing Ltd.*

259. Worcester 'A' and Caughley 'B' mugs, as shown in Plate 258, above, depicting the blue-printed 'La Prominade Chînoise' design found with the 'La Pêche' design, above (see Page 133). Note the shape of the umbrella, the height of the two trees behind the standing figure, the length of the bird's tail and the foreground.

260. Worcester version of the cabbage-leaf jug (see Plates 276–80 and Page 138) bearing the 'Parrot and fruit' pattern with cross-hatching in the foreground rocks 'A', compare with Caughley 'pull' shown in Plate 40. Indistinct disguised numeral mark '3' or '7'. *c.* 1775–80. *Victoria & Albert Museum (Crown Copyright).*

261. Worcester tea canister form (see Plate 309) decorated with *hand-painted* version of the Caughley printed 'Temple' pattern (see Plate 16 and Page 17) with Worcester 'waster'. $6\frac{3}{4}$ in. high. *c.* 1770–80. *Author's Collection.*

262. Worcester 'B' and Caughley 'A' butter dish stands decorated with the popular 'Fence' pattern (see Plates 263 & 288 and Pages 132 & 135). $6\frac{1}{4}$ in. dia. Worcester stand 'B', blue-printed shaded crescent mark, Caughley 'A' blue-printed 'C' mark. *c.* 1775–85. *Godden of Worthing Ltd.*

A   B

263. Worcester blue-printed butter tub and cover of the 'Fence' pattern (see Pages 132 & 135). Note the thin long leaf on the cover. $4\frac{1}{10}$ in. dia. Blue-printed, shaded crescent mark. *c.* 1770–80. *Godden of Worthing Ltd.*

264. Worcester scale-blue ground butter tub and stand, painted with typical exotic birds. Blue 'square' mark. *c.* 1770. *Messrs Sotheby & Co.*

Worcester Butter Tureens

265. Worcester oval butter tureen and stand, decorated with the blue-printed 'rose' pattern (see Page 135). Compare with the Caughley example shown in Plate 93, and note the long narrow applied leaves on this Worcester specimen. Stand $7\frac{1}{5} \times 5$ in. Blue-printed, shaded crescent mark. *c.* 1770–80. *W. W. Warner (Antiques) Ltd.*

266. Scale-blue ground Worcester butter tureen of the same basic form as that shown in Plate 265 above. The applied twig handles, leaves and flowers vary from specimen to specimen but note the long, thin leaves. Blue 'square' mark. *c.* 1770. *Messrs Sotheby & Co.*

267. Worcester blue-printed coffee pot bearing the 'vase' or 'bat' pattern (see Plates 236–40 and Pages 119, 122 & 136). Note the stud-like knob, not found on Caughley examples. 9¼ in. high. Blue disguised numeral mark '6'. *c.* 1775–85. *Godden of Worthing Ltd.*

268. Worcester blue-printed coffee pot bearing the 'fruit and wreath' design (see Plates 43 & 299 and Page 134). Compare the handle and height of this cover with the Caughley specimen illustrated in Plate 104. 9½ in. high. Blue disguised numeral mark '5'. *c.* 1775–85. *Victoria & Albert Museum (Crown Copyright).*

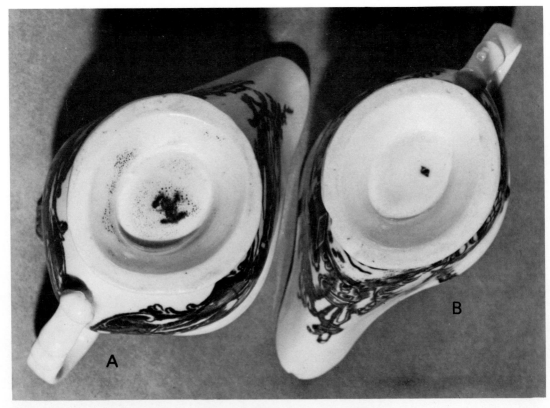

269. Base of a Worcester 'A' and a Caughley 'B' cream boat, showing a disguised numeral mark and bubbled glaze on the fatter Worcester example, and a blue-printed 'S' mark on the slim Caughley specimen (see also Plate 270, below).

270. Side view of Worcester 'A' and Caughley 'B' cream boats (marks shown in Plate 269, above) showing the slight differences between the Worcester specimen, with the disguised numeral mark, and the 'S'-marked Caughley example. Note especially the different handles, and see Page 136. Worcester boat 'A' $4\frac{1}{10}$ in. long. *c.* 1775–80. *Author's Collection.*

271. Worcester blue-printed pierced cress dish and stand, bearing the pine cone design (see also Plate 12 and Page 136). Stand 9½ in. dia. Blue-printed, shaded crescent mark. *c.* 1775–80. *Godden of Worthing Ltd.*

272. Worcester blue-printed chocolate cup and saucer of a shape also made at Caughley (see Plates 101–2 and Page 137). Saucer 6 in. dia. Blue-printed, shaded crescent mark. *c.* 1775–80. *Dyson Perrins Museum, Worcester Royal Porcelain Co.*

273. Detail of Worcester 'A' and Caughley 'B' chocolate cup handles (see Plates 101–2 & 272 and Page 137), noting especially the larger 'kick' at the top of the Caughley handle, and the manner in which the head at the base of the Worcester handle comes away from the cup.

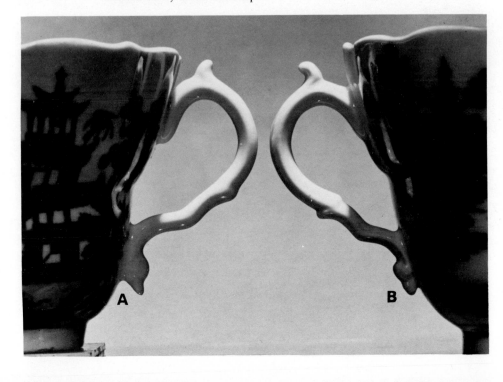

274. Caughley 'A' and Worcester 'B' standard shape of fluted cup (as found in teasets such as those shown in Plates 275, 308 & 309). Note the greater inward 'kick' to the Caughley handle and factory 'waster', and straighter outline to the Worcester cup (see Page 137). Worcester cup 'B' bears the blue crescent mark, Caughley cup 'A' bears the blue 'S' mark. *c.* 1780–5.

275. An attractive Worcester fluted teaset showing standard shapes and above cup form (see also Plate 309). Teapot $4\frac{5}{8}$ in. high. Blue 'W' factory mark. *c.* 1770–80. *Victoria & Albert Museum (Crown Copyright).*

276. Caughley unglazed (bubbled) cabbage-leaf jug, showing oval lemon-like shape of the main body. Note also mask spout with open eye with clear eye-lid and pronounced lips. 9 in. high. *c.* 1780. *Author's Collection.*

277. A Worcester porcelain cabbage-leaf jug which has become warped in the firing. Shown to contrast the basic rotund shape with the more oval Caughley form shown above. The mask spout also has slit eyes (see also Plate 278). 8¾ in. high. Cursive 'W' mark. *c.* 1770-5. *Godden of Worthing Ltd.*

278. Factory 'wasters' showing Caughley 'A' mask-head spout with open eye and thick, well marked lips. Compare with Worcester 'B' unglazed 'waster' showing clearly the slit eye. Note also the lack of eyebrows and less accentuated lips (see also Pages 138–9).

279. Worcester blue-printed cabbage-leaf jug, with rotund body and slit eyes to the mask-spout (see Plates 277 & 280 and Pages 138–9). 7 in. high. *c.* 1775–80. *Author's Collection.*

280. A fine Worcester enamelled cabbage-leaf jug (for many years included in the Caughley case at the Victoria & Albert Museum) with Worcester version of mask-head spout and handle (see Pages 138–9), and compare with Colour Plate VIII and Plates 67–71, 276–9. 9 in. high. *c.* 1770–80. *Victoria & Albert Museum (Crown Copyright).*

281. Detail of Worcester 'A' mask-head spout from jug shown in Plate 282 below, and 'B' detail of Caughley spout from 1780 jug shown in Colour Plate III. The differences between these masks is the same as Plate 278 but notice especially the eyebrows on the Caughley mask 'B', which do not show on the Worcester example.

282. Worcester blue-printed mask-head jug (detail of spout shown in Plate 281, above). Compare with the Caughley examples shown in Plates 134–6 and see Pages 138–9. 7 in. high. Blue-printed shaded crescent mark. *c.* 1770–80. *Godden of Worthing Ltd.*

A

283. Worcester moulded leaf dish, note especially the relief moulded feature at 'A', which does not appear on Caughley dishes of this general form (see Plate 137 and Page 139). $7\frac{3}{4}$ × $6\frac{3}{4}$ in. *c.* 1770–5. *Godden of Worthing Ltd.*

284. Worcester moulded leaf dish of a shape apparently not made at the Caughley factory. $10\frac{1}{2}$ in. long. Blue-printed, shaded crescent mark. *c.* 1770–5. *W. W. Warner (Antiques) Ltd.*

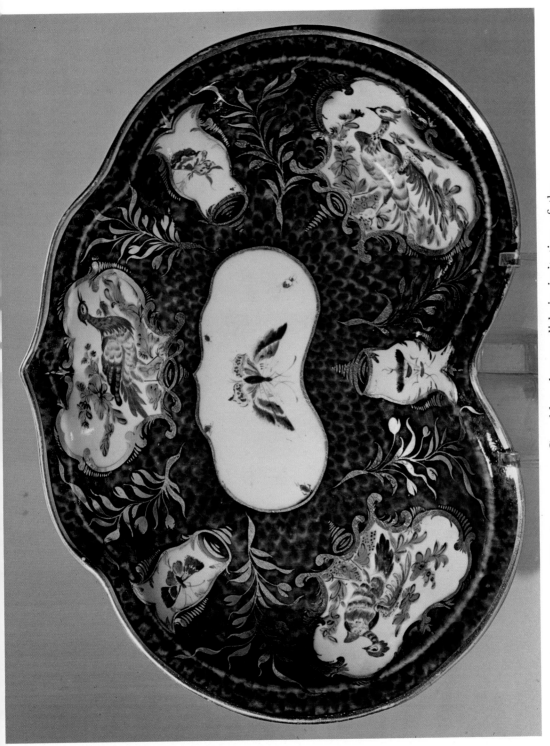

IX. A very rare Caughley dessert dish in imitation of the better-known Worcester scale-blue ground wares (see Page 4). The enamel decoration and gilding perhaps added outside the Caughley factory. $10\frac{3}{4}$ in. long. Underglaze blue 'S' mark. c. 1780–5. *Author's Collection.*

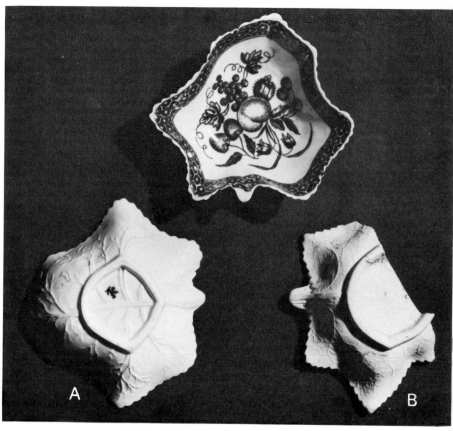

285. Worcester blue-printed leaf dish, with underside of a matching dish shown at 'A'. The unglazed fragment 'B' is from the Caughley site, and matches marked Caughley finished examples. Note the totally different moulding of the veins and stalk (see Pages 139–40). Worcester example $3\frac{1}{2} \times 4$ in. *c.* 1775–85. *Author's Collection.*

286. Worcester 'A' small leaf dish, decorated in underglaze blue, shown with a Caughley version 'B'. Note the undulating top edge to the Worcester example and the longer stalk to the Caughley specimen (see Page 140). Caughley leaf $2\frac{4}{5}$ in. wide. Blue 'S' mark. *c.* 1775–85. *Author's Collection.*

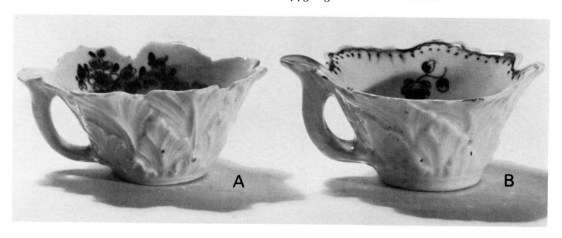

287. Worcester blue and white milk jug of a basic shape also made at Caughley (see Plate 143) and Lowestoft. This piece is most important as it bears the post-1783 Worcester impressed 'Flight' mark as well as a shaded crescent (see detail of base), showing that blue printing of this type was continued into the 1780's (see Pages 127 & 140). $4\frac{5}{8}$ in. high. *c.* 1783. *Victoria & Albert Museum (Crown Copyright).*

288. Worcester 'sparrow-beak' milk jug 'A' with Caughley version 'B'. Note the low settling 'belly' on the Worcester specimen (see Page 140). $4\frac{1}{2}$ and $4\frac{3}{4}$ in. high. Blue-printed, shaded crescent and 'S' initial marks. *c.* 1775–85. *Godden of Worthing Ltd.*

A   B

X. A blue-printed Worcester tankard bearing the 'La Pêche' and 'La Promenade Chînoise' patterns (see Plates 258-9). Dated 1780, so showing that the Worcester factory was producing these blue-painted wares at this rather late date. 5⅘ in. high. Blue-printed, shaded crescent mark. *Godden of Worthing Ltd.*

289. Worcester mustard pot bearing the Worcester version of the Fisherman pattern (see Page 142). Note the stud-like knob not used at Caughley. $3\frac{1}{2}$ in. high. Blue-printed, shaded crescent mark. *c.* 1775–85. *Sotheby & Co.*

290. Caughley 'A' and Worcester 'B' blue-printed mustard pots. Note the different heights and position of base of handles, and also the thicker leaves on the cover of the Caughley pot (see Page 141). Caughley pot $3\frac{3}{4}$ in. high, Worcester 4 in. high. Blue-printed 'C' mark and shaded crescent mark. *c.* 1775–85. *Godden of Worthing Ltd.*

A   B

291. Worcester moulded salad bowl of a form also made at Caughley (see Plate 167 and Page 142). Decorated with underglaze blue prints. 10 in. dia. Blue-printed disguised numeral mark '8'. *c.* 1775–85. *Sotheby & Co.*

292. Worcester sauce boat of a basic form made also at Caughley (see Plate 172). Decorated with the Worcester version of the 'Fisherman' pattern. Note the wavy, loose fishing line (see Pages 131 & 143). 6¼ in. long. Blue-printed disguised numeral mark '8'. *c.* 1775–85. *Godden of Worthing Ltd.*

293. Two Worcester moulded sauce boats, hand-painted in underglaze blue. 5½ and 7 in. long. Blue-painted open crescent marks. *c.* 1765-75. *Godden of Worthing Ltd.*

294. Rare Worcester deep shell-shaped dish of a form not apparently made at the Caughley factory. Blue-printed centre. 1¾ in. high, 5¼ in. across. Blue-printed, shaded crescent mark. *c.* 1770-5. *Author's Collection.*

295. Worcester blue-printed spittoon or 'saffer pot' (see Page 144). Note the finely turned foot, and compare with the Caughley specimens shown in Plates 165 and 166. $4\frac{1}{4}$ in. high. Blue-printed, shaded crescent mark. *c.* 1770–80. *Godden of Worthing Ltd.*

296. Caughley unglazed 'waster' spoon-tray 'A', with Worcester version 'B' below. Note the Worcester 'Fisherman' pattern (see Pages 131–2 & 144), different outline and thin section, in comparison with the Caughley 'wasters' above. Worcester tray 'B' $6\frac{1}{5} \times 3\frac{1}{2}$ in. Blue-printed, shaded crescent mark. *c.* 1775–85. *Author's Collection.*

297. Worcester overglaze printed sugar bowl and cover, bearing the well-known 'Tea party'
print. Note the Worcester stud-
like knob. 5 in. high. *c.* 1765–75.
*Victoria & Albert Museum (Crown
Copyright).*

298. Worcester blue-printed
patty or 'tart pan'. Compare
the shape with the Caughley
version shown in Plates 184 and
185. 5¼ in. dia. Blue-painted,
open crescent mark. *c.* 1765–75.
Godden of Worthing Ltd.

299. Worcester blue-printed teapot, bearing the 'Fruit and wreath' pattern (see Page 134) $4\frac{3}{4}$ in. high. Blue-printed shaded crescent mark. *c.* 1770-80. *Bulwer Collection. Castle Museum, Norwich.*

300. Worcester teapot enamelled with Chinese figures in a style employed at several English factories. $5\frac{3}{4}$ in. high. *c.* 1770-5. *Godden of Worthing Ltd.*

301. Worcester teapot with matching tea-bowl and saucer, enamelled in a style copied from Chinese porcelains imported into Europe. Note the Worcester stud-like knob. Teapot $5\frac{1}{2}$ in. high. *c.* 1770-80. *Godden of Worthing Ltd.*

302. A rare Worcester teapot with the general outline midway between the standard early globular shape (as Plates 299–301) and the later, barrel-shaped pots (as Plates 303–11). $4\frac{3}{4}$ in. high. Blue-printed, shaded crescent mark. *c.* 1770–5. *Author's Collection.*

303. Part of a Worcester teaset bearing the Worcester version of the 'Fisherman' pattern (see Pages 131 & 146). Note Worcester form of spoon-tray, tea canister and teapot (compare with Plates 296, 189 & 201 and see Pages 144 & 146). Blue-printed, shaded crescent mark. *c.* 1770–80. *Godden of Worthing Ltd.*

304. A superb blue-printed Worcester teapot, showing the reverse side of the standard 'Birds in tree' pattern (see Plates 39 & 141 and Page 134). Note the handle and graceful spout and compare with Caughley form as illustrated in Plate 62. 4¾ in. high. Blue-printed, shaded crescent mark. *c.* 1770–80. *Godden of Worthing Ltd.*

305. Representative pieces from a blue-printed Worcester tea service of 'Temple' pattern (see Plate 241 and Page 119). Note the Worcester stud-like knobs and teapot handle. The blue-printed disguised numeral mark '7' is seen on upturned teapot stand. *c.* 1775–85. *Godden of Worthing Ltd.*

306. A superbly enamelled Worcester barrel-shaped teapot, with typical handle, spout and stud-like knob. $5\frac{1}{4}$ in. high. *c.* 1780. *Godden of Worthing Ltd.*

307. A Worcester teapot and stand which has often been illustrated as Caughley. Note the Worcester spout and handle, and thinly potted stand (compare with Plates 62, 201 & 312 and see Pages 145 & 146). $4\frac{3}{8}$ in. high. *c.* 1775–85. *Victoria & Albert Museum (Crown Copyright).*

308. Representative pieces of a fluted Worcester tea service. Note the creamer handle and compare with the standard Caughley form (Plate 145) and also the teapot handle, spout and stud knob, and cup outline and handle (see Plate 274). The teapot has twenty-four convex flutes (see Page 145). *Sotheby & Co.*

309. Representative pieces from a finely decorated fluted Worcester tea service showing typical forms which may be contrasted with the Caughley versions. Teapot 5¼ in. high. *c.* 1770-5. *Delomosne & Son, London.*

310. Three pieces from a blue and gold Worcester tea service. Note the stud-like knobs and creamer form—not used at the Caughley factory. Teapot $5\frac{1}{2}$ in. high. *c.* 1775–85. *Godden of Worthing Ltd.*

311. Representative pieces from a fluted Worcester service decorated in blue and gold, showing Worcester, not Caughley, shapes. Teapot $5\frac{1}{4}$ in. high. Blue painted, open crescent mark. *c.* 1775–85. *J. Waring, Brighton.*

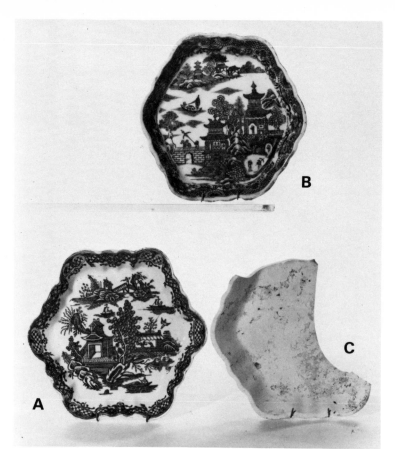

312. Worcester teapot stand 'A', bearing the 'Argument' pattern (see Page 120) shown with the Caughley 'Temple' pattern stand 'B', and below the Caughley site 'waster' 'C'. Note the different outline and thickness (see Page 146). Worcester stand 'A' blue-printed disguised numeral mark '7'. *c.* 1775–80. *Author's Collection.*

313. Worcester blue-printed tea canister bearing the Worcester version of the popular 'Fisherman' design (see Pages 131 & 146) and of a form not made at the Caughley factory. $4\frac{3}{4}$ in. high. Blue-printed, shaded crescent mark. *c.* 1775–80. *Author's Collection.*

314. Caughley 'A' white and gold sugar or cream tureen, as found in early dessert services (see Page 147) and a Worcester example 'B'. Note differences in the applied leaf on the cover, the Caughley example being thicker in the potting than the crescent marked Worcester specimen. 4¾ in. high. *c.* 1770–5. *Godden of Worthing Ltd.*

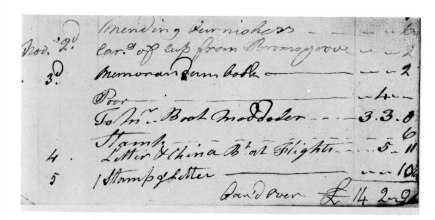

315. Extract from Chamberlains' cash book showing payment for china bought from Flights in November 1791.

316. Extract from Chamberlain sales book showing Worcester 'Temple' pattern teawares, sold in February 1790 (see Plates 241 & 305).

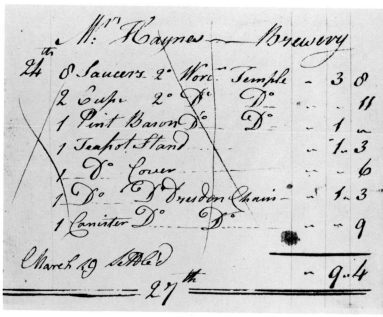

317. Extract from Chamberlain account of February 1790 showing 'gilt' Pleasure Boat (Fisherman) pattern and 'Worc' Temple' pattern teawares (see Plates 241 & 305 and Pages 130–1). *Plates 315–17, Worcester Royal Porcelain Co. Ltd.*